The Lawyer's Guide to Succession Planning

A Project Management Approach for Successful Law Firm Transitions and Exits

John W. Olmstead, MBA, Ph.D., CMC

Cover design by Kelly Book/ABA Publishing

Printed in the United States of America.

19 18 5 4 3 2

Library of Congress Cataloging-in-Publication Data

ISBN: 978-1-63425-350-5
e-ISBN: 978-1-63425-351-2

Discounts are available for books ordered in bulk. Special consideration is given to state bars, CLE programs, and other bar-related organizations. Inquire at Book Publishing, ABA Publishing, American Bar Association, 321 N. Clark Street, Chicago, Illinois 60654-7598.

www.ShopABA.org

CONTENTS

PREFACE

November 2014 was a major milestone for me—thirty years since I started my legal management consulting practice, forty-six years since I started working with attorneys. I have spent my entire working life managing and working with attorneys. Along the road, I completed my MBA and, later, a PhD in business with a concentration in organizational psychology.

I first started in legal management in 1968 with the United States Air Force Judge Advocate General (JAG). After nine years in legal administration and a terminal assignment as assistant chief court administrator with The Judge Advocate General's (TJAG) office based in Washington DC, I jumped into the field of law firm legal administration. Upon joining my first law firm as a legal administrator, I assumed that my nine years' experience adequately prepared me for my new venture. Boy, was I wrong. Now I was working for a business organization whose primary measure of success was to make money and turn a profit and if I was going to be successful, I had to contribute toward firm profitability. This was a major departure from the focus of a governmental law department. I could no longer hold on to the security of the chain of command and I now had to deal with a completely different style and approach to management. I discovered very quickly that lawyers in law firms have their own style of management, whether dealing with clients, one another, or the problems they face administering the needs of the firm.

After three years, I joined a larger law firm as director of administration and was with this firm for four years, after which time I received my calling and took the plunge and started my legal management consulting practice Olmstead & Associates. Since 1984 I have worked with hundreds of small- to mid-size law firms across the United States and internationally. Initially engagements were more along process and operational lines. Over the years, my engagements evolved into succession and exit planning, strategy and competitive business models, governance, and partnership matters including partnership admission, compensation, mergers, and acquisitions. During the past ten years, as a result of the aging attorney population, my work with attorneys helping them successfully design and implement succession strategies, my articles and blogs on aging and succession, and approximately 80 percent of my engagements have been succession/exit planning projects—helping attorneys come to grips with retirement and successfully transitioning from and exiting their practices.

The purpose of this book is to provide guidance to firms of all sizes, especially smaller firms, and share succession and transition processes, approaches, and step-by-step action plans for solo practitioners, sole owners, and members of larger law firms. The book discusses what to do and what not to do and how to go about it, as well as providing case studies, sample action plans, sample succession plans, sample agreements, and other documents.

I hope you will find this book interesting and informative and that it will help those facing, contemplating, or eventually facing succession, transition, and retirement come to terms and effectively plan and implement effective succession, transition, and exit strategies.

Good luck on your journey!

ACKNOWLEDGMENTS

Completion of this book would not have been impossible had it not been for the help and support of numerous people.

I would like to thank my editor with ABA Publishing, Kevin Commins, who guided me through this process. During the course of the project, he proved to be a friend as well as my advisor and his help and assistance was truly instrumental in moving me forward to the successful completion of this project. I thank him for all that he shared with me during the long journey and all that I learned from him.

My special thanks to Dr. Thomas J. Venardos for initially getting me interested in writing and publishing a book and then for his ongoing encouragement, coaching, and mentoring. Without his backing over the years, success would not have been possible.

I would also like to thank Deborah K. Olmstead, my communications manager, spouse, and accountability partner, for her assistance in coordinating the project, document proofing, timeline nagging, and putting up with me during the trying moments of this project.

Thanks to all of the attorneys and others who took the time to read through preview copies of the book.

INTRODUCTION

Law firm succession, transition, and exit planning is one of the hottest management challenges facing attorneys whether they are a partner in a law firm, a sole owner of a firm comprising other employed attorneys and staff members, or a solo attorney in practice with no other attorneys in the firm. Talent is a law firm's strategic asset, yet it is an area most neglected by law firms of all sizes.

Many solo and sole owner attorneys as well as larger law firms are in "reactionary mode" and have not adequately prepared for transition of clients, firm leadership, and management. A firm's very survival may well depend upon coming to terms with succession and transition, and doing so early. Over the past five years, law firm practice succession, transition, and exit planning has become our busiest practice area and ranks at the top of the charts regarding practice management questions and concerns raised by practicing attorneys. According to the 2013 Altman Weil Law Firms in Transition Survey, respondents reported the following (Clay 2013, 38):

- Senior partners don't want to retire (77.6 percent respondents reported);
- Senior partners don't want to transition clients and give up current compensation (73.2 percent respondents reported);
- Only 27 percent of law firms with fifty or more lawyers have formal succession plans; and
- Forty-five percent of the survey respondents cited that aging, mortality, retirement, and succession are uncomfortable topics and awkward for senior partners to discuss with their partners.

This book is a guide designed to help ignite the process and get you thinking about aging and mortality as well as what you are going to do with your life and your practice after you retire. It will ask you to come to terms with aging and accept, rather that deny, the fact that eventually you will retire from the practice of law, either voluntarily or involuntarily. Succession, transition, and exit planning are all about getting "unstuck" and getting your head out of the sand. I will present demographics and case studies to help you feel a sense of urgency and a desire to begin formulating specific goals and action plans for your life and law practice. While this book can help get you started down the path of succession and transition, you may need professional help along the way from advisors such as accountants/tax advisors, law firm management consultants, financial planners, insurance agents, business attorneys, spiritual advisors, and accountability coaches or partners. Do not try to take this journey alone. Obtain professional help and guidance along the way.

Throughout this book I will highlight the demographics of the profession, the importance of early succession planning, and the implications and consequences of failure to address succession and transition. I will discuss both challenges and how to come to terms with aging and eventual retirement, using various other law firms as examples. In addition, I will provide stories and case studies of firms that have failed to address succession, as well as those that have managed to successfully deal with both succession and transition. I will also discuss:

- Where and how to start succession planning;
- Firm size, issues, and impact upon succession and transition;
- Finding candidates and opportunities;
- Strategies and approaches;
- Valuation;
- Buy-in/buyout/compensation;
- Developing the succession and transition plans;
- Implementation of the strategies and plans;
- Key documents and agreements; and
- Ethical issues.

It is my intention and desire that readers will find this book a useful toolkit that helps senior attorneys and their respective law firms get "unstuck" and assists them in coming to terms with retirement, succession, and transition by prompting them to think about and have open discussions at home with family members and at the firm with partners and other stakeholders.

An effective succession and transition strategy involves coming to terms with aging and retirement, developing a timeline, and identifying transition candidates either internally or externally. There is an old saying at IBM—what gets planned and what get measured is what gets done. You have worked hard to build your practice. Your practice may or may not have value depending upon the steps you take and when you take them. Start early.

CHAPTER 1

Reasons for Early Retirement and Succession Planning

As a senior, I know first-hand what it is like to face aging and retirement. I started thinking about it five years ago, putting in place personal and practice plans. Following a five-year procrastination after initially meeting with our estate-planning attorney, my wife and I finally made the time to have the discussions that we needed to have to finalize our estate-planning documents. We eliminated all personal debt and monthly payments and started acquiring what we actually needed rather than what everybody else has. I began thinking about my management consulting practice and while I decided that I wanted to continue to work as long as I am able, I started refocusing my practice into areas more fitting a senior citizen and reduced my emphasis in other areas. While my original goal was to work less, I have actually been working more, but in the areas that I enjoy and that are less stressful and more profitable. I should have begun the process much earlier, but I simply did not want to think about getting older. Therefore, I understand why attorneys procrastinate and are in no hurry to begin thinking about and planning for the succession and transition of their practices, whether they are solo practitioners, solo owners, or partners in larger firms.

Law firm succession and transition is a big deal and will become even more so over the next decade. The pending retirement of the baby boomer generation and the unrelenting challenge of finding and keeping talented staff can have grave consequences for law firms that fail to develop a succession strategy. Steps that you take or do not take five years or earlier prior to your actual retirement will determine whether your practice, clients, employees, and your legacy transitions to another generation. For a small or solo practice, these steps may determine whether your practice has any goodwill value at all. Early planning will pay dividends. Many firms are in "reactionary mode" and have not adequately prepared for transition of firm leadership and client relationships. A firm's very survival may very well depend upon the quality of its succession/exit plan.

Many are asking, "What do I do with this practice?" "Is there value or goodwill?" "Where and how should I start?"

Demographics

According to a Standard and Poor's analysis on aging, "No other force is likely to shape the future of national health, public finances and policymaking as the irreversible rate at which the world's population is aging" (Mrsnik 2010, 1). The US Department of Health and Human Services reports that the sixty-five and older population increased by 15 percent between 2000 and 2010 and projects that it will increase by another 36 percent over the next decade; the eighty-five and older population is projected to increase by 19 percent between 2010 and 2020 (A Profile of Older Americans 2012, 3). Within the next twenty years, more than ninety million people (baby boomers) in the United States and Canada will be retiring. Economist and demographic expert Robert Avery, from Cornell University, predicts that baby boomers will transfer 10 trillion dollars to later generations—the largest generational transfer of wealth in the history of humankind (Avery 1993, 11). The vast majority of this wealth is held as stock in more than twelve million privately owned businesses, and during the next ten to fifteen years, more than 70 percent of these companies will change hands.

Unprecedented Number of Attorneys Approaching Retirement

Given these trends and projections, in the upcoming years we can expect the legal profession to include more practitioners who are seniors. The numbers reported in the Lawyer Statistical Report prepared by the American Bar Foundation are indicative of this trend. According to the report, 25 percent of the lawyer population was fifty-five and older in 1980. By 2005 the percentage increased to 34 percent. Likewise, the median age of lawyers increased during that time from thirty-nine to forty-nine years old (Lawyer Demographics 2013). **Sixty-five percent of law firms' equity partners are in their late fifties or early sixties.** *Over the next ten years there are going to be many senior partners in firms of all sizes retiring, transitioning, and exiting their practices.*

Law firms will have a larger population of senior lawyers who will be approaching retirement and will need to develop strategies for transitioning their legal and leadership skills as well as their client relationships and market presence. Since clients of law firms, both individual and institutional business clients, advise us that they "hire the lawyer," individual relationships are a key component of all client relationships and firms, and thus sole owners must find ways to cross-pollinate and successfully transition these relationships. Firm leadership and management roles will need to be transitioned as well. Successors must be groomed for both roles. This will take effort, time, and commitment.

Implications and Consequences of Failure to Plan for Succession and Transition

Failure to manage succession proactively and plan for the exit of senior attorneys can result in:

- Loss of key clients;
- Loss of senior legal talent and leadership;

- Inability of firm owners, especially founders, to effectively capitalize on goodwill and sweat equity built up over the years;
- Unfunded retirement for partners and/or owners;
- Failure to protect family wealth in the event of unexpected life-changing events;
- Failure to protect partners, employees, and clients from unexpected life-changing events;
- Defections and firm breakups caused by younger lawyers unwilling to finance departing partner buyouts from future earnings; and
- In the case of solo and small firms, having to turn out the lights and close the door with little or no compensation for the sweat equity and goodwill of the practice.

Many small and midsize law firms are setting up formal succession plans for the simple reason that their founding partners are nearing retirement age. The founders want to ensure that their firms:

- Have the leadership and management in place to continue on to the next generation;
- Are able to retain existing client and referral relationships and sources of business and revenue for the firm; and
- Are willing and able to finance their buyouts.

Succession/Transition/Exit Strategies

Succession is not limited to a single course of action. It involves evaluating different aspects of the firm and identifying systems, processes, and policies that need improvement in order to position your firm or practice succession regardless of your exit strategy. Options for succession typically include:

- Selling or merging the firm or practice;
- Internal transition;
- Practice continuation with other firms; or
- Turning out the lights and closing the practice.

Case Studies

Johnson Law Firm (Fictitious Names Used)

A CASE STUDY OF A SOLE OWNER THAT FAILED TO PLAN HIS SUCCESSION

Robert Johnson was born and raised in the Chicago suburbs. Like many attorneys, he always wanted to be a lawyer. His father, now deceased, practiced law for thirty years. Upon graduation from high school, he immediately attended a private liberal arts college in northern Illinois and graduated with honors with a BA in history. After a short summer break, Robert started law school at the University of Illinois School of Law. He graduated from law school after three years, with a class ranking roughly in the middle of his class.

Inspired by his father, Robert wanted to practice in a small firm and eventually be a partner or owner. After law school, he immediately joined a three-partner general practice law firm as an associate at the age of twenty-six. Initially Robert worked in each of the firm's practice areas. However, early on he discovered that he did not enjoy litigation and his real interest and passion was estate planning and estate administration. Robert worked long hours building up his skills and book of business in these areas. After three years with the firm, Robert became a partner.

Robert worked hard as a partner and after four years, his fee origination (client finding) and generation (individual production/working attorney) numbers were substantially greater than the fee origination and generation of the other partners. However, his compensation, based on his ownership interest percentage of 25 percent, was the same. Robert brought up the subject of compensation on numerous occasions, but his partners were unwilling to make any changes to Robert's pay. He was also unhappy with the direction of the firm and the inability of the partners to agree on core values, common goals, and future direction of the firm. Robert wanted to invest in the firm, grow the firm, and provide new and innovative client services. His partners, however, were only interested in preserving the status quo, taking home as much money as possible each year, and not making any changes whatsoever. Partner meetings were infrequent and nonproductive. The partners simply could not agree on anything. After ten years in partnership, Robert had had enough and decided to start his own law firm with a personal commitment to never go into partnership with another attorney ever again.

After a series of confrontations with his partners concerning clients and staff who would leave the firm with Robert, final compensation, buyout of Robert's ownership interest, and other matters, Robert launched his new practice in leased office space with himself and one staff member. Sixty percent of the firm's clients eventually followed him to his new firm. Within two years of starting his new

(*continued*)

practice, Robert was taking home twice the compensation that he was in the other firm. Robert enjoyed his newfound freedom, the independence, and the additional compensation that he was receiving from his practice. As his practice grew and he got busier, he added staff and eventually, other attorneys. Robert always hired lawyers to be worker bees and never required them to develop clients, as he wanted to retain total control and thus not have to make his associates partners. At one point Robert had three associates but none of them lasted longer than a year or two, leaving for positions in other law firms. A couple of the associates who left started their own law firms.

Fast-forward twenty years. Robert is now sixty and suffering from Alzheimer's. He has three legal assistants and two associate attorneys. The associates are newbies, each out of law school less than three years, are risk averse, have no client book of business, and have no desire to own a law firm. As Robert's physical health has declined, his mental acuity has declined as well. However, rather than examining possible succession alternatives, Robert has continued to practice, and the quality of his services to clients has declined. Clients have become aware of this and as a result, many have taken their business to other law firms. Recently, Robert's wife, who also serves as the firm's office manager, approached several law firms regarding possible sale of the practice. All of the law firms that she has approached have rejected her proposals, advising her that since the firm is "uniquely Robert" and without a lengthy transition, they do not believe that there is sufficient value to warrant a practice acquisition. Four weeks ago, Robert's wife approached both of the associates, and both advised her that they did not wish to acquire this or any other law practice. Soon after, both associates gave their notice and advised that they were joining other law firms in the area. Based upon the medical advice of Robert's doctor, he has decided to close the practice and has asked his wife to handle the logistics of closing it down. Robert's failure to plan for his succession and transition has resulted in:

1. Loss of compensation for the goodwill of his practice and the sweat equity that he invested because of the need for a hasty practice sale;
2. A one-generation law firm;
3. Loss of peace of mind for Richard's family and employees;
4. Failure to provide continuity for clients and employees; and
5. Failure to continue the legacy of the firm that Robert built.

Had Robert reconsidered his attitude of having partners, hired and groomed entrepreneurial associates with a desire to own a law firm, institutionalized the firm's brand to be less uniquely Robert, and put in place both a short-term practice continuation plan and a long-term succession plan, the story may have ended differently.

Price, Jones, Jacobson, and Brown (Fictitious Names Used)

A CASE STUDY OF A FIRST-GENERATION PARTNERSHIP THAT FAILED TO ADDRESS SUCCESSION AND CLIENT, LEADERSHIP, AND MANAGEMENT TRANSITION

John Price, Mary Jones, and Paul Jacobson worked together as in-house attorneys for a major oil company in the energy section of the company's fifteen-attorney law department. Each had been an attorney for ten years and had been with the company for about the same amount of time. When the company started downsizing the law department, although not initially part of the initial cuts, the trio believed that they should start thinking about their futures. After countless meetings, they ultimately decided to start an energy boutique law firm and form a partnership. Since none of them had any experience working in or managing private law firms, they did the following:

- Read all the articles and books on law firm management they could find;
- Retained professional advisors, including a business attorney, accountant, law firm consultant, technology consultant, and insurance consultant;
- Learned the fundamentals of business, marketing, and client relationship management;
- Invested time and money on client development;
- Hired and invested in top-quality lawyer and staff talent; and
- Worked long hours and did whatever it took to deliver top results for their clients.

By admitting what they did not know, learning all they could on their own, and listening to their advisors, within five years the firm had successfully built a formidable statewide reputation as an energy boutique competing on a level with the large law firms.

As the firm grew, they brought in associate attorneys to serve as "worker bees" and handle the work. At the five-year point, they had six lawyers, three partners, and two associates. About six years after they founded the firm, the three partners decided to make one of the associates, Richard Brown, an equity partner. While Richard did not have a book of business, the firm felt that he was a good lawyer and a hard worker and deserved partnership. At this time, the partners agreed to the terms of Richard Brown's buy-in and amended the partnership agreement, with each partner having an equal share in the partnership. Partner compensation was based upon partnership interest percentages. An executive committee consisting of the three partners managed the firm.

Things were going well for the firm. The partners enjoyed their work and their independence, and were having fun. They were making more money in their

(*continued*)

ten-attorney firm than partners were making in some of the much larger law firms. The firm had a well-diversified, solid book of institutional clients, some of whom had been with the firm for many years. The firm had a team of great lawyers and support staff, a strong reputation, and a practice envied by many law firms across the state.

Time seemed to fly and on the firm's twenty-fifth anniversary the three founding partners, John, Mary, and Paul, now each sixty years old, announced that they intended to retire within the next year. Richard, the fourth partner and now fifty, was shell-shocked and advised the other partners that he did not want to be the "last man standing" and the only partner in the firm going forward. Each agreed that a succession plan should be implemented immediately.

The law firm engaged our firm, and we expressed the following concerns:

- John, Mary, and Paul had unique qualifications and expertise in the energy field that would be hard to replace and their withdrawal from the firm could result in loss of key clients and substantial revenues.
- Either the firm would have to transition one or both of the two non-equity partners promoted last year, recruit and hire a lateral partner, or merge with another law firm.
- The two non-equity partners would need to bulk up their professional profiles, dramatically improve their business development skills, enhance their relationships with existing clients, and develop new sources of clients.
- A three- to five-year timeline would be desirable to properly transition clients and managerial roles.

The partners agreed to admit the two non-equity partners as minority equity partners. Richard was completely on board with the plan. A transition plan was developed and the firm began implementing the plan. However, after six months, Richard announced that he was not interested in going forward with the transition and would leave the firm once the other three partners retired. Both the four senior partners and the two junior partners agreed that the junior partners could not retain the clients or continue the firm without an infusion of senior-level talent. The senior partners refused to extend their retirement timelines. With only six months remaining, the firm tried to find suitable laterals and merger firm candidates, to no avail. There was simply not enough time. After five months of searching, the partners decided to dissolve the firm.

The firm joined the ranks of one-generation law firms that were unable to transition to second generation. Had the firm hired more rainmakers, balanced their talent mix, and begun planning earlier, the outcome may have been different.

Adams Jennings LLP (Fictitious Names Used)

A CASE STUDY OF A SECOND-GENERATION LAW FIRM THAT BUNGLED THE TRANSITION OF A LARGE CLIENT

Adams Jennings LLP, a 260-lawyer firm in the Midwest, was in its second generation. The firm represented clients in all major industries and in all major practice areas throughout the United States. Of the 260 lawyers, a hundred were equity partners, forty were non-equity partners, and 120 were associates. The firm billed itself as a full-service firm and touted a large core of Fortune 500 clients on its client roster.

In the firm's first generation, it grew quickly from a handful of lawyers to over one hundred. Other than one merger with a small firm, the firm's growth was almost completely organic internal growth. The founders and subsequent first-generation partners did an excellent job of transitioning clients and management roles to the next generation of partners. However, as the economic recession of 2008 took hold, the firm became increasingly concerned about growth and new sources of fee revenue. Consequently, the firm became very aggressive in its search for new practice areas and portable books of business.

In 2009 the firm voted to merge with an intellectual property practice consisting of a founding partner (James Harrison) in his sixties with seventeen other equity partners and ten associates. The total book of business was 12 million dollars a year in fee collections. While intellectual property was a new and unknown practice area for the firm, the integration of the merger seemed to go fairly well. However, the new intellectual property practice operated as a separate silo, with little oversight of the practice. The firm's biggest mistake was that it did not understand who really controlled the book of business. As it turned out, the sixty-year-old Harrison had more control over the clients than originally thought.

Two years after the merger, Harrison announced that he would retire in five years. He started his five-year phasedown in accordance with the provisions of the firm's retirement program. Over the five-year period, his work schedule and compensation was reduced 20 percent each year. Harrison only made token client introductions to the other partners in the firm, for clients that he was he relationship attorney. These introductions were made to partners who joined the firm with Harrison in the Intellectual Property Group. Other partners outside of the Intellectual Property Group were simply not engaged in the phasedown and transition. Harrison sailed through his phasedown, collected his retirement payout, and withdrew from the practice and moved to Florida. He had no interest in an Of Counsel relationship.

(*continued*)

Soon after Harrison's withdrawal, since his client influence had been much stronger than believed, the client defections began. Other partners in his group who had joined the firm with him simply did not control the "business books" as it was initially assumed, even though they were designated as relationship attorneys. Within one year after Harrison's withdrawal, 50 percent of the clients had switched their business to other law firms, resulting in a revenue loss of 6.5 million dollars per year.

This situation could have been avoided had the firm done a better job:

1. Determining strategic fit of intellectual property practice area with the firm's other areas of practice;
2. Performing the initial merger due diligence regarding control of client relationships;
3. Integrating the practice group;
4. Injecting other attorneys into the practice group; and
5. Actively managing Harrison's phasedown.

CHAPTER 2

Coming to Terms with Aging

Several years ago I was giving a presentation to an Association of Legal Administrators (ALA) Chapter. After the presentation an administrator approached me and asked, "what kind of financial incentives can we put in place to encourage some of our senior attorneys to retire?" I responded by saying, "help them identify some hobbies." While my comment was partly in jest, many attorneys, especially baby boomers, have invested so much into their careers and law practices that they have not had either the desire or the time to invest into other areas of interest. Their work has been their life, often to the exclusion of family, friends, and other interests and pursuits. *These lawyers avoid thinking about aging and retirement like the plague.* Often their goal is to work forever, which is a common goal expressed to me by senior lawyers. Six out of ten Baby Boom generation lawyers that I am working with on succession engagements tell me that they want to work as long as they possibly can. Some would like to retire but need the money and cannot afford to stop working. Others love what they do and simply do not want to retire.

On the flipside, I have Generation X (adults born between 1961 and 1981) lawyers approaching their forties who are wanting to begin planning for their succession and retirement. Many of these Gen X lawyers have saved for retirement and are retiring in their fifties. Gen Xers are often highly educated, active, balanced, happy, and family oriented. In 2012 the Corporation for National and Community Service ranked Gen X volunteer rates in the United States at "29.4% per year," the highest compared with other generations. This is a generation that values change, human dignity, and individual freedom, the need to combat corruption, dictatorships, and abuse, and the need for stability, love, tolerance, and human rights for all. For Gen X, there is more to life than work. This is a generation that believes in work–life balance.

Many Baby Boomer lawyers have been so busy living the good life that they have not given any serious thought as to what will happen when the time comes for them to stop working. Coming to terms with aging and retirement can be a difficult thing. It requires us to come face to face with our own mortality, which is an uncomfortable subject for all of us. Some senior lawyers have been doing a good job of investing and saving for their retirement through pension, profit sharing, and 401k plans. However, financial preparation is one of the easier components to put in place to ensure a happy retirement.

The Stress of Retirement

In his book *The Retiring Mind*, Robert Delamontagne, PhD, states, "retirement often causes major emotional upheavals on the same level as the death of a loved one, loss of a job, or a financial crisis caused by a bad investment. I have come to learn that this emotional distress is often subtle in nature. It doesn't announce itself with fanfare, but sneaks up and taps you on the shoulder"(Delamontagne 2010, 3–16).

The more difficult components of retirement include:

- Coming to terms with aging and the fear of getting older;
- Deciding how to spend your time once you quit working;
- Identifying other interests;
- Preserving your self-esteem after retirement;

- Planning your retirement; and
- Dealing with the stress of retirement.

Achievement Addiction and Preserving Self-Esteem

Many lawyers, more so than various other professionals, are high achievers who are married and addicted to their law practices. They believe that their self-worth is reduced if they are not accomplishing something important. Psychologists refer to this as "achievement addiction." In his book *The Psychology of Retirement*, Derek Milne advises that surveys in the United States suggest more than 60 percent of retirees "un-retire" and continue to engage in some form of paid work, then "re-retire" or "semi-retire" later on in their retirement (Milne 2012, 11–15). A major challenge for lawyers who have an achievement-focused personality will be to find ways to replace the sense of accomplishment that they have experienced from the practice of law once they retire. While playing golf may be a worthwhile recreational activity for those who enjoy it, it will not be enough to fulfill the needs of those with an achievement-focused personality. These individuals will require activities where they can contribute and make a difference and continue to fulfill their self-actualization and self-esteem needs. Activities such as teaching, consulting, volunteer work, and community leadership often satisfy these needs.

Identifying Other Interests

Many of us have heard some of the stories of unhappy retirees, ranging from poor health, depression, and premature death. Years ago when my mother passed away, my father's boss asked my father how he could help. My father told him, "*Keep me working.*" My father's boss did so, and my father worked every day of his life until he passed away at eighty-four. Dad used to tell me that when you enjoy your work and your work is your hobby, it is not work. For some people the best way to retire may be to continue working.

For others, rather than being a time of easing back and retiring into old age or continuing to work in one's old job or career, it can be a time of personal growth and an opportunity to explore other interests, callings, and vocations. It can be a time of freedom to do what you always wanted to do but could not because you had to earn money and the pressure of work prevented you from pursuing the dreams and interests that were in tune with your values and beliefs. Here is a list of a few areas that you might want to explore:

1. Teaching courses at a local law school or university
2. Pro-bono work
3. Writing
4. Photography, gardening, travel, or other hobbies
5. Serving as a director on a for-profit or nonprofit board
6. Counseling
7. Volunteering

Planning Your Retirement

One way to begin to visualize getting older, your mortality, and retirement is to think about the amount of time that you have left on this earth. For instance, say you are sixty-five and may live to be eighty. Thus, you have fifteen years left and this is your planning horizon. Retirement planning is deciding on how to use this time. It is about the process of determining what you will do in your retirement and putting a plan into practice. As the amount of time left to you decreases, its value increases to the point where it will be more valuable than monetary assets. It will be more valuable that a new house, a new car, a new boat, or a chest full of cash. Time enjoying life, being with your family, and spiritual renewal will become more important than earning money. The greatest change when you retire is how you will use your time.

Retirement planning begins with taking the time to think about how you will use your time. If you live fifteen years beyond your retirement, you will have approximately 28,800 hours that will have to be filled with retirement activities (five days a week, eight hours a day, forty-eight weeks, for fifteen years) Start by creating an interest activity list, a time plan, and then DECIDE, PLAN, and ACT.

Options include:

1. Continue working in your present situation;
2. Continue to work for compensation but in another occupation; or
3. Retire and pursue recreational and other retirement activities without compensation.

Two Short Stories—Two Lawyers Who Wanted to Work Forever

The first story occurred five years ago. I was engaged to referee a dispute between the founding partner of a sixteen-attorney firm and the other partners. Five years earlier the founding partner and the other partners agreed on a five-year phasedown program for the sixty-five-year-old founding partner. Each year he would reduce his work schedule, and his draw would be reduced in proportion. He would transition his client and management responsibilities to other partners in the firm. The founding partner and other partners signed an agreement that was not mentioned or discussed again for five years.

Near the end of the fifth year, at the annual partner's meeting, the partners asked the founding partner what his plans were after he left the firm at the end of the year. The founding partner was shell-shocked, taken aback, and in denial. He had simply not thought about the matter again since the document was signed five years ago. He filed his copy and got busy with day-to-day life. His response to his partners was, I am not leaving. His partners' response was that this was our agreement and we expect you to withdraw from the firm by the end of the year. The founding partner responded that he would blow up the firm, start a new firm, and take a majority of the clients with him. The founding partner and the partners were at an impasse and I was engaged to help.

For three months, since the parties were not speaking with one another, I conducted shuttle diplomacy and held separate meetings with the founding partner and the other partners. During one of my early meetings with the founding partner, he stated, "I built this firm, I love coming into the office, this firm has been my life, and I don't have anywhere to go." I quickly realized that the founding partner was not a candidate for full retirement. He received his energy and self-esteem from his law practice and his role in the firm and in the community. For years, the founding partner had not provided legal services to clients. His primarily roles had been that of managing partner and he was the firm's primary rainmaker and innovator.

After numerous meetings with the founding partner and the other partners, the following points were settled:

1. His partnership interest was purchased in accordance with the initial agreement;
2. His managing partner duties were transitioned to another partner in the firm;
3. The role of director of business development was created for the founding partner, who would serve an Of Counsel capacity, with compensation to be based upon a minimal salary supplemented with a commission for new business originated; and
4. Specific performance expectations and accountabilities for the founding partner were outlined.

At the end of the day, the issues were resolved and an accommodation was made for a partner who did not want to retire. While he is no longer a partner, he still has a role, is still contributing, and has preserved his self-esteem.

The second story occurred two years ago. At that time, the senior partner was seventy-five years old, with numerous health issues. He is partially blind in both eyes, experiences memory loss, has difficulty walking without a cane, and falls asleep at his desk for most of the afternoon. He has lost several clients and others have complained about his client service and requested other attorneys be assigned to their matters. A year ago, the senior partner's wife passed away. They had no children. The senior partner has no other family, no outside interests—the firm is his life and he considers it his home. The other partners have asked the senior partner about his retirement plans and he remains evasive, continuing to push out the timeline. His partners do not have the heart to thrust him out, so the cycle of poor lawyer morale, poor productivity, financial underperformance, and client dissatisfaction continues. This lawyer wants to continue to work forever whether he should or not.

CHAPTER 3

What Other Firms Are Doing

A decade ago, only the more proactive, well-managed law firms had in place programs and provisions for senior partner succession and transition. A majority of firms simply had not addressed or even given serious thought to the eventual retirement and exit of their senior partners. However, in the last five years, I have seen a lot of interest in succession, transition, and exit planning. The avalanche of baby boomers reaching retirement age has fueled this interest. Firms from the largest to the smallest are getting proactive and actively addressing succession and transition of senior partners. Some are putting in place formal programs, while others are at least addressing succession and transition informally using ad hoc approaches.

The Altman Weil 2013 Transition Survey gives us a glimpse of what other law firms are doing. Here are a few highlights from their survey concerning responding law firms (Clay 2013, 38):

- 26.9 percent have formal succession planning programs in place;
- 48.9 percent have informal ad hoc approaches to succession planning;

- 18.4 percent are working on succession planning programs; and
- 5.8 percent are not doing anything with regard to succession planning.

The appropriate approach to succession planning will depend upon firm size, type of practice, age of the lawyer or lawyers in the firm, and readiness and willingness of other lawyers in the firm to assume equity ownership positions.

Two Detailed Case Studies

The following case studies illustrate approaches that some of our law firm clients have taken.

Case Studies

Bigger, Better & Best (Fictitious Names Used)

A CASE STUDY OF A NINE-ATTORNEY LAW FIRM WHOSE THREE FOUNDERS WANTED TO RETIRE AND NEEDED A SUCCESSION AND TRANSITION PLAN

Paul Bigger and George Better graduated in the top of their law school class and upon graduation, joined the same large law firm in Chicago. Both worked in the firm's prestigious litigation department and performed the typical discovery support work that associates do in large law firms, beginning with document reviews and later graduating to preparation of pleadings and taking of depositions. After ten years with the firm, the two attorneys, now non-equity partners, were now trying cases, bringing in clients, and controlling small books of business. The firm recently announced a freeze on admitting new equity partners. Paul and George had worked together on some large cases and they were frustrated that after ten years they had not made partner. They began meeting and discussing starting a litigation boutique firm offering big firm know-how, in a small boutique firm package, at small firm prices. On January 2, 1990, they launched their new firm, Bigger & Better. Paul and George formed a partnership, with each having an equal interest. Compensation was based upon partnership interest, and each partner shared equally in firm profits.

The firm was very successful at obtaining quality clients and began hiring additional lawyers. After eight years, the firm had a roster of top-tier Fortune 500 clients and five attorneys. Revenues and profits per partner were on par with large firms in Chicago. In 2004 the firm admitted Joanne Best as an equity partner with an equal interest. Joanne paid $75,000 for her equity interest over twelve months.

Ownership shares were now one-third each, with compensation based on partnership shares. The firm continued to do well. Joanne worked hard, generated working attorney fees close to Paul and George's, and developed a solid book of business. The firm added two additional associates.

In early 2012, the firm created a non-equity partner tier and promoted two associates, Brenda Cox and Jim Brown, to non-equity partner. Brenda and Jim were good workers and generated adequate working attorney fees. However, neither had a book of business, nor were they demonstrating the ability to bring in clients. Associates received a base salary, $40 per hour for each billable hour over 1,800 annual billable hours, and a discretionary bonus. Non-equity partners received the same compensation packages that the associates received. In addition, non-equity partners also received, on cases where they were the responsible attorney, 10 percent of the working attorney fees of other timekeepers logging time on the matter.

In the fall of 2012, there was a surprise announcement. Paul and George, both now sixty, hoped to retire in the next few years and wanted to begin succession planning. They asked me to assist them with the process and advised me that Joanne, who was ten years younger, would be willing to be part of the firm's transition. However, Joanne would not be an owner by herself and would want other partners to share the burden of ownership. The firm envisioned extending equity partnership offers to the two non-equity partners, Brenda and Jim. The firm's partnership agreement provided for the terms of the buyout of the equity partners. The firm also had precedent for buy-in terms from when Joanne bought in.

I spent a day with the partners at their office and met with all the other lawyers individually. Later the three partners joined me for a day at our offices. I reviewed with them my thoughts and the following observations:

1. Brenda and John have a long way to go in terms of maturity and experience in order to be able to retain existing clients and obtain new clients;
2. Brenda and John are grinders generating working attorney dollars. They need to become minders (client relationship managers) and eventually finders (originate new client business). A key question is whether, with the unique skillsets of Paul and George, Joanna, Brenda, and John will be able to retain a majority of the existing clients;
3. The equity partners need to help Brenda and John bulk up their individual professional brands;
4. The equity partners need to begin assigning Brenda and John as responsible attorney on more client matters and doing all they can to inject Brenda and John into client relationships; and
5. The equity partners need to put in place a succession and transition plan as soon as possible.

(*continued*)

Paul, George, Joanne, and I discussed their various options, including:

1. Internal transition by admitting one or both of the two non-equity partners to equity partnership;
2. Bringing in a lateral partner and admitting to equity partnership;
3. Merging with another firm; or
4. Selling the fixed assets, paying all the bills, billing out the work in process, collecting the receivables, helping the employees find jobs in other law firms, and closing the doors.

We discussed the mechanics of developing a succession/transition plan and I advised that the WHO dictates that WHAT. In other words, many law firms find that they start down one path and end up on another. Not all non-equity partners and associates want to own a law firm. Not all lateral and merger candidates will be a good fit for the firm and its culture. The key is the right relationship and sometimes that takes the form of making someone at the firm a partner, bringing in a seasoned lateral, or merging with another firm. Therefore, succession/transition plans have to be flexible. Often the key is not getting stuck in creating complex succession plans at the onset. The firm should establish timelines, outline a general course of action, generate some momentum, and see where that leads the firm. Then, once the firm can see what direction it is going in, they can begin to build their plan.

I advised the partners that it takes time to implement a successful transition of clients and management roles and suggested a five-year timeline. I suggested to Paul and George that the next step would be to determine their retirement dates. I also asked them to think about their retirement dates and get back to the rest of us. Two weeks later, they informed us that they were unwilling to stay on for five years and that their retirement date would be in three years.

The equity partners considered and discussed their options and all agreed that they preferred to go the route of internal transition. While firm legacy was not an important issue, the partners wanted continuity for their clients and continued employment for their employees. The partners reviewed financial performance for the past five years and added Brenda and Jim's compensation and benefits back to the profit pool to determine an appropriate initial partnership interest percentage for Brenda and Jim. The partners decided to offer Brenda an 8-percent partnership interest and Jim a 7-percent interest for an initial cash capital contribution of $25,000 each, with additional contribution required when they would acquire additional shares in the future.

The equity partners and I met with Brenda and Jim to feel them out and see if there was a tentative interest in equity ownership. We discussed with them Paul, George, and Joanne's future goals and provided them with financial summary of revenue, expenses, and net income. We discussed what equity partnership would mean, the upside potential of being an equity partner, the initial capital contribution, and other matters. The equity partners asked Brenda and Jim to think about whether they were tentatively interested and if so, to get back with the partners within the next few weeks. The equity partners also advised Brenda and Jim that if one or both expressed a tentative interest, the firm would prepare a detailed proposal, which would include five years of firm tax returns and financial statements, partnership agreement, building lease, and a detailed client and management transition plan. Ten days later Brenda and Jim advised the equity partners that they were interested and would like to take the next step.

The equity partners asked me to start putting together the proposal package and a week later I received an e-mail from Paul and George advising me that Joanne, the third equity partner, advised them that she had second thoughts and did not want to participate in a transition with Brenda and Jim. Burnt out and stressed, Joanne wished to retire at the same time as Paul and George. Based upon this turn of events, Paul and George advised Brenda and Jim that they were putting equity partnership on hold and were considering other options such as possible merger with a larger firm.

The equity partners and I had several discussions and concluded that due to the youth and limited minding and finding abilities of Brenda and Jim, the best option for the firm would be to merge with a large firm with extensive litigation experience. Jointly we developed a short list of potential large firm candidates and a list of what we were looking for from a potential merger. We discussed a strategy for initial approach and I prepared a Confidential Descriptive Memorandum for the firm to use as an initial contact package "leave behind." We then decided to focus on two firms from the short list and Paul and George initiated contact with both firms. To Paul and George's surprise, both firms were very receptive, and Paul, George, and Joanne met with partners from both firms. After two meetings with each firm, financial statements and other documents were exchanged and the due diligence commenced. For Paul, George, and Joanne the most important factor was cultural fit. Money was a secondary consideration. They wanted a home for their clients, attorneys, and staff. Early on, Paul, George, and Joanne took a liking to the first firm they met with—we shall call the firm Adams & Jones. The firm had ninety attorneys, of which only six were equity partners. The firm was still in its first generation and controlled by its founding partners. While a larger firm in comparison to Big, Better & Best, Adams & Jones still possessed a small-firm personality and culture. The partners at Adams & Jones were impressed with Bigger, Better & Best's talent, clients, and financial performance. The firm's client roster included top-tier Fortune 500 companies and their partner earnings were on par with those of Bigger, Better & Best. Discussions progressed rapidly, due diligence was performed, and a decision was made to merge. On January 1, 2014, the firms merged.

(continued)

The merger agreement included the following terms:

- The name of the merged firm would be Adams & Jones.
- The existing equity partners of Big, Better & Best would be admitted as non-equity partners.
- The existing non-equity partners of Big, Better & Best would be admitted as non-equity partners.
- Since the office of Big, Better & Best was in a different city and in a city of strategic importance for Adams & Jones, the office would continue operations.
- All existing employees of Big, Better & Best would become employees of Adams & Jones.
- Big, Better & Best would retain fees from existing accounts receivable and work in process on the books prior to the date of the merger.
- Adams & Jones would purchase existing fixed assets.
- Adams & Jones would lease office space in the building presently owned by Big, Better & Best and would have a right of first refusal on the future purchase of said building.
- The three equity partners of Big, Better & Best would retire in three years and would be paid a referral fee (client origination fee) of 20 percent for all business originated for two years after their retirement.
- After retirement, the three equity partners of Big, Better & Best would have the option to continue as Of Counsel with Adams & Jones under the terms of an Of Counsel agreement, with terms to be determined at the time of exercising the option.
- The compensation of the three equity partners of Big, Better & Best would be based upon the net profits of their office.
- The non-equity partners and associates at Big, Better & Best would be paid salaries commensurate with their existing salaries. Future compensation increases would be based upon the compensation system of Adams & Jones.

As of this writing, the merger has been in effect for fifteen months and is going well. Paul, George and Joanne are looking forward to their retirement, buying homes in the Southwest, and pursuing post-retirement interests.

Law Office of Mary Allison (Fictitious Names Used)

A CASE STUDY OF A SOLO ATTORNEY THAT AFTER TWO UNSUCCESSFUL ATTEMPTS TOOK A PHASED APPROACH TO A MERGER WITH A SMALL SOLE OWNER PRACTICE

Upon graduation from law school, Mary Allison landed a job in a small law firm owned by Michael Brown. Michael's practice was limited to estate planning, estate administration, and real estate. Michael was in his early fifties and it was his hope that Mary might be his eventual successor. Mary was Michael's first associate. She worked hard for the next five years, on Michael's matters as well as her own. After seven years with the firm, Mary was bringing in enough business that she only had time available to work on her own matters. She was generating 50 percent more fee revenue than Michael and bringing in more business. On several occasions, Mary brought up the subject of partnership but Michael advised her that he was not interested in having a partner. Mary felt that she was not being adequately compensated, had no voice in the firm, and little control over her future. After ten years, Mary left the firm and started her own firm concentrating on estate planning, estate administration, and real estate. She brought along her clients and the paralegal who had worked for her at Michael's firm for the past ten years.

Mary was a natural and her firm was successful from startup. She was a good attorney and had an excellent bedside manner. She truly cared for her clients, which was evident from the repeat business and client referrals. Mary built up a strong referral source base of banks, financial planners, accountants, attorneys, insurance agents, church members, and community leaders. Other than her website and annual holiday cards, no other marketing investments were necessary. Mary enjoyed being a "solo" and had no desire to grow any larger than herself, her paralegal, and her staff assistant. She never had the need to hire another attorney, as with the help of her paralegal, she was able to handle the business by herself.

Fast-forward the calendar thirty-five years to 2013. Mary is now seventy. Her husband passed away a year ago and her children are living out of town. Her paralegal is sixty but needs to work another ten years as her husband is deceased and she needs the income. Mary is having some health problems but is still in relatively good health. She loves her clients, enjoys her work, and wants to continue working as long as she can. However, Mary realizes that she will not be able to continue working forever and needs to begin planning for the eventual succession and transition of her practice.

Mary retained our firm to assist her with succession planning and advised me that her long-range goals, in order of priority, were:

1. To take care of her clients
2. To provide continued employment for her paralegal
3. To receive fair compensation for her practice

We discussed various options, including:

1. Hiring and mentoring a young associate who could eventually buy into the practice
2. Selling the practice
3. Merging with another firm
4. Forming an Of Counsel relationship with another lawyer or law firm

(*continued*)

Mary quickly ruled out hiring an associate and mentoring. She believed that she had neither the time to devote nor a sufficient volume of business to support an associate's salary. Since Mary wanted to continue to practice as long as possible, she did not want to sell her practice prematurely due to the ethical requirements and restrictions that would have to be satisfied with a practice sale. She was open to an Of Counsel relationship or merger with another law firm.

Mary had been talking with another attorney, Sally, who had recently left her in-house position with a bank trust department, regarding a possible future relationship where Sally would provide backup coverage for Mary's practice and eventually buy Mary's practice at such time that Mary should decide to retire. I interviewed Sally and had some concerns. I did not believe that Sally had the desire or entrepreneurial ability to own and manage a law practice. However, Mary liked Sally and wanted to work out an arrangement. I suggested a "pilot test" and we structured an affiliate "Of Counsel"–type relationship designed to explore whether the relationship could work. In essence, the "Affiliation Agreement" (Of Counsel) provided:

1. Sally would work at Mary's office one day a week, on Mary's matters;
2. Over time Sally would be introduced to Mary's clients and referral sources;
3. For services provided for Mary's clients, Sally would be paid an hourly rate; and
4. For business that Mary referred to Sally that Mary did not handle or business that Sally referred to Mary, Sally would be paid a referral fee of 20 percent.

Mary and Sally signed the agreement. Two weeks later Mary called me and advised that the arrangement did not work out and they had terminated the relationship. As I suspected, Sally had no real interest in ever owning a law practice and this had become obvious to Mary as they moved forward with the relationship. While Mary was disappointed, she was also gratified that she had started with an exploratory relationship rather than jumping "feet first" into a partnership or other relationship.

We then placed online ads and commenced a search for other candidates. We were looking for other solo attorneys with an established estate planning/administration practice. After meeting with three potential candidates, Mary focused on one candidate, Kathy, who had an established practice in another city approximately fifteen miles away. Kathy was in her early forties and her practice, in addition to handling estate planning and estate administration, handled elder law as well. Both practices generated approximately $300,000 in annual revenues. They visited each other's offices, met each other's staff, and had lunch on three different occasions. Mary and Kathy really liked each other and believed that they could make it work. Kathy's practice was located in a less affluent community and her practice had reached a plateau. She believed that the acquisition of Mary's practice could really jump-start her practice in five years. Mary believed that Kathy would be a good fit for her clients and would provide solid employment for her paralegal.

Mary was cautious after her recent experience with Sally. Mary and Kathy executed the same "pilot test" Affiliation Agreement that Mary and Sally had executed. The relationship proceeded well and they began working together. In addition, since Mary did not handle elder law matters, she began referring those matters to Kathy and received a 20-percent referral fee for those referrals. After six months, we met to discuss the next step. Mary wanted to merge, but Kathy was not ready for a merger. Mary was still unclear about her actual retirement timeline but suggested that she wanted to work another five years. Therefore, she was uncomfortable with actually selling the practice at this time. Kathy and Mary agreed that Kathy would become "Of Counsel" with Mary's firm and Mary would promote the relationship to her existing and prospective clients. Mary and Kathy also agreed to the terms for the purchase of Mary's practice when Mary decided to sell her practice in the future. Mary retained a business attorney to draft a formal "Of Counsel" agreement. The "Of Counsel" agreement contained similar provisions as the Affiliation Agreement, but with a lot more legalese. It also contained a right of first refusal for Kathy to purchase the practice when Mary decided to sell in accordance with terms outlined in an attached Practice Sale Agreement. The terms of the Practice Sale Agreement provided for a 50,000-dollar payment at closing and 20 percent of practice revenue for five years with the 50,000-dollar payment serving as a credit against future payments that would be due. Mary and Kathy signed the agreements.

The relationship continued to go well. Mary's clients liked Kathy and Mary's paralegal and Kathy worked well together. Mary now had backup and coverage and was able to take more time off. Kathy received additional revenues in the form of payments for her time spent on Mary's matters and elder law referrals. Mary received referral fees from the elder law matters referred to Kathy. However, after one year, the relationship fell apart and Mary and Kathy terminated their relationship. The problem resulted from Mary's unwillingness to commit to a retirement timeline and micromanaging Kathy and treating her as an associate rather than a peer business owner.

After the relationship fell apart, Mary contacted me and advised me of what had happened. I scolded her and advised that if she did not commit to some sort of a specific timeline and recognize that since her goal was "succession and transition" she should not try to enforce her approach on another attorney, she might not find anyone interested in working with her. She began searching

(*continued*)

again and met with a few candidates, with no success. Finally, I introduced her to Brian, the owner of an estate planning/administration/elder law firm in a community approximately twenty miles away. Unlike the other candidates that Mary had met with, Brian had a larger practice that included four other attorneys and five staff members. Brian's practice had hit a revenue plateau at 1.1 million dollars and he was looking to expand his practice into other communities. After several meetings, Mary and Brian advised me that they wanted to merge their practices. Based upon Mary's past record of accomplishment, I suggested a two-phased approach. A four-month "Of Counsel" relationship to explore feasibility and compatibility would constitute Phase I and a merger of the practices would constitute Phase II. The same Of Counsel agreement with the right of first refusal and related sale agreement that was used with Kathy was executed for the exploratory Phase I. A preliminary term sheet outlining the possible terms of the merger was prepared and discussed. Mary and Brian agreed that they would further develop the terms for the merger as they progressed through Phase I.

The relationship went well and after four months, Mary and Brian merged their practices. Since both firms were proprietorships, Brian formed an LLC, Mary merged her firm into the LLC, and they executed an Operating Agreement, which, among other things, established ownership interests, capital contributions, compensation, and Mary's retirement payout after three years. Mary and Brian continued to operate and manage their respective offices until Mary retired, at which time Brian took over and staffed Mary's office with an associate attorney. A few details of the merger included:

- Mary retained the cash in bank and collected and retained cash from her accounts receivable, and work in process;
- Mary's fixed assets were sold to the LLC at appraised value and credited to her capital account;
- Mary's was admitted with a 40-percent membership interest;
- Compensation was based upon a "profit center" approach, with each office being treated as a separate profit center;
- Mary agreed to retire within three years after the date of the merger and her payout would be based upon 20 percent of gross practice revenue from her practice location for five years; and
- Decision making and voting was based upon ownership interest.

This time Mary got it right. The merger was successful and Mary is now retired, in her third year of her five-year payout, and enjoying her retirement.

Other Case Illustrations

In addition to the approaches outlined in the two previous case studies, here are somc approaches taken by some of our other client firms:

- Two-lawyer partner firm sells off a non-legal tax preparation practice (one practice area) that generated $300,000 a year in gross fee revenues to a CPA firm. The practice area was sold for $300,000, with $250,000 paid at closing and the balance paid over a three-year period with a provision for sale price deduction if a certain percentage of clients defected. It took one year to find a suitable candidate through advertising placed in the state CPA Society print and online journal and to effect the sale.
- Sole owner three-attorney Social Security disability practice sells shareholder interests to an associate over time. While the owner, who was in his early fifties, wanted to continue to working for another ten years or so, he hoped to take a phased approach to transition and get a pair of "golden handcuffs" on an associate or two. He started with an associate who had been with the firm for many years. A valuation methodology (using a multiple times average of gross revenue over the past five years) was created to determine an initial buy-in value. An initial buy-in amount was determined with an initial pay-in amount, with the remainder paid in over a period of three years. This entitled the associate to a 10-percent interest and after the pay-in amount had been fully paid off, the associate could, with the consent of the owner, acquire additional interest based upon the same valuation methodology and the five-year average gross revenue figure at that time. Other associates considered worthy of equity ownership would also be able to participate in the program in the future.
- Sole owner of a three-attorney estate planning and elder law LLC firm admits two associates to membership and retires a year later. Each associate initially made a 25,000-dollar capital contribution for minority interests. The firm deposited these funds into a special working capital savings account for use after retirement of the owner. After one year, the owner retired and received a cash distribution

for the balance of his capital account and retirement payments for three years based upon 1.5 times his five-year IRS 1040 Schedule C earnings. His shares were distributed evenly to each associate. The associates also signed a lease for office space, which the owner owned through a separate LLC. The lease provided a right of first refusal to purchase the building at a future date. The owner continued to work for the firm as Of Counsel.

CHAPTER 4

Where and When to Start

The most important ingredient of a successful succession, transition, and exit strategy is to start early. In Chapter 1, I presented case studies of three firms that waited until it was too late. Waiting too long can result in the following consequences:

- Loss of key clients;
- Loss of senior legal talent and leadership;
- Inability of firm owners, especially founders, to effectively capitalize on goodwill and sweat equity built up over the years;
- Unfunded retirement for partners and/or owners;
- Failure to protect family wealth in the event of unexpected life changing events;
- Failure to protect partners, employees, and clients from unexpected life-changing events;
- Defections and firm breakups caused by younger lawyers unwilling to finance departing partner buyouts from future earnings; and

- In the case of solo and small firms, having to turn out the lights and close the door with little or no compensation for the sweat equity and goodwill of the practice.

As you begin the planning process, you will have to:

Come to Terms with Aging and Eventual Retirement

At a personal level, you should admit to yourself that, regardless of your current age, you are getting older and you will eventually retire—one way or another. The sooner you begin thinking about this, the better prepared you will be. I have many clients who have started their succession/transition planning in their mid-forties and early fifties. Unfortunately, however, many have waited until their mid-sixties and early seventies. For these folks there has been little time to make adequate preparation and often, adverse consequences have resulted. At an absolute minimum, you should start your succession/transition planning *five years* before you plan to begin your transition. It simply takes this long to put your house in order, to locate or groom succession/transition candidates, find a candidate law firm interested in your practice, and transition clients and management responsibilities. Here are a few ideas to help you get started:

Multi-Owner Firms

1. Stop giving succession and transition lip service—if you are serious, put in place organizational systems that will facilitate the process.
2. Put in place a firm strategic plan that incorporates a succession plan.
3. Host a partner brainstorming retreat to address key questions surrounding your firm's plan and identify a course of action that will be supported by all.
4. Make long-term plans for the firm.
5. Ensure partner accountability.
6. Implement funded retirement plan for partners and other employees in the firm.

7. Consider Key-Personal life insurance to fund buyout of ownership interests of partners who die or become disabled.
8. Execute partnership/operating/shareholder and buy–sell agreements.
9. Consider unfunded buyout plans that that are ully paid by the end of the wind-down or transition period.
10. Urge partners to think about and plan for retirement. They should start early and begin on a wind-down program at least five years before they are ready to retire or exit. Each partner should decide when they want to exit the practice and begin a disciplined phase-down (wind-down) in which legal skills, leadership and management, and client relationships are transitioned to the next generation of attorneys in the firm.

Sole Owner and Solo Practices

1. Decide when you want to retire and leave your firm.
2. Determine how much cash or annual cash flow you need when you exit the firm.
3. Fund a retirement plan in the early years of your practice and project how much income it will generate at various exit points.
4. Determine to whom you would like to transfer the practice. (Family members in law school, other attorneys in the firm, another firm, etc.)
5. Based on future cash flow, ascertain how much the firm is worth today. Value the practice.
6. Begin implementing management strategies that will maximize the future value of the firm—before you exit and afterward.
7. Institutionalize the firm, so that it is not uniquely you.
8. Determine whether the firm is even saleable.
9. Draft and implement a succession/exit plan. Ensure that it incorporates safeguards for your clients, employees, and family if the unexpected happens to you.
10. Take steps to protect your family's wealth.
11. To retire and exit successfully, you need:

    A plan—a roadmap that outlines the process and helps you decide on where you want to go and how you will get there.

Timeline—a disciplined implementation timetable keyed to your succession/transition/exit plan.

Start Early—Getting ready for exit takes time. Start early—five to eight years before you are ready to retire or exit.

Decide—When do you want to leave the practice?

Decide—How much cash you will need when you exit?

Decide—To whom you want to transfer the practice?

At a firm level, especially if you are a member of a multi-partner firm, start sharing your ideas and plans with your partners. Have an ongoing dialog with your partners. Review the firm's partnership/operating/shareholder agreement. If the firm has a succession/transition plan, review it. After going through these documents, determine how the firm's policy regarding retirement will affect your retirement timeline, compensation, and payout. Does the policy require mandatory retirement at a certain age? Ascertain whether the policy provides for phasedown. How does the phasedown handle management and client transition? Is there an "Of Counsel" provision after retirement? Reach an agreement with your partners concerning your retirement timeline, client and management transition, and retirement payout or return on invested capital.

Review Your Personal Financial Situation

Often the reason many lawyers work into their seventies and eighties is not that they do not want to retire—it is that they financially must continue to earn an income. They failed to save for retirement. In their younger years, they spent all they earned on elaborate homes, expensive cars, expensive vacations, and numerous other luxuries and now they simply do not have the savings to support full retirement. Review your financial situation and determine whether your savings will support full retirement and at what age. If your savings are not adequate, determine what you can do to change the situation between now and when you plan on retiring. If you have waited too long to save for retirement, determine the lifestyle you will live and if there is a financial shortfall, how you will earn the additional income. This may affect your retirement date or require you to continue to work after retirement.

Explore Post-Retirement Interests and Develop Plan for Pursuing These Interests

Begin thinking about your legacy—how you want to be remembered, and your contribution to family, friends, and society. Think about other interests outside of law. If law has been your life, consider looking into some hobbies. Experiment with a few. If you must still earn income, think about how you will earn that income. Think about other forms of employment using your legal training or a completely different occupation. If you do not need to earn income, think about volunteer activities.

Establishing General Goals and Timelines

Think about your retirement as a project or a case. Start with the end date in mind and develop your other goals and timelines. The end date will be the date you want to leave the firm. Examples of possible dates might include:

- The date you want to leave the firm;
- The date you become Of Counsel;
- The date you retire;
- The date you begin transitioning your management responsibilities;
- The date you begin client transition;
- The date you begin your phasedown;
- The date you announce your decision to your partners;
- The date you admit associates to equity partnership or merge or sell your firm (sole owner firm);
- The date you commence search for candidates to sell to or merge your firm with (solo practitioner);
- The date you prepare a confidential descriptive memorandum regarding the firm and its goals concerning sale or merger;
- The date you value the firm; and
- The date you commerce firm management and other improvements designed to improve the future value of the firm.

CHAPTER 5

Firm Size: Challenges, Issues, and Impact upon Succession and Transition/Exit

The size of the firm will present different retirement succession, transition, and exit challenges. Firm size will affect the number of moving parts, specific steps that a firm will have to take, and the overall timeline. Solo practitioners and sole owners will have the most moving parts and face the greatest challenges.

Solo Practitioners

Solo practitioners have the greatest challenge since they have no associates or anyone in place to transition the practice to. Therefore, the practitioner must hire and groom an associate that could buy the firm or become a partner and eventually buy out the owner's interests, sell the firm to another firm, or merge with another firm. Other options would be to become Of Counsel with another firm or simply close down the practice. This takes time.

Hiring and Grooming an Associate

Hiring and grooming an associate can be problematic for the solo. If he does not have sufficient business and the associate does not originate business, the associate will be an expense and the owner's net earnings will suffer. Other issues include:

- The associate may have no interest in owning a law firm. He or she may simply want to be a lawyer, have a job, and not be a business owner.
- The owner could invest several years in mentoring and training an associate, only to lose the associate to another firm in two or three years. The owner's succession/transition/exit plan is now out the window and he or she has to start all over again, with less time remaining to do so.
- The owner may not have the time or inclination to groom and train an associate.

Sell the Firm to Another Lawyer or Law Firm

The owner can sell the firm to another lawyer or law firm. This option works best when the practitioner is actually ready to retire and quit practicing. Often this is not the case and the restrictions on sale of law practice levied by a state's rules of professional conduct, in particular Rule 1.17, may make this option undesirable. Locating desirable candidates will take time and a well-planned search process may have to be initiated. Our experience has been that this can take a year or longer.

Solo practices are often very personal practices with little annual repeat business. Clients of law firms advise us that they hire the lawyer and not the law firm. This makes buyers very cautious due to their concern that the clients and referral sources will not stay and the revenues will not materialize after the owner sells the practice. Therefore, many buyers are not willing to pay cash for a law practice. Our experience has been that most of these practices are sold with payouts over time based upon a percentage of revenues collected over a certain number of years. Usually, the seller stays on in a consulting capacity for a year to help ensure that clients and referral sources stay with the new owner.

Merger with Another Firm

Merger with another lawyer or law firm is another option. This is often a better option for solos that want to gradually phasedown yet continue to practice for a few more years. In essence, they join another firm as an equity or non-equity partner, member, or shareholder and subsequently retire from that firm under pre-agreed-to terms for the payout. The odds are improved for clients and referral sources staying with the merged firm and the merged firm is more committed than a buyer might be under a payout arrangement based upon collected revenues. The solo practitioner has more flexibility in regard to the ability to continue to practice longer, reduced stress, additional support and resources, and gradual phasedown to retirement.

Of Counsel with Another Firm

Forming an Of Counsel relationship with another firm is an option that many solos are taking. Sometimes it is a final arrangement where a solo winds down his or her practice and then joins another firm as an employee or independent contractor. He or she is paid a percentage of collected revenue under a compensation agreement, with different percentages depending upon whether the practitioner brings in the business, the types of services that he or she brings in, or the types of services the firm refers to the practitioner. In other situations, an Of Counsel relationship is used as a practice continuation mechanism that provides the solo with additional resources and support if needed. An Of Counsel relationship can also be used to "pilot test" a relationship prior to merging with another firm. We have had several law firm clients that have taken a phased approach to merger, with Phase I being an Of Counsel "pilot test" exploratory arrangement and Phase II being the actual merger.

Sole Owners

Sole owners are practitioners who have no partners or shareholders but have associates and staff employees. While typically this might be a firm of an owner and a handful of associates and staff, this is not always the case. Our firm has law firm clients that are much larger. For example:

- A twenty-five attorney plaintiff firm with seventy-five staff employees in California with one owner;
- A twenty-four attorney insurance defense firm in Massachusetts with one owner;
- A fourteen-attorney firm with fifty-five staff employees in Missouri with one owner;
- An eight-attorney collection/foreclosure firm with forty staff employees in Ohio with one owner; and
- A six-attorney insurance defense firm in Florida with one owner.

Unlike solo practitioner firms, these firms have associate attorneys on board and often this is the best option for an owner's succession/transition/exit strategy if the owner has hired the type of lawyers that want to own a law firm. Sometimes this is not the case. Often when the practice is larger, the value the owner is seeking is difficult for one associate to swing on his or her own. In these cases, it often makes sense to bring more than one associate in to the equity ownership circle. If internal succession by virtue of sale or admission to equity ownership is not a valid option, the owner can pursue one of the options discussed earlier for the solo practitioner.

Larger Law Firm

In a larger firm, there are other partners in place to transition clients and management responsibilities. Unless the retiring partner has a unique practice niche, the firm usually does not have to go on the hunt for merger candidates or associates to groom. This eliminates many of the challenges and issues that solo practitioners and solo owners face. The initial challenge in a larger firm is to determine who the successor or successors will be to transition clients and management responsibilities. This may be no easy task, especially if the firm is in its first generation and the retiring partner is one of the founders.

Client Transition

In larger firms, clients are more likely to be large, sophisticated ones, possibly Fortune 500 companies, which refer many matters to the firm during the course of a year. Often such clients may be both a *blessing and a curse* for the firm. A blessing in that their business provides the firm with huge legal fees during the course of a year. A curse in that their business represents a large percent of the firm's annual fee collections and a significant business risk if the firm were to lose the client. An effective client transition is critical, takes time, and must be well planned.

Recently I was doing a telephone interview with the general counsel of a Fortune 500 company, which was a client of our law firm client. I asked him if there was an opportunity for the law firm to get additional work in a practice area in which the company had no previous experience with the law firm and, if such an opportunity existed, what the firm needed to do to earn the additional business. Here is his response:

- "Obviously, we currently have other law firms handling that work. However, we have been evaluating those relationships and may be making some changes. There is room for other law firms to earn our business in the practice areas that you have discussed with me.
- I am aware that the law firm does other work other than what we have been using them for—but I am not sure exactly what those areas are.
- In order to begin to forge a relationship into these other service areas:

    1. I need to know specifically what they do;
    2. I need to know who does it;
    3. I need to know how well the person(s) do it;
    4. I need to have a well-established relationship with the person—trust, respect, like the individual, etc.;
    5. I suggest that we start by having the partner in the firm that I have a relationship with begin educating me on the firm's other practice areas and begin introducing me to the other players in the law firm; and
    6. We hire lawyers—not law firms."

Successful client transition—moving clients from one generation to the next—is a major challenge for larger firms. Shifting clients is not an individual responsibility but a firm responsibility. To effectively transition clients the individual lawyer, with clients, must work together with the firm to ensure the clients receive quality legal services throughout the transition process. Both the individual lawyer and the firm must be committed to keeping clients in the firm when the senior attorneys retire. Potential obstacles include:

- The firm's complacency regarding the relationship between the responsible attorney and the client;
- Clients who are uncomfortable with other lawyers in the firm doing their legal work;
- Other lawyers in the firm not being familiar with the client's business;
- Senior attorneys who do not include younger attorneys in meetings with clients; and
- The point lawyer not identifying the appropriate lawyer successor to the client.

Management Transition

In larger firms, partners may have management responsibilities as well as client responsibilities. A retiring partner may be a managing partner, executive committee chair or member, or serve as a chair or member on other firm committees. Retiring partners will have to transition these responsibilities to other partners in the firm.

Transitioning client relationships and management responsibilities effectively can and, where possible, should, take a number of years—preferably five years—typically not less than three years. For this reason, many firms use five-year phasedown programs for retiring partners. These plans provide detailed timelines and action steps for transitioning client relationships and management responsibilities.

CHAPTER 6

Strategies and Approaches

As I discussed in Chapter 5, the biggest challenge for many firms is finding the right WHO.

The *who* dictates the *what*—the actual succession/transition/exit strategy. In other words, many law firms find that they start down one path and end up on another. Not all non-equity partners and associates want to own a law firm. Not all lateral and merger candidates will be a good fit for your firm and culture. The key is the right relationship and sometimes, that takes the form of making someone at the firm a partner, bringing in a seasoned lateral, merging with another firm, or selling the practice. Therefore, succession/transition plans have to be flexible and often the key is to not get stuck in creating complex succession plans at the onset. Establish timelines, outline a general course of action, generate some momentum, and see where that takes you. Then build the plan when you can see where the firm is headed.

Unless the retiring partner in a larger firm has a unique practice that requires the firm to conduct a search for lateral or merger candidates, larger firms will not have to embark on a search. However, solo practitioners and, often, sole owners, will have to explore their options and conduct a search for the following:

- Associate candidates who can be groomed for either partnership or to buy the practice;
- Associates and lateral partner candidates;
- Merger candidates;
- Of Counsel candidates; and
- Practice sale candidates.

This search and exploration often is the most time consuming and difficult part of the process and often the options identified through this process ends up dictating the succession/transition/exit strategy.

Associate Candidates

If a firm has associates, does the firm have the right associates on the bus for the long term? In other words, has the firm hired associates who want to be business owners and own a law firm? Many owners and senior partners in law firms are approaching retirement age and are beginning to think about succession strategies. As they examine their associate lawyer ranks, some partners are often surprised to learn that there may be few takers. While their associates may be great lawyers, they may not bring in business and may not be interested in ownership or partnership. Such firms have hired a bunch of folks that just wanted jobs and have no interest in owning a law firm. While this hiring approach may have satisfied the firm's short-term needs—it may fall short in the long term.

Hiring Associates for the Long Term

Years ago, it seemed that all the associates working in law firms wanted to become a partner in the law firm. This has changed because of the new mix of women and men graduating from law schools and entering the legal profession, changing attitudes toward work–life balance, other opportunities outside law firms, and additional variables. While partnership/ ownership is still important to many, do not assume that all the associates that a firm hires hire will even want to be equity partners—especially if it means a hefty capital contribution and signing personal guarantees for a large amount of firm debt. Has the firm really discussed with their associates their interests in equity ownership individually and as a group? Recently, an associate whom the firm had written off advised me that while she was not interested in equity partnership now due to her present situation in life, she would be in maybe five years, especially if others were brought in as well—in other words, she did not want to have the responsibility alone and be an equity owner by herself.

I suggest that law firms talk with their people and see where they really stand. Help them to begin developing client development and business skills. Depending on you and the other partner's retirement timelines, law firms may have to consider other options such as laterals or merging with another firm.

A key suggestion is to look for entrepreneurial associates when hiring. The desire for ownership of a business is often in a person's blood. Do not start the interview with a discussion from law school until the present. Dig deeper into hobbies, family, and so on that will provide clues as to whether you may be hiring someone who just wants a law job or someone that eventually wants to own or be a partner in a law firm.

Implement a Law Firm Associate Career Progression/Partnership Admission Program

A common complaint that I hear from interviews of associates is lack of feedback on short-term performance and what it takes to "make partner" and how they are progressing toward eventual partnership. During a recent interview, an associate listed the following major points of interest:

1. What does it take to become a partner—consideration criteria? What do I have to do?
2. What is the timeline for consideration?
3. How am I doing? Am I partnership material?
4. What does partnership mean in this firm?
5. What are the mechanics of admission? (Is there a buy-in?)

I suggest that law firms consider developing what I call a Law Firm Associate Career Progression/Partnership Program and put it in writing. Here is an approach that firms might take:

1. Determine whether the firm wants more partners/owners and if so, how many. Evaluate the appropriate ratio.
2. Consider non-equity partners as a first step and determine what that means.
3. Establish a minimum number of years for consideration.
4. Determine competencies and expectation for associate development and document.
5. Develop an associate performance evaluation form and conduct formal annual evaluations.
6. Develop partner admission criteria (associate to non-equity and non-equity to equity partner) and document.
7. Write up an overall program document and include as attachments the competencies document, the performance evaluation form, and the admission criteria document.
8. Present the program to associates in a live meeting format to launch the program.

Regarding equity partnership, make the criteria tough and require a buy-in or capital contribution. Most firms, for the equity partnership tier, should require business development and a client following.

Associate Performance Evaluations

One of the most frequent complaints I hear during interviews with associates in law firms of all sizes is lack of specific detailed feedback, unclear or non-existent expectations concerning their performance and future career progression, and vague informal performance reviews.

Here are a few suggestions:

1. Institute a system where associates, especially when they are new, have a chance to work with all of the partners in the firm.

2. A managing partner should solicit feedback from partners, meet monthly with each associate, and discuss their performance during their first two years of employment with the firm.
3. Annually conduct formal performance reviews with each associate. Before the review obtain specific feedback from each of the partners and have each partner complete a written review of each associate using the associate performance rating form. Ask each associate to conduct a self-evaluation using the firm's associate performance rating form and then conduct a review with each associate. The review should be detailed, specific, and developmental, with specific goals and timelines established. Document the review in the associate performance rating form.
4. Consider developing an associate career progression program (partnership track) and committing it to writing. The program should outline the timeline for first consideration for partnership, competencies and performance factors, what partnership means in your firm, how an associate becomes a partner, buy-in or capital contribution requirements, voting, and so on.
5. Be honest and open with associates—do not try to be Santa Claus. Tell them the truth, have the difficult discussions, and make the tough calls. Be accessible.

Mentoring Law Firm Associates: Getting the Basics Right

A law firm's greatest asset is its people, and its associates are the firm's future. Lack of mentoring is one of the biggest complaints that we hear from associates in on-site interviews. While your firm may be too small for a comprehensive formal mentoring program, the firm should at least explore an informal program. Start with baby steps and go from there.

The keys to successful mentoring relationships involve the mentor and mentee deciding on the logistics up front. Many potential mentoring pairs fail to form because the parties did not agree on the little things up front. Below are tips designed to help both participants in formal and informal programs:

1. **Meeting schedule:** Decide on an approximate meeting schedule. Suggest that meetings be scheduled at least once a month.

2. **Means to schedule meetings:** Share the best way to get on each other's calendar.
3. **Scheduled meetings:** Do not wait until the end of one meeting to schedule the next. Always have the next two or three meetings on the calendar.
4. **Length of program/partnership:** For formal programs, the firm may suggest a length of time to meet (usually a year). For informal mentoring, suggest having a date on the calendar to review goals and examine the relationship.
5. **Confidentiality:** Mentors and mentees need to discuss what confidentiality means to them. It is the foundation of trust, which is the basic currency of mentoring.

Associates and Lateral Equity Partner Candidates

Your firm believes you have identified the right person, or one you *believe* is the right person, for partnership. However, just because the associate has been a good associate does not mean that the associate will be a good partner—the relationship will be different. At least the associate is somewhat of a known quantity since you know the associate and have worked with the associate for several years.

Here are a few ideas that you might consider:

1. Outline goals and expectations for the relationship;
2. Meet with your associate/lateral candidate and identify his/her goals and expectations for the relationship;
3. Determine how much control over the practice and decision making you and or the firm is willing to give up;
4. Determine how much and for how long you are willing to make less if the associate/lateral candidate does not bring in business or you don't initially have enough work;
5. Determine whether the associate/lateral candidate will be expected to bring in business, and what the timeline is;
6. Think about the firm you want to build—firm-first or lone ranger (team-based or individual practices);
7. Decide on firm name: whether it will or should change, the impact on image and clients, and so on;

8. Decision as to capital contribution or buy-in: yes or no, how much, and a timeline for payment;
9. Ownership percentages;
10. Voting;
11. Compensation; and
12. Withdrawal arrangements.

Once you reach agreement on these issues and general terms, craft a suitable partnership or operating agreement that you can both live with.

Should You Consider a Lateral?

Initially, consider and decide upon the actual goals and objectives that you hope to achieve by bringing in the lateral and your particular requirements and specifications for the candidate. Start by focusing on the person, then move to the other areas that must be considered. It is critical that you get the right person.

Here are a few ideas to help you get started:

1. Do some research on the law firm that the candidate is with now in order to understand the culture and environment in which he/she has been working, potential conflicts, referral issues, and so on.
2. What are the reasons that he/she is considering leaving the firm?
3. What is the candidate's experience and professional history?
4. What practice area does he/she work? Clients served?
5. Can the candidate bring in clients?
6. Is the candidate's practice compatible with your practice and needs?
7. Assemble a candidate financial profile—billings and collections for past five years; working, originating, and billing attorney figures; realization; write-offs; and so on. (If you can't get financials, get what you can—at the very least, get tax returns of the candidate to determine what he/she has been making.)
8. Access the financial health portfolio of client, if clients will be coming along with the candidate.
9. Determine whether a level of synergism will result because of the arrangement.
10. Does a deal make business sense?

Do You Really Want Partners?

You may want to ask yourselves whether you want employees or partners. What is the criteria for becoming an equity partner? Is client development part of that criterion? Should they contribute capital? If they are not adding value to the firm in terms of growth, you are diluting the earnings pool and reducing the size of the pie for yourselves. Personally, I think in small firms criteria for becoming an equity partner should include a client development requirement/expectation and a capital contribution. They should have some skin in the game, contributing capital and signing up for their share of the liabilities. I also believe they should then be included in the inner circle.

Capital Accounts

Typically, a buy-in or capital contribution is not required for non-equity partners, nor do I recommend such. Often, non-equity partners are salaried and may participate in some form of an incentive bonus system tied to individual, team, or firm financial performance. They are also not required to assume any responsibility for any of the firm's financial liabilities or debts.

If you intend on bringing in the associates/laterals as equity partners, this is another matter. I believe that all new equity partners should be expected to contribute capital and have some "skin in the game." Whenever a firm admits a new partner, the firm should require the new partner to contribute capital. Increasingly, a partner's capital requirement should bear a relationship to the partner's ownership interest and share of profits. You may want to allow new partners a reasonable period to fund their capital accounts—say five years—or help them arrange favorable terms at your bank to finance their capital accounts. Some firms use bank credit lines instead of capital contributions to pay routine firm expenses and partner draws during periods when cash flow is tight. It has been my experience that many firms that follow this practice have ongoing financial challenges and problems. *The reality is that many firms are under-capitalized.* Make the criteria tough and resist the temptation to make everyone a partner.

Merger Candidates

Another option would be to merge with another firm. It all comes down to whether the relationship is right for you and your firm. While mergers can be a valid option, making them work is often another matter. Our experience has been that one-third to one-half of all mergers fail to meet expectations due to cultural misalignment and personnel problems. Do not try to use a merger or acquisition as a life raft, for the wrong reasons and as your sole strategy. Successful mergers are based upon a sound integrated business strategy that creates synergy and a combined firm that produces greater client value than either firm can produce alone.

There can be a whole list of reasons for failure, including poor financial performance, attorney defections, loss of key clients, and leadership and management issues. However, it has been our experience that most failures have been the result of poor cultural fit—the wrong WHO. The merging firms—after they have moved past conflict checks and excitement about new client potential—jump immediately to an examination of practice economics and the financials. They fail to perform proper due diligence on the people. It is critical that firms ensure that cultural due diligence is a key component of the merger assessment process. Philosophies, personalities, and lifestyles should be generally compatible. The partners should like each other and have a common vision of the firm's future, and the deal should make sense. *The question is not the what (merge) but the who (people).*

You should do all the due diligence that you can (starting with the people), then move through the rest of the process. Right reasons for merging might include:

- Improve the firm's competitive position;
- Increase specialization by obtaining additional expertise;
- Expand into other geographic regions;
- Add new practice areas;
- Increase or decrease client base; and
- Improve and/or solidify client relationships.

Start by thinking about the reasons that your firm wants to merge and your objectives. Ask yourself the following questions.

- Do you want to practice in a large firm? If not, what is the largest firm in which you would want to practice?
- What is driving the desire to merge?
- If the desire to merge is being driven by a desire to retreat from internal problems, what have you done to address these issues internally?
- Is your name, or the existing firm name, being part of the firm name important to you?
- What are your expectations and objectives for a merger?
- What are you looking from a merger partner?
- Make sure that you look for a complimentary fit. If you are weak in firm leadership, management, and administration, look for a firm that is strong in these areas. Strong leadership, management, and administration may be hard to find in a firm that has fewer than twenty-five attorneys.

Getting Started Preparing for a Merger

Start with determining your merger objectives. Why do you want to merge? What do you hope to achieve? Is merger compatible with your strategic plan? What size of firm are you considering?

Once you are sure that merger exploration, in general, makes sense, you should ensure that your house is in order. In other words, what can the firm be doing to enhance its value and/or marketability? For example:

- Do you have a business or strategic plan? If not, how will you convince a potential merger partner that you have a plan for the future and know where you are going? Maybe now is a good time to work on that plan.
- Work on and clean up your financials. Improve the financial performance of your practice. Eliminate dead wood. Write off uncollectable accounts receivable and work in process.
- Avoid entering into long-term commitments that might make your firm undesirable to another firm. For example, new long-term leases, risky client matters/cases, loans, admission of new partners, unfunded partner buyouts/retirements, and so on.
- Enhance firm image where you can.
- Develop a first-class firm profile.

Next, develop a merger project plan and begin working the plan. Try to generate enough leads that you can explore merger with several firms rather than engaging in "random merger talks," which often result in isolated merger offers with you having no framework for comparison. Use an outside consulting firm if you need help organizing, identifying candidates, and managing the process.

Once you have merger candidates identified, the real work begins. Here is a general outline of the process:

Merger Assessment (Due Diligence)

Philosophies, personalities, lifestyles, do the partners like each other?, why does the merger make sense?

- Firm Name
- Conflicts
- Economics
- Partner Compensation System Comparisons
- Retirement, Voluntary Withdrawal, Expulsion Policies
- Management Structure
- Practice Compatibility
- Practice Philosophies
- Work Ethic
- Firm Structure
- Associate Management

Merger Implementation

If the two firms decide to proceed with a merger, then the process of merger implementation begins. Start with a term sheet and if the two firms can come to general agreement on terms, execute a merger agreement and put a merger implementation plan in place. Then work the plan. If the merging firms are of similar size (as opposed to a large firm acquiring a smaller firm), a lot of infrastructure work will need to be done, ranging from IT systems, management structure, space, and so on to accommodate the larger entity.

Of Counsel Candidates

"Of counsel" is an approach that many firms are also taking in a variety of forms and formats as well. Of counsel is a lawyer who is employed by a firm to do work but is not an associate or a partner. The American Bar Association defines an "Of Counsel" as follows:

- A part-time practitioner who practices law in association with a firm, but on a basis different from that of the mainstream lawyers in the firm. Such part-time practitioners are sometimes lawyers who have decided to change from a full-time practice, either with that firm or with another, to a part-time one, or sometimes lawyers who have changed careers entirely, as for example former judges or government officials, or attorneys who transition from corporate/in-house practice to law firm practice;
- A retired partner of the firm who, although not actively practicing law, nonetheless remains associated with the firm and available for occasional consultation;
- A lawyer who is, in effect, a probationary partner-to-be: usually this is a lawyer brought into the firm laterally with the expectation of becoming partner after a relatively short period of time; or
- A permanent status in between those of partner and associate, having the quality of tenure, or something close to it, and lacking that of an expectation of likely promotion to full partner status.

These four examples underscore that Of Counsel should not be used to designate more casual relationships that involve: the occasional consultation; the co-counseling of a single case, even if it is of long duration; "a relationship involving only occasional collaborative efforts among otherwise unrelated lawyers or firms"; or a relationship based solely on making or accepting referrals. The name of a lawyer who is Of Counsel to a firm should not appear in the name of the firm unless the lawyer who is Of Counsel is a retired name partner of the firm.

I am seeing Of Counsel arrangements used more and more frequently as a succession/transition/exit strategy and employed in the following ways:

Pre-Merger—Phase I Pilot Test

In Chapter 3 I discussed in a case study how the Law Office of Mary Allison used Of Counsel as a pilot test to explore and test a couple of relationships with other lawyers and law firms, which kept her from making a grave mistake. On her third try, Mary used an Of Counsel relationship as a Phase I four-month exploration before moving to a Phase II merger with a firm. This time she got it right and the merger has been successful. Of Counsel can be used by solo practitioners, sole owner firms, and larger firms to "test the water" before entering into more formal relationships.

Practice Phasedown and Joining Another Firm

Some solo practitioners, as well as partners in larger firms, may want to join up with another firm but do not want to formally merge or become partners. The relationship feels like a merger. However, in essence they sort of close down their practice and join another firm as an employee under a compensation plan that typically pays them a percentage of their working attorney collections and client originations while working with the firm and, sometimes, a continued referral percentage for client originations for a couple of years after their departure from the firm. While working for the law firm they may have the title of Of Counsel, Special Counsel, Senior Counsel, or even Non-Equity Partner.

Vehicle for Collaboration

Some solo practitioners and sole owners want to keep practicing and are not interested in joining another firm. However, they realize that on occasion they need access to additional resources and support. Of Counsel relationships between two firms can be an effective tool for facilitating collaboration and can provide a solo or sole owner, in their older years, with additional flexibility that can allow them to continue to practice longer but in a more stress-free manner.

Vehicle for Practice Continuation

A practice continuation arrangement is an arrangement typically in the form of an agreement made between an individual lawyer or a small law firm and another lawyer or law firm. The arrangement describes a course of action to transfer a lawyer's practice and sets payment for its value. In the event of vacation, temporary or permanent disability, or death, a practice continuation arrangement protects the practice, the business interests of the lawyer or law firm's clients, and the financial interest of the lawyer and his or her family. There are different kinds of practice continuation arrangements. Typically, a lawyer enters into a one-on-one agreement with another sole proprietorship, partnership, or professional corporation in the community. Agreements can range from simple "dual coverage for each other" for vacation or other temporary absences to sale of the practice in the event of long-term disability or death.

Lawyers and law firms are using Of Counsel arrangements more and more and for a variety of purposes. Ensure that you review your state's rules of professional conduct to confirm that you are in compliance as well as with your legal malpractice carrier before entering into an Of Counsel relationship with another lawyer or law firm.

Practice Sale Candidates

Practice sale is an approach that is available in most states. Typically, there are very specific requirements and procedures that a lawyer or law firm must follow in accordance with a state's rules of professional conduct. Many states have followed or adapted the following American Bar Association's Model Rule 1.17 regarding sale of a law practice:

ABA Rule 1.17 Sale of Law Practice

A lawyer or a law firm may sell or purchase a law practice, or an area of law practice, including goodwill, if the following conditions are satisfied:

a. The seller ceases to engage in the private practice of law or in the area of practice that has been sold (in the geographic area) (in the jurisdiction) (a jurisdiction may elect either version) and in which the practice has been conducted;
b. The entire practice, or the entire area of practice, is sold to one or more lawyers or law firms;

c. The seller gives written notice to each of the seller's clients regarding:
   1. the proposed sale;
   2. the client's right to retain other counsel or to take possession of the file; and
   3. the fact that the client's consent to the transfer of the client's files will be presumed if the client does not take any action or does not otherwise object within ninety (90) days of receipt of the notice.

   If a client cannot be given notice, the representation of that client may be transferred to the purchaser only upon entry of an order so authorizing by a court having jurisdiction. The seller may disclose to the court in camera information relating to the representation only to the extent necessary to obtain an order authorizing the transfer of a file.

d. The fees charged clients shall not be increased because of the sale.

Check your state's rules of professional conduct beforehand and determine whether a sale is permitted in your state and, if so, what the requirements and restrictions are that must be met and satisfied. If you want to continue to practice in some capacity, make sure the rules allow you to continue to do so.

We have worked with solo practitioners who have sold their practices. However, I also see many lawyers starting off thinking that they will sell their practice, then ending up going one of the following directions:

1. Admitting an existing associate to partnership and then having the associate buy out the owner's partnership interest in a retirement payout.
2. Bringing in an associate and mentoring and grooming them, admitting the associate to partnership when he or she is ready, and then having the associate buy out partnership interest in a retirement payout. Sometimes partnership interests are sold gradually over time.
3. Merger with another law firm.
4. A wind-down of the practice and then Of Counsel relationship with another firm with a client transition/payout arrangement.

Many solo practitioners are often taken aback by the inflexibility of some of the various state rules of professional conduct concerning sale of law practices and find the above approaches more flexible.

However, there are occasions when a sole practitioner or solo owner is ready to retire and selling the firm is the most feasible option. Here are a few ideas for getting started:

1. Prepare a detailed project plan or timeline.
2. Decide when you want to retire and leave your firm.
3. Begin implementing management strategies that will maximize the future value of the firm.
4. Institutionalize the firm so that it is not uniquely you.
5. Determine whether your state permits the sale of a law practice.
6. Review and be aware of your state's rules concerning sale of a law practice.
7. Determine how much cash or annual cash flow you need when you exit the firm.
8. Determine whether your practice is sellable.
9. Establish a rough value for the practice.
10. Establish an initial asking price and specific terms for sale of your practice.
11. Prepare a Confidential Descriptive Memorandum outlining the particulars of your practice and a Non-Disclosure Agreement.
12. Prepare a buyer candidate profile highlighting what you are looking for in a buyer candidate.
13. Prepare a buyer candidate search plan outlining how you will find candidates interested in your practice.
14. Determine whether you will conduct the candidate search yourself or will use outside assistance.
15. Begin the candidate search and monitor.
16. Negotiate with potential buyers.
17. Close the sale.
18. Implement the sale in accordance with your state's rules of professional conduct and begin the transition.

CHAPTER 7
Finding Candidates and Opportunities

In Chapter 6, I discussed different succession/transition/exit strategies and approaches that law firms and lawyers may take when contemplating retirement and phasing down their practices. I suggested that the WHO often dictates the WHAT and this is for some, especially solo practitioners and sole owners, the most time-consuming and difficult part of the process. For some larger firms, this may also be true as well. The search and grooming process takes time and patience. For some practitioners, finding the right transition candidate—the right WHO—may mean the difference between successfully transitioning the practice and closing the doors.

Successful candidate searches often take a year or longer. Start the process early and allow ample time for conducting the search, vetting the candidates, and performing appropriate due diligence. This applies to all transition candidates, whether they be present or future associate candidates, lateral candidates, merger candidates, or Of Counsel candidates.

Existing Equity/Non-Equity Partners and Associates

Larger firms should begin their search within their firm. If the firm has other equity partners, this would be the starting point. A larger firm may have a succession plan or provisions with their partnership/operating/shareholder agreements that provides a mechanism for succession and transition. If so, a retiring partner should review these documents, meet with his or her partners, and discuss retirement goals. Once a timeline has been determined, the firm should develop a shortlist of equity partners in the firm that are best suited for client and management transition. Here are a few ideas:

Client Transition

1. Other equity partners who perform work for the same client, similar clients, or industry team;
2. Other equity partners who work in the same practice area;
3. Other equity partners who have worked with the client and have a past positive relationship with the client;
4. Other non-equity partners or associates worthy of equity partnership who perform work for the same client, similar clients, or industry team;
5. Other non-equity partners or associates worthy of equity partnership who work in the same practice area; and
6. Other non-equity partners or associates worthy of equity partnership who have worked with the client and have a past positive relationship with the client.

Management Transition

1. For the managing partner position, other equity partners who have served as managing partner in the past;
2. For the managing partner position, other equity partners serving on the management/executive or other committees;
3. For the managing partner position, other equity partners who have served on the management/executive committee or other committees;
4. For the managing partner position, other equity partners who have demonstrated leadership capabilities;

5. For other committees and practice group chairs, other equity partners who are serving or have served in management and leadership roles in the past; and
6. For other committees and practice group chairs, other non-equity partners and associates who are serving or have served in management and leadership roles in the past or have demonstrated leadership capabilities.

After the firm has identified and selected succession/transition candidates, the firm should establish the timeline and put in place a detailed plan with specific action steps for implementing the client and management transition. In larger firms, this frequently occurs within the context of a five-year phasedown program.

Associates and Lateral Partner Candidates

Solo and sole owner practitioner firms that do not have any equity partners or non-equity partners often have to look, as a first-step strategy, to associates and lateral partner candidates to affect their succession/transition/exit strategy. Solo practitioners will have to look outside the firm and sole owner practitioners may look within the firm by considering on staff associate attorneys or non-equity partners or may have to look outside the firm for associate or lateral partner candidates who can been groomed as successors. Here are some ideas for conducting an effective search:

Determine the Desired Candidate Profile

1. Think about what you are looking for in a candidate;
2. Consider whether you have the time, willingness, and ability to train and groom a new associate attorney;
3. Consider your past associate retention history;
4. Consider the level of experience you are looking for;
5. Consider whether a portable book of business is part of your criteria;
6. Consider whether the candidate should have experience owning a law practice or other business—business sense;
7. Prepare a candidate profile;

8. Prepare a candidate job description;
9. Determine how you will find qualified candidates;
10. Prepare job advertisements; and
11. Place candidate advertising.

Locating and Finding Candidates

1. Start looking in your own back yard—work your network and ask around;
2. Review print and online law school postings;
3. Review print and online bar association postings;
4. Review online law school and bar association Listservs;
5. Review other print and online postings;
6. Place online and print advertising;
   a. Craigslist
   b. Law schools
   c. Bar association
   d. Legal publishers
   e. Monster.com
   f. Local newspapers—print and online
7. Consider using a legal recruiter—if other efforts are unsuccessful—especially if looking for a seasoned lateral with a portable book of business;
8. Develop a system for monitoring and storing inquiries;
9. Use telephone interviews as initial screen device; and
10. Use outside assistance if your time and availability is limited.

Our firm and our clients have had success using all of the above listed approaches for locating qualified candidates.

Merger Candidates

For larger firms that have a talent shortage or need to increase their book of business or solo practitioner and sole owners' merger is often an appropriate strategy and approach. It all comes down to finding the right firm, the right culture, and the right fit. The search process can take time as well. Here are some suggestions to help get the process started:

Determine the Desired Merger Candidate Profile

1. Determine what you are looking for in a merger candidate;
2. Determine size of firm;
3. Determine desired firm culture—team-based firm versus lone ranger firm of individual practitioners operating under an eat-what-you-kill compensation system;
4. Determine desired practice specialties;
5. Prepare a merger candidate profile;
6. Prepare a confidential descriptive memorandum for your firm providing an overall overview of the firm and a non-disclosure agreement;
7. Prepare a vetting checklist;
8. Determine how you will find candidates; and
9. Prepare a project or action plan for the merger search project.

Locating and Finding Merger Candidates

1. Using the Internet and Google, start by thinking about possible target law firm candidates;
2. Prepare a merger candidate short list based upon firms that your firm has worked or have had contact with;
3. Prepare a merger candidate short list based upon firms that your firm is aware of but has not worked with nor had any contact with—cold leads;
4. Decide on an initial contact strategy for each target firm and who in your firm will initiate contact;
5. Begin contacting target firm and setting up initial meetings;
6. Maintain a constant and consistent flow with prospective merger candidates rather than fits-and-starts;
7. Work toward a specified target goal and maintain a timeline to avoid project drift;
8. If your firm is unable to maintain a constant and consistent flow, consider outside assistance; and
9. If your firm is unable to identify suitable target candidates, consider some of the advertising vehicles, including legal recruiting firms, which I listed earlier under finding associate and lateral partner candidates.

My experience has been that for small law firms the most successful approach for locating merger candidates has been developing the short list and looking in their own backyard. However, other approaches, including advertising, have worked as well. If the firm decides to use advertising, the firm may want to keep from divulging the firm name too early in the process.

Of Counsel Candidates

A firm does not usually go on the search for Of Counsel candidates; often the firm ends up there. In other words, an Of Counsel relationship becomes a method of implementing or formalizing a relationship. As discussed in Chapter 6, an Of Counsel relationship may be used as a Phase I pilot test to explore a possible merger, practice sale, practice continuation, or other relationship. The search often begins as a search for a merger or practice sale candidate, with Of Counsel used as the implementation mechanism. Specific search strategies include all listed strategies for associate, lateral, merger, and practice sale candidates.

Practice Sale Candidates—Potential Buyers

Solo and sole owner practitioners often have to sell their practices to another lawyer or law firm. As with a merger, a successful practice sale comes down finding the right firm, the right culture, and the right fit. The search process can take time as well. Here are some suggestions to help get the process started:

Determine the Desired Buyer Candidate Profile

1. Determine what you are looking for in a buyer candidate;
2. Determine size of desired buyer firm;
3. Determine desired buyer fee revenue level;
4. Determine desired buyer client type and mix;
5. Determine desired geographical location;
6. Determine desired firm culture;
7. Determine desired practice specialties;
8. Prepare a buyer candidate profile;
9. Prepare a confidential descriptive memorandum for your firm, providing an overall overview of the firm and a non-disclosure agreement;

10. Prepare a vetting checklist;
11. Determine how you will find buyer candidates; and
12. Prepare a project or action plan for the buyer search project.

Locating and Finding Buyer Candidates

1. Using the Internet and Google, start by thinking about possible target buyer candidates;
2. Prepare a buyer candidate short list based upon firms that your firm has worked or have had contact with;
3. Prepare a buyer candidate short list based upon firms that your firm is aware of but has not worked nor had any contact with—cold leads;
4. Decide on whether you will use a middleman such as a business broker, law firm management consultant, accountant, and so on, and what role the middleman will play;
5. Decide on an initial contact strategy for each target firm and who will initiate contact;
6. Review print and online bar association postings;
7. Review online law school and bar association Listservs;
8. Review websites of law firm management consultants, business brokers, and so on looking for law firms to acquire;
9. Review other print and online postings;
10. Place online and print advertising;
    a. Craigslist
    b. Law schools
    c. Bar association journals and newsletters
    d. Legal publishers
    e. Monster.com
    f. Local newspapers—print and online
    g. Law firm management consulting and business broker websites
11. Consider using a law firm management consultant, business broker, or other middleman—if other efforts are unsuccessful;
12. Develop a system for monitoring and storing inquiries;
13. Use telephone interviews as initial screen device;
14. Begin contacting target firms and setting up initial meetings;

15. Maintain a constant and consistent flow with prospective buyer candidates rather than fits-and-starts;
16. Work toward a specified target goal and maintain a timeline to avoid project drift; and
17. If your firm is unable to maintain a constant and consistent flow, consider outside assistance.

As with mergers, if the firm decides to use advertising, the firm may want to keep from divulging the firm name too early in the process.

A Short Story—A Law Firm That Sold a Practice Area (Fictitious Names Used)

This story occurred three years ago. A two-partner firm in a small rural town in a southern-tier state, Jones & Brinks, engaged me to help them address succession issues. The senior partner's father and now the senior partner, Michael Jones, continued the firm, founded in the early 1900s by the senior partner's grandfather. Twenty years ago, Michael brought in John Brinks as a lateral partner. While Michael had a varied general practice with specific focus on litigation, John brought transactional expertise to the firm. In addition to his law credentials, John was also a CPA and had worked in a large CPA firm in a large city before becoming an attorney. John focused his practice on general business and corporate transactional work as well as tax law.

After a couple of years the firm decided that with John's expertise in tax, the firm should offer tax return preparation and bookkeeping services for clients. The law firm hired a CPA, Mary Wilson, to manage the practice area. Mary managed the tax return preparation and bookkeeping practice area and brought in clients as well. She acquired staff accountants and clerical staff as well as computers, tax software, and other resources as needed to support the practice. The accounting staff members were cross-trained as paralegals and legal assistants and supported traditional legal services during the non-tax-season. The tax return/bookkeeping practice area was very successful, filing 500 tax returns a year and generating more than $300,000 a year in fee revenue.

The firm contacted me in the fall of 2012 seeking assistance concerning succession and transition. Michael was seventy, John was sixty-four, and Mary had announced that she planned to retire in the next couple of years. In the short-term, Michael and John were concerned about what to do with the tax preparation and bookkeeping practice. They also were interested in assistance concerning what to do with the law practice in the long term.

The firm provided me with financial statements and reports as well as other documents. Michael, John, Mary, and the legal and accounting support staff completed online questionnaires that I provided for my review. I then visited the law firm for a day, reviewed the operations of the firm, and interviewed Michael, John, Mary, and all of the support staff employees.

During a dinner meeting with the two partners, we discussed their retirement goals as well as succession and transition strategies. Michael and John advised that they wanted to continue to work as many years as possible; however, both recognized that they needed to be thinking about the long-term succession of the firm. Michael believed that a law firm is such a personal practice that there is no value beyond the tenure of the individual lawyer and that it would be hard if not impossible to find succession/transition candidates in their small rural community. I responded that you never know if you do not look and sometimes you have to look beyond your own backyard. We discussed various short-term and long-term options and agreed that the firm's first priority was to sell the tax return preparation and bookkeeping practice to an accounting firm. Our firm would help with the search process.

Michael, John, and I discussed the ideal buyer candidate and I prepared a candidate profile. We established an initial asking price and terms and agreed that our target candidates were small local CPA firms. I prepared a confidential descriptive memorandum and a non-disclosure agreement. Michael, John, and Mary were unable to identify any potential buyer candidates, so we decided to place blind-confidential advertisements. I placed an advertisement with Craigslist and the state CPA Society's print and online journal in January 2013 and we continued to run the CPA Society's print and online journal ad for over a year. I received inquiries from both sources directed to my e-mail address for initial screening and response.

Upon receiving an e-mail inquiry, I spoke with the interested party over the phone and if we determined there was a mutual interest, I e-mailed a non-disclosure agreement, after approval by Michael and John. Upon receipt of the signed non-disclosure agreement, I e-mailed the confidential descriptive memorandum providing details concerning the firm. (The identity of the law firm or the attorneys was not revealed prior to sending the non-disclosure agreement.) I maintained a communication log; coordinated, screened, and monitored inquiries; and liaised with Michael and John and recommended candidates for Michael and John to meet.

In February 2014 Michael and John sold the tax return/bookkeeping practice area to a husband and wife CPA couple who were looking to start their own CPA practice. They saw the advertisement in the CPA Society online journal. Michael and John sold the practice for $300,000—$250,000 paid at closing and the remaining $50,000 paid over the next three years. The CPA firm acquired the fixed assets, clients, and the employees; leased space from the law firm; and leased the employees to the law firm during the non-tax-season. The relationship worked well, and John and I proved to Michael that a dedicated and consistent search strategy could make the difference between value and no value for a professional practice. Advertising can work. The CPA couple was not even from the local area.

CHAPTER 8
Valuation

In Chapter 6, I outlined the following succession/transition/exist strategies:

- Associate candidates who can be groomed for either partnership or to buy the practice;
- Associates and lateral partner candidates;
- Merger candidates;
- Of Counsel candidates; and
- Practice sale candidates.

Whether the firm is considering equity ownership for a non-equity partner, associate, or lateral hire, the firm will have to address the questions of value. The same will be true if the firm is considering merger or practice sale. In other words, what is the firm worth? As a firm considers its succession/transition/exit goals and strategies, the firm should perform, or have performed, a valuation of the practice, whether a formal valuation or simply an initial estimate. This will give the firm a feel for the value of the practice. A comprehensive valuation is one of the cornerstones of the succession/transition/exit planning process. Without a good idea of what your firm is worth, it is impossible to make informed succession/transition/exit planning decisions. Without a valuation you will not be able to plan for retirement, do comprehensive tax planning, formulate a good estate plan, or understand the full extent of various exit options. A business valuation affects virtually every component of the succession/exit planning process, including:

- **Retirement**
  How much will the transfer of ownership shares provide for retirement?
- **Estate Planning/Tax**
  Impact upon estate planning. How much estate tax exposure is attributable to the firm?
- **Life Insurance**
  Is life insurance adequate given the value of the firm?
- **Buy–Sell/Shareholder/Partnership Agreements**
  What value should be included in buy–sell agreements for transfers and buyouts? Will a valuation formula work? Should the agreement call for a formal independent valuation?
- **Financial**
  How much loan collateral might be available? How much is the firm worth in a sale, merger, or internal transfer?

You cannot begin to formulate a succession/transition strategy without a baseline valuation.

Getting the Valuation Process Started

Unless you have a financial background and experience in law firm valuations, you will need help from an outside source. Professionals who can assist with valuations include:

- Law firm management consultants;
- Exit planning professionals;

- Certified public accountants;
- Commercial appraisal firms; and
- Attorneys.

Select a professional to work with who has experience with valuing law firms similar to yours and has extensive familiarity with law firms.

Once you have selected a professional to work with, collect and provide the following information to your advisor:

- Headcount and census data for the past five years;
- Financial statements for the past five years;
- Income tax returns for the past five years;
- Attorney compensation data for the past five years;
- Documents outlining/illustrating long-term commitments;
    - Pension obligations
    - Loans payable
    - Leases (building lease)
    - Other commitments
- Copy of last malpractice insurance application;
- Copies of the following reports:
    - Accounts Receivable Report
    - Contingency fee case inventory pipeline report of projections
    - Summary Work in Progress Report
    - Timekeeper Productivity Report
    - Cash Receipt Fee Allocation Report
    - Area of Practice Productivity Report
    - Cash Requirements Report showing unpaid payables and other liabilities
    - A copy of the firm budget
- Documents explaining the present partner and associate compensation system, bonuses, production of partners for the past five years, etc.;
- Documents related to succession plans of the firm;
- Partnership Agreement, Buy–Sell Agreement, etc.;
- Strategic or business plans;
- Marketing plan;

Determining Value

There is no one "right answer" when valuing a law practice. There are different types of valuations performed by different advisors for different reasons. Valuations can be extensive or ballpark estimates. If you are planning on transferring your ownership interests now (within a year or two), it is a good idea to get more than a ballpark idea of value. However, if you are three to five years away from transferring your ownership interests, a ballpark estimate should suffice for planning purposes. You should update this ballpark estimate annually.

While law firm owners and partners would like a simple "plug and play" approach to establishing a value for their firms, such an approach does not exist in the real world. Too many variables come into play. However, the following four valuation approaches/methods are standard practice and an understanding of these approaches can give you a better idea of the process:

Valuation Approaches/Methods

Asset-Based Valuation

The asset-based valuation method is based on the premise that the value of the firm is best determined by adding the value of all the firm's assets and subtracting the liabilities, leaving the net value of its assets. An asset-based valuation is further segmented into five approaches:

1. Book value;
2. Replacement cost;
3. Appraised value;
4. Liquidation value; and
5. Market value.

Because most law firms maintain the financial records on a cash-based method of accounting, their cash-based financials are adjusted to accrual-based financials for valuation purposes since the largest assets of a law firm are typically accounts receivable and work in progress. Asset-based valuation methods ignore the importance of a firm's earnings and cash flow. For this reason, this valuation approach generally is not used to determine the market value of a firm, particularly in the case of a practice sale.

Multiple of Annual Gross Revenue

A multiple of annual gross revenue rule-of-thumb approach is simple and direct. Multiply one year's gross revenue by a multiplier. The result will be the stream of income's value. I usually suggest that you average the firm's gross fee revenue over the past five years to even out any peculiar ups or downs in the revenue stream. Then multiply this average year's gross fee revenue by a given multiplier. The multiplier varies with the industry and even with geographic location. Accounting firms, for example, are valued at 1.0–1.5 times (100–150 percent) annual gross fee receipts. A well-established standard is still in its infancy in law firms. Some argue that the multiplier for the rule-of-thumb method for law practices should be between 0.5 and 3.0. However, based upon what I have seen in recent sales of law practices, the multiplier for the rule-of-thumb method for law practices is ranging between 0.3 and 1.0 (30–100 percent) of annual year's gross fee revenue. Another way to look at it would be 0.60–2.0 (60–200 percent) times net income (based upon partnership method of accounting and not including owner's compensation as an expense). Whether the multiplier is in the lower or higher level of the range depends on the following:

- How much repeat business is expected;
- The nature of the law practice;
- The number of clients;
- The transferability of client relationships;
- Dependency on only a few large clients; and
- Whether the firm has been "institutionalized" or is a personal practice and uniquely the owner.

If there is a great deal of repeat business and client loyalty can be transferred, the multiplier will be higher. In the sale of a law practice, a portion of the clients and referral sources will not stay with the practice, because of the close personal relationships usually developed. This factor must be considered when determining the multiplier. If the firm is dependent on a few large clients, the multiplier will be lower.

Comparable Firm Transactions

This method involves researching what other law firms similar to your firm are being sold for in the marketplace and then applying that data to your valuation. Since law firms are privately held, access to this sort of information is difficult to obtain. Therefore, this method of valuation is of limited value. However, even if limited information is available, such information can be used to supplement other method(s) being used to value your firm.

Discounted Cash Flow

Valuation experts often consider this a superior method of valuation since it is based on projected future financial performance of the firm, rather than historical financial performance. This method used estimates of a firm's future cash flows and the expected rate of return a buyer would reasonably expect on those cash flows.

Typically, combinations of two or more valuation methods are used when valuing a law practice and there are pros and cons of each method.

Is There Goodwill?

There is currently a lot of discussion on the question of whether there is goodwill that has value in a law firm and whether law firms are even marketable. The short answer is, it depends. Clients of law firms often advise us, "we hire the lawyer—not the firm." If this is the case, will these clients stay with the firm if the lawyer with whom they have the relationship is no longer with the firm? Law firm management consultants typically refer to the following types of law firm goodwill:

- Personal or professional goodwill
- Practice goodwill

Personal goodwill is the value associated with an individual lawyer in your firm and practice goodwill is the value associated with the firm as an entity or organization that goes beyond the reputation of the individual attorney(s). Personal goodwill ceases when you are no longer with the firm—practice goodwill continues after you are no longer there.

Practice goodwill is what future partners or buyers are interested in and what impacts value. Unfortunately, many law firms have a lot of personal goodwill and little practice goodwill. These firms need to be finding ways to institutionalize their firms to enhance practice goodwill and incorporate these strategies into their succession/exit plans.

The Bottom Line

In the final analysis, the value of the practice is what your partners will agree to or what an outside buyer will pay for the practice. The valuation process is simply a tool to use to help you get to this point.

Typical Approaches in Actual Practice

Valuation approaches typically depend on whether the succession vehicle being considered is an internal or external transition. In other words, is the firm considering admitting a partner or shareholder, a merger with another firm, or a practice sale? Firms use different strategies for different situations.

Internal Transition—Partnership/Shareholder Admission

Law firms that are considering admitting new partners or shareholders often do not consider the actual value of the firm in determining buy-ins when a new partner, shareholder, or member is admitted to the partnership, corporation, or limited liability company. Often a new partner or shareholder is asked to make a capital contribution based upon the firm's cash-based capital (cash-based net asset value) in alignment with the new partner or shareholder's interest percentage. Accrual assets such as accounts receivable and work in process are not considered. The value of goodwill is also not considered. Some have no capital accounts or capital requirements and admit new partners and shareholder with no buy-in or capital contribution.

Mergers

When a merger of equal-size firms is contemplated a valuation of the two firms is often done. When the merger involves a larger firm acquiring a smaller firm, billing rates, fee revenues, attorney performance, and so on are the deciding factors. Cash accounts, accounts receivable, and work in progress are typically retained by each firm prior to the merger. Fixed assets contributed to the merged firm are credited to respective capital accounts. Each partner/shareholder as required contributes additional capital based upon ownership interests acquired in the merged firm. Goodwill only plays a role in the decision to merge in the first place, the ownership interests allocated to each of the partners/shareholders, and the approach to compensation.

Practice Sale

Valuation plays a key role when selling a practice to an outside party such as another lawyer or law firm. The external lawyer or firm has no "sweat equity" invested in the firm and there is not the loyalty to a long-term dedicated associate or another partner. There is greater risk in the sale of a practice both to the seller and to a potential buyer. Without the emotional ties, the sale of a practice will be based much more on the economics, a valuation of the practice, and both the price and the terms of the sale. While many practices sell based on various forms of earn-outs, a solid valuation incorporating the value of cash and accrual assets as well as practice goodwill is the starting point.

CHAPTER 9

Buy-In/Buyout/Compensation

In Chapter 8, I discussed valuation and the various approaches taken based upon different situations. Valuation should determine a new partner's/shareholder's buy-in as well as, buyouts of partners/shareholders, and play a role in compensation. However, this is not always the case. Here are a few illustrations:

Buy-In

Equity Partner/Shareholder/Member Admission

In a typical business, buying an interest in a closely held company would be tied to the value of the business and a per share price determined for the stock. After a formal valuation, a share price would be determined and this share price would decide the buy-in amount required. If the total shares added up to a thousand and the business was valued at 1 million dollars, the value per share or share price would be a thousand dollars per share. A new shareholder buying a 50-percent interest in the company would acquire 500 shares at a share price of $1,000 per share and would pay $500,000 to buy in to the company. While this may be an oversimplification, the point is that the value of the company is a determining factor in the buy-in or investment. When a shareholder sells their interest, they sell their stock in the same manner.

Law firms and other professional service firms are different from a typical closely held company. Their stock in trade is the skills and abilities of their professionals and their assets are their intellectual capabilities. Acquiring or retaining an attorney's talent, skills, and book of business is usually more important that the monetary buy-in. The number of shares (partnership interest) initially offered as well as additional shares (interest) offered in the future is tied to the value that the attorney contributes to the firm from the sweat of their brow. An attorney earns ownership interests through work. Capital contribution, if required at all (buy-in) is tied to these ownership interests. Here is a summary of typical arrangements for new equity partners, shareholders, or members admitted to a partnership, professional or other corporation, or limited liability company:

- **No capital contribution or buy-in**
  Some firms have no capital accounts for any of the equity owners. They use their line of credit and bank borrowing for all their working capital requirements. Other firms do have capital accounts for the equity owners but simply waive the requirement for a new partner. I do not agree with this approach. I believe that an equity owner should have some stake in the game and bear the same risks and rewards as the other equity owners. They should contribute capital that lines up with their ownership interest and they should be a signatory on the firm's lease, credit lines, and other obligations.
- **Fixed capital contribution—same for all equity owners**
  Another approach taken by some firms is that each equity owner has an equal ownership interest with the same capital contribution or stock purchase. Compensation and allocation of firm profit is determined under a different compensation plan based upon performance. Typically, contributions range from $25,000 to $75,000.

- **Capital contribution—based upon ownership interest and tied to cash-based net asset value**
  This is the most common approach with the capital contribution or stock purchase based on the ownership interest an owner has and the cash-based net asset value of the firm. This does not include the value of accounts receivable or unbilled work in process—the accrual-based assets. An equity owner contributes additional capital when needed in proportion to their ownership interest. Likewise, there is a return of capital if capital requirements or ownership interests are reduced. While this approach is more affordable for a new equity owner, the capital contribution, or buy-in, is not tied to the value of the firm as the firm's largest assets—accounts receivable and unbilled work in process—are ignored.
- **Capital contribution—based upon ownership interest and tied to cash-based and accrual-based net asset value**
  This approach involves a capital contribution or stock purchase based on the ownership interest an owner has and the cash-based and accrual-based net asset value of the firm. This includes the value, adjusted for doubtful accounts, of accounts receivable and unbilled work in process—the accrual-based assets. Client case-by-case value assignments or other methods are used with contingency fee cases. An equity owner contributes additional capital when needed in proportion to their ownership interest. Likewise, there is a return of capital if capital requirements or ownership interests are reduced. While this approach is more appropriate and tied more closely to firm value, it is often unaffordable for a new equity owner.
- **Capital contribution—skin-in-the-game contribution**
  Sometimes the initial capital contribution or stock purchase is a "skin-in-the-game" seat-of-the-pants buy-in with no tie-in whatsoever to the value of the firm or the capital investment by the other equity owners. The firm wants to simply bring another lawyer into the equity ranks and wants a little "skin-in-the-game" investment from the lawyer. The equity owners want the buy-in to be affordable and their real interest is in the skills, talent, and the book of business of the lawyer they are considering for equity ownership.

- **Buy-in based on firm valuation—accrual-based net asset value plus multiple for goodwill**
  This approach has been used in situations where a solo owner founder wants to sell his interests to one or more associates in the firm and wants some return for the sweat equity and the firm brand that he has built over the years. A value for the firm as a whole is determined including some value for goodwill (often using a multiple times gross revenue as discussed in Chapter 8) and then a value for a percentage point is calculated. The associate then buys partnership interest or stock based on the percentage points or shares of stock being initially offered/sold. Typically, the associate makes an initial payment and pays the balance over a year to two, interest free, supported by a capital note. Over time, the owner sells the associate additional ownership interests under the same arrangement. When the owner retires or otherwise withdraws from the firm he or she, or their estate in the event of death, sells his or her remaining interests under the same arrangement.

Mergers

Law firms approach buy-in in different ways as well, but the most common approach I see in smaller firm mergers is as follows:

1. Each firm retains and collects their own accounts receivable and work in process;
2. Each firm sells their fixed assets to the new firm in exchange for a credit to their capital account (or stock shares);
3. Each equity owner is provided a certain negotiated ownership interest based upon past performance and anticipated future performance including reputation, experience, billings/collections, and client book of business;
4. A capital contribution or stock purchase is required in the merged firm based upon the cash-based net asset value of the merged firm and the partner, shareholder, or member's ownership interest.

When accounts receivable and unbilled work in process are pooled and included in the merged firm, the capital contribution or stock purchase would reflect these amounts as well.

Buyouts

Withdrawal of Equity Partners, Shareholder, and Members

Withdrawal of an equity partner, shareholder, or member can be a challenge in many ways. It is often an emotional time, whether the withdrawal be the result of simply leaving to go with another firm or a result of retirement, death, or disability. The firm will have to deal with replacing the skills and experience of the equity owner and transition client relationships and management responsibilities. Finally, the firm will have to buy out the departing equity owner's interests. Hopefully, the firm has planned for such events in advance and memorialized the terms for such payouts in a partnership, shareholder, operating, and buy–sell agreements. Common buyout or payout approaches include:

- **Return of Cash-Based Capital Account/Stock**
  Some payout arrangements simply provide for payment of the equity owner's earnings entitlement to date and return of his or her cash-based capital account. The departing partner receives no interest in the accrual-based assets—accounts receivable and unbilled work in process.
- **Cash-Based Capital Accounts Plus Interest in Accounts Receivable and Unbilled Work in Process**
  Other payout arrangements provide for payment of the equity owner's earnings entitlement to date, return of his or her cash-based capital account, and his or her ownership share of accounts receivable and unbilled work in process. Accounts receivable and unbilled work in process values are often discounted based on an aging schedule with doubtful accounts excluded and later added back in if actually billed and collected. Payouts are paid out as follows:
  - Cash-based capital account paid either upon withdrawal or within ninety days;
  - Interest in accounts receivable and unbilled work in process paid over three to five years; or
  - Interests in accounts receivable and unbilled work in process paid when billed and collected.

- **Cash-Based Capital Account Plus Interest in Cases When Concluded—Contingency Fee Cases**
  Contingency fee cases present a unique valuation and buyout challenge, as they are often impossible to value until the cases are concluded. When a firm has a large portfolio of contingency fee cases, payout arrangements provide for payment of the equity owner's earnings entitlement to date, return of his or her cash-based capital account, and his or her ownership share of cases in progress. The value of cases in progress is determined either by mutual agreement or on a case-by-case basis when cases are concluded. Payouts are paid out as follows:
  - Cash-based capital account paid either upon withdrawal or within ninety days;
  - Interest in cases in progress is determined on date of withdrawal by mutual agreement and paid over three to five years; or
  - Interests in cases in progress, tied to a percentage of completion of the case before and after the withdrawal of the equity owner, and determined on a case-by-case basis when each case is concluded. The withdrawing equity owner is paid when the firm receives settlement proceeds from the case.
- **Cash-Based Capital Account Plus Retirement Payout in Lieu of Ownership Interest**
  Some firms have a different payout arrangement for retirement and pay the retiring equity owner their undistributed earnings entitlement to date, return of cash-based capital account, and a retirement payout over a period of time—typically five years. Undistributed earnings are paid out to the retiring shareholder upon retirement or within thirty days and the cash-based capital account is paid within six months to one year. This retirement payout is in lieu of buyout of ownership interest. Often the retirement payout is in the form of a multiple of 1.0–2.0 on an average of the owner's highest three to five earning years. For example, if a partner/shareholder/member's average highest three years is $300,000 and a multiple of 1.5 is used, then the retirement payout would be $450,000 paid out over five years—$90,000 per year.

Mergers

Buyouts of withdrawing equity owners in a merged firm may take the form of any of the buyout approaches listed for equity partners, shareholders, and members. I hope that the terms for withdrawal and retirement were spelled out and memorialized in the merger agreement as well as partnership, shareholder, operating, and buy–sell agreements that were executed before the merger took place. I have seen in some situations where the merger is part of a succession strategy for one of the law firms, a special goodwill buyout provision in the form of a payment for client origination—10–20 percent of collected fees for a period of two to three years after retirement.

Of Counsel

An Of Counsel relationship with another law firm is an approach often taken by solo and sole owners. There is actually no buy-in or buyout of a capital account or other assets unless fixed assets are sold to the other firm. The solo or sole owner winds down their practice and then begins practicing with the other firm as an employee or independent contractor and is paid in accordance with a negotiated compensation agreement. While the compensation agreement may provide an hourly arrangement, the approach that I have seen most often is a percentage of collected fees—working attorney and client-originated fees. Upon retirement, the solo/sole owner may receive payment for client-originated fees for a period of two to five years ranging from 10 to 20 percent.

Challenges and Considerations

While I have presented a general overview of various buyout approaches, there can be numerous hurdles and challenges to overcome in actual practice. Here are just a few of them:

1. Should all forms of withdrawal be handled in the same manner? In other words, should the buyout be the same for an equity owner leaving the firm to join or start another firm as it is for a retiring equity owner?
2. Should a founder be paid additional consideration for starting the firm and the goodwill and value of the firm brand?

3. Should the next generation of equity owners be saddled with unfunded retirement obligations of prior generation senior equity owners?
4. What impact should affordability have upon equity owner buyouts and how should it be addressed?
5. Have unfunded retirements outlived their day and should they be eliminated from consideration?

Compensation

As solos, solo owners, and small firms implement their succession strategies and team up with other firms, the subject of equity owner compensation becomes a key consideration variable. In fact, the compensation systems that are in place tell a lot about each firm's culture and fit. Are the firm's team firm-first firms or lone ranger firms? Firms must ask themselves what kind of firm they want to be—team based or lone ranger (group of space sharers or partnership of individual firms). Eat-what-you-kill systems might be appropriate for lone ranger firms. However, such systems are not appropriate for law firms wanting to build and create a team-based practice since such systems typically reinforce "lone ranger" behavior resulting in a "me first versus firm first" orientation.

Compensation systems should do more than simply allocate the pie—they should reinforce the behaviors and efforts that the firm seeks from its attorneys. Many firms are discovering that desired behaviors and results must go beyond short-term fee production and must include contributions in areas such as marketing, mentoring, firm management, and so on to ensure the long-term viability of the firm.

Various types of approaches to equity owner compensation include (Cotterman 2004):

- *Subjective Plans* that review the performance of each partner and subjectively determine a relative value for each partner. These plans require evaluation of the individual, comparing the evaluation against those of all other partners and relating the determinations to available funds. Some firms use a democratic process in which each partner participates, while others use a committee to perform the evaluation. Increasingly, partners are required to submit personal business plans each year that must be approved by the partnership, executive, or compensation committee.

- Formula—*Objective Plans* that use a formula to assign value to various criteria to determine compensation. Approaches can range from eat-what-you-kill plans that focus only on a partner's individual production to plans that assign values to the full range of compensation criteria. Some eat-what-you-kill plans employ a profit center approach in which each partner is set up as a department in the accounting system, fee revenue is assigned based upon generation, and indirect and direct overhead is allocated based upon a predetermined usage formula. Other eat-what-you-kill systems focus only on revenue by allocating fee credits for generation (production of work) and for origination of business, weighting the two factors, and determining compensation based upon the results.
- *Combination Plans* are hybrid plans that combine elements from subjective and formula plans.
- *Bonus Pools* are being used to supplement the above plans and reward individuals or groups of lawyers for extraordinary performance.

Subjective or combination plans are most appropriate for firms desiring to build and reinforce a team-based practice. They focus on the long as well as the short term and all contributions (compensation criteria) to the firm. They also require more work from firm management. While total formula plans are increasingly falling in favor, they can be appropriate in lone ranger firms that only want to eat what they kill—nothing more.

As lawyers and firms look to join other firms, they will find almost as many different approaches to compensation as firms they are considering. Listen to what the compensation systems are telling you about the candidate firms and whether you will be a good fit. When I am having an initial first call with a new law firm client and I want to have a quick understanding about the firm and its culture I can get a feel by asking one question—how do the equity owners pay themselves?

CHAPTER 10

Developing the Plans

In Chapters 6 and 7, I stated that the WHO usually dictates the WHAT. For some, especially solo practitioners and sole owners, this is the most time consuming and difficult part of the process. For some larger firms this may also be true as well. The search and grooming process takes time and patience. For some practitioners, finding the right transition candidate—the right WHO—may mean the difference between successfully transitioning the practice and closing the doors. The key is the right relationship and sometimes that takes the form of making someone at the firm a partner, bringing in a seasoned lateral, merging with another firm, or selling the practice. As you begin to develop your succession/transition plan keep it flexible at first. Establish some basic timelines and develop a general course of action. Resist the temptation to develop a comprehensive plan until you have a sense of the direction the firm is headed. Then built out the plan.

The type of plan will depend upon where you are in the process, size of your firm, type of clients—institutional versus individual clients—and whether you have associates or other non-equity or equity owners in the firm. Here is a general outline and discussion of some of the plans that we have used with client law firms.

Succession/Transition/Exit Project Action Plan

In larger firms where there are heirs apparent, other equity owners, the starting point may be simply writing an internal succession/transition plan and commencing its implementation. In smaller firms with no heirs apparent, the starting point is often a succession/transition/exit project action plan. The key is to approach succession and transition like managing a project or a litigation case using project management concepts and tools. Effective project management is the discipline of getting things done and requires a different approach than managing current operations. A project such as succession and transition happens one time only and has a clear beginning and end. A successful project is completed on time and according to a schedule and it has a clear definition, a plan, and a control system. A project plan is a document with milestone and due dates, start dates, tasks and action items, required resources, and names of those responsible for different tasks and action items. The plan is then used to manage the succession/transition/exit project and related processes. The key is to have a continuous flow, generate momentum rather than fits and starts, and have assigned

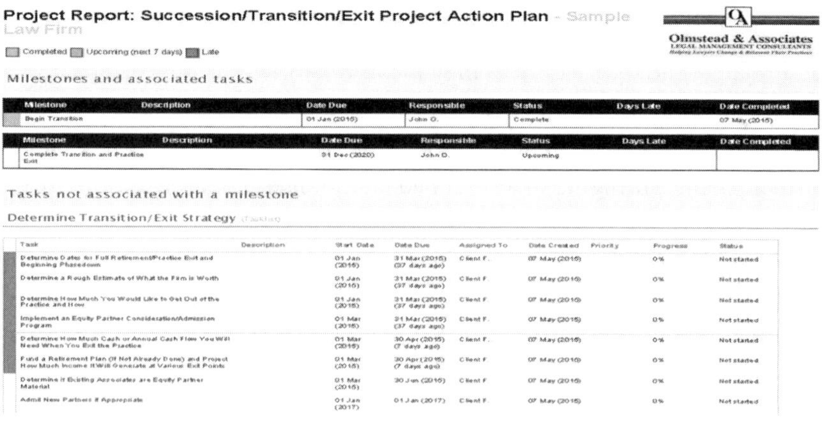

Project Report: Succession/Transition/Exit Project Action Plan - Sample Law Firm

Olmstead & Associates
LEGAL MANAGEMENT CONSULTANTS
Helping Lawyers Change & Reinvent Their Practices

Completed | Upcoming (next 7 days) | Late

Milestones and associated tasks

Milestone	Description	Date Due	Responsible	Status	Days Late	Date Completed
Begin Transition		01 Jan (2015)	John O.	Complete		07 May (2015)

Milestone	Description	Date Due	Responsible	Status	Days Late	Date Completed
Complete Transition and Practice Exit		31 Dec (2020)	John O.	Upcoming		

Tasks not associated with a milestone

Determine Transition/Exit Strategy (Tasklist)

Task	Description	Start Date	Date Due	Assigned To	Date Created	Priority	Progress	Status
Determine Dates for Full Retirement/Practice Exit and Beginning Phasedown		01 Jan (2015)	31 Mar (2015) (37 days ago)	Client F.	07 May (2015)		0%	Not started
Determine a Rough Estimate of What the Firm is Worth		01 Jan (2015)	31 Mar (2015) (37 days ago)	Client F.	07 May (2015)		0%	Not started
Determine How Much You Would Like to Get Out of the Practice and How		01 Jan (2015)	31 Mar (2015) (37 days ago)	Client F.	07 May (2015)		0%	Not started
Implement an Equity Partner Consideration/Admission Program		01 Mar (2015)	31 Mar (2015) (37 days ago)	Client F.	07 May (2015)		0%	Not started
Determine How Much Cash or Annual Cash Flow You Will Need When You Exit the Practice		01 Mar (2015)	30 Apr (2015) (7 days ago)	Client F.	07 May (2015)		0%	Not started
Fund a Retirement Plan (If Not Already Done) and Project How Much Income It Will Generate at Various Exit Points		01 Mar (2015)	30 Apr (2015) (7 days ago)	Client F.	07 May (2015)		0%	Not started
Determine if Existing Associates are Equity Partner Material		01 Mar (2015)	30 Jun (2015)	Client F.	07 May (2015)		0%	Not started
Admit New Partners if Appropriate		01 Jan (2017)	01 Jan (2017)	Client F.	07 May (2015)		0%	Not started

Figure 10.1 Sample Succession/Transition/Exit Project Action Plan

responsibilities and accountability. A project action plan is designed to accomplish this. Below is an illustration of the format of such a plan:

Appendix A includes a more detailed illustration of a succession/transition/exit project action plan.

Internal Succession/Transition/Exit Plan

The succession/transition/exit project action plan provides the roadmap for keeping things moving and managing the overall project. However, in a larger firm with multiple partners, shareholders, or members, succession and transition involves transitioning client relationships and management roles. Such transitions take time. Many larger firms have five-year phase-down retirements for this reason and require equity owners to properly transition clients and management responsibilities. Some firms tie retirement pay or compensation to completing a successful transition program.

Appendix B is a Partner (Owner) Transition Plan for a sample law firm. The plan provides the following:

- The Transition Partner becomes a Transition Partner as of the commencement of the phasedown and begins client and management transition at that time and ending on his retirement date, at which time he retires and withdraws from the partnership. The transition period constitutes a reduction in work and transfer of responsibility over a period of five years.
- Compensation of the Transitioning Partner is proportionately reduced by the amount of reduction in the Transitioning Partner's present work schedule. For example, if a Transitioning Partner works a reduced work schedule of 75 percent of his/her present work schedule, then his/her compensation shall be reduced by 25 percent. The Transitioning Partner shall report to the executive committee no later than December 1, what his/her work schedule for the preceding year shall be and the executive committee, after setting the draw of all partners, including the Transitioning Partner, shall then reduce the draw/compensation of the transition partner accordingly. This schedule may be reevaluated quarterly at the discretion of either the Transitioning Partner or the Executive Committee.

- Transitioning Partner is responsible for the collection of his/her accounts receivable and billing of his/her Work-in-Process throughout the entire transition phase unless delegated to his/her Co-Responsible Partners.
- Transitioning Partner's purchase price (payout) is to be calculated immediately prior to the beginning of the transition period and in the same time and in the same manner in accordance with the Firm Partnership Agreement, and will be paid only upon the completion of the transition period.

The value of an internal succession/transition plan is that it provides a mechanism for the firm to outline a general timeline for a senior partner's retirement, a process to effect an orderly transition of clients and management responsibilities, and a vehicle for starting initial discussions.

Practice Continuation Arrangement/Plan

While many lawyers and law firms are beginning to think about long-range succession issues and the need for long-range succession plans, many have not yet addressed the shorter-range issues. I find that often solo and sole owner practitioners are in a "reactionary mode" and have not adequately prepared backup plans in the event that, in the short term, prior to retirement, something would happen to them.

At a recent presentation on succession/exit planning, a lawyer asked me, "what if something happens to me today or tomorrow . . . what is my backup plan?" While my presentation had focused on the longer-term retirement succession issues, I had failed to address issues such as short-term illness, disability, death, and even vacations. For example:

- How would the firm keep operating?
- Who would take care of the client's needs?
- How would the firm's staff be taken care of?

Sound practice continuation arrangements can solve this dilemma and preserve practice value and can help prevent a lawyer's spouse or immediate heirs from facing a hasty sale or disposition of the practice in an emergency. A practice continuation arrangement can also give lawyer practitioners, their staff, and their families peace of mind.

What Is a Practice Continuation Arrangement/Plan?

A practice continuation arrangement is an arrangement, typically in the form of an agreement or contract made between an individual lawyer or a small law firm and another lawyer or law firm. The arrangement describes a course of action to transfer a lawyer's practice and sets payment for its value. In the event of vacation, temporary or permanent disability, or death, a practice continuation arrangement protects the practice, the business interests of the lawyer or law firm's clients, and the financial interest of the lawyer and his or her family.

Approaches

There are different kinds of practice continuation arrangements. Typically, a lawyer enters into a one-on-one agreement with another sole proprietorship, partnership, limited liability company, or professional corporation in the community. Agreements can range from simple "dual coverage for each other" for vacation or other temporary absences to sale of the practice in the event of long-term disability or death.

Typical Components of Continuation Agreements

There are many components to a practice continuation agreement. It is important that temporary disability, permanent or total disability, and retirement are outlined and defined appropriately.

Permanent disability is total disability due to poor health, either physical or mental. In contrast, temporary disability is defined as a physical or mental disability that does not last more than approximately six months. Retirement is defined as the exit from the practice of law on an immediate or phase-out basis.

Temporary disability. The agreement should call for the successor firm to provide employees to assist in the practice's daily business. The employees generally would be attorneys and staff. However, an attorney or attorneys must be available in the successor firm to review the work of paralegals and staff and provide the necessary experience and background to make needed decisions. The attorney(s) would be in contact with and under the supervision of the temporarily disabled practitioner. Each of the two law firms would negotiate a compensation arrangement for the assisting firm. The agreement would provide for a conclusion of the arrangement once temporary disability ends. The temporarily disabled practitioner probably would give advance notice of his return, but the agreement would not require it.

Permanent disability or death. The provisions called for in these cases are much more detailed. They must allow for an orderly transfer of firm clients to the successor firm with no assistance from the practitioner and for the beginning of predetermined regularly scheduled payments to his heirs.

Payment for the Practice

A practice continuation agreement's provisions for the sale of a practice must contain a reasonable valuation and a realistic payment structure. What lawyers really want is to leave to their surviving spouses or heirs something from all the years of hard work it took to build the practice. To accomplish this end, selling the practice at a buyer-friendly price may be necessary. Law practices can lose value very quickly, so timing is vital.

One approach would be to list each client in the agreement and assign individual values that equal the total valuation agreed on for the practice. Payment for each is made to the lawyer's heirs from cash received by the successor firm from billings to these clients for future services. The agreed-on percentage of current collections to be paid depends on the contract's term. If the term were five years, then 20 percent of each collected amount would be paid each year. The maximum amount to be paid for any client is its agreed-on value. If the client terminates the successor firm's services, payments for that client cease.

The surviving spouse or heirs do not participate in any future client growth once the practice continuation agreement takes effect. Be careful about executing a note since it fixes the price for consideration and prevents payments that correspond with cash flow. It is inflexible to client loss. The buyer could end up paying for a client it may not keep.

Notification

The predecessor firm should notify all clients of the agreement in accordance with their state bar requirements and assure them there will be no interruption of services when the practice changes hands. It is important to ensure that the surviving spouse or heirs are aware of the existence of the practice continuation agreement and understand its provisions. In addition, the attorney for the predecessor lawyer's estate should be familiar with agreement terms, if he or she did not draft and negotiate the agreement.

An Investment—Well Worth Your Time

Lawyers must invest time and effort to find suitable successors for their firms and to create useful, equitable, practice continuation agreements. The key is finding the right person or firm. The investment of time is a good investment, however, because a good practice continuation arrangement will ensure that if a lawyer is unable to continue managing the practice, the value he or she has built over the years will not be lost. An orderly transfer of a practice to another lawyer or law firm is a substantial financial benefit to the lawyer's family. At the same time, through the handpicked successor, the lawyer fulfills his professional responsibility to his clients. Lawyers who do not have these agreements should learn more about preserving the value they have created.

CHAPTER 11
Implementation of the Strategies and Plans

Strategies, plans, and ideas are great but useless if not implemented. Lawyers love to plan and debate but often fail to implement. I have started many engagements with law firms that have retained management consultants in the past. I often ask how it went and they advise me that they had a good experience; the consultant provided good ideas, and a great report. I then ask what they implemented and am told "very little." Many firms have elaborate strategic plans sitting on their shelves collecting dust. Law firm solo practitioners, sole owners, and multi-owner firms need to be aware of this problem and address it head on in their succession/transition/exit plans. In larger firms, failure to implement can result in loss of clients and ineffective transition of management roles and responsibilities, leading to reduced long-range effectiveness of the firm. Solo and sole owner firms can also have the same fate. However, the impact can be more dramatic. Failure to implement in solo and sole-owner firms can make the difference between firm owners recognizing value from the firm upon his or her exit or no value at all.

The key question is how will the solo, the sole owner, or partners manage the work of the succession/transition/exit project while continuing to practice, serve clients, and manage the firm. How will they balance billable client production with the non-billable time that a succession/transition/exit project will require? Otherwise, the project will drift, will not be prioritized, and will fail to receive the proper attention to keep it moving forward. Newspaper reporters are taught to ask the following questions when working on a story:

- Who
- What
- Where
- Why
- When
- How

To succeed at managing a succession/transition/exit project, you will need to ask, answer, and address many of the same questions.

WHO

Who will lead, direct, and manage the project? In a solo or solo-owner firm, this may be the owner or an outside consulting firm retained to lead, direct, and manage the process. In a larger law firm, this may be the management or executive committee, a managing partner, or a transition committee formed for such purposes. Larger firms may also retain a consulting firm as well. Other outside advisors such as certified public accountants, financial planners, and insurance professionals may also be involved. Specific roles, expectations, and accountabilities should be developed for everyone inside and outside the firm who will be working on the project.

WHAT

What is the specific nature of the project? The law firm should define the succession/transition/exit project specifically. Will the project involve looking into all possible transition/succession/exit options or will it be limited to a single specific option, such as sale of the practice to another law firm, admission of a non-equity partner or associate to equity ownership, or merger with another firm? Define the specific scope of the project and put it in writing in the form of a succession/transition/exit project charter or project plan. Define desired outcomes.

WHERE

If the firm has multiple offices, which office location is the primary focus? In the case of a practice sale or merger, in what geographical areas should the candidates be presently located? Will the project team have to be located in the same area as the law firm? Can the law firm and team members be located in different locations? Will the law firm require face-to-face team meetings? Will the meetings be able to be held remotely?

WHY

Why is the succession/transition/exit project necessary? Why is the project being considered? What are the consequences for failing to start and successfully complete the project: loss of key clients? Loss of retirement payout and/or sweat equity from the practice? Why is it important to start the project now rather than later?

WHEN

When should the succession/transition/exit project start? When should the project be completed? What are the key milestone dates, specific tasks, and specific task start and completion dates? Examples of two milestone dates in a larger firm that has a transition/phasedown plan might be

1. Start phasedown—January 1, 2015
2. Retire—December 31, 2019

HOW

The HOW involves the how of managing the project. In other words, some of the basic project management tools used to keep the project:

- Focused
- On schedule and on time
- Fluid and moving forward

The HOW also involves deciding upon and implementing the succession/transition/exit strategy that achieves the goals of the solo, sole owner, or equity owners in a larger law firm. Usually the project planning HOW leads to the specific strategy and implementation HOW. The strategy and implementation HOW might involve selling the practice, admitting a non-equity partner or associate to equity ownership, or merger with another law firm. In the case of a larger law firm, it may involve the specific transition and phasedown activities.

Goals Are Critical to the Process

Goals are critical to success of any succession/transition/exit planning project. Here are ten requirements for quality goals:

1. Your most important goals must be yours;
2. Goals must be meaningful;
3. Goals must be specific and measurable;
4. Goals must be flexible;
5. Goals must be challenging and exciting;
6. Goals must be in alignment with values;
7. Goals must be well balanced;
8. Goals must be realistic;
9. Goals must include contribution; and
10. Goals need to be supported.

Goals should be *SMART* goals, where:

S = specific

Goals should be straightforward and emphasize what you want to happen. The specifics help you focus your efforts and clearly define specific tasks and actions steps in the project plan. The specifics entails what you are going to do, why the plan is important, what you want to accomplish, and how you are going to manage the process and the implementation of the chosen succession/transition/exit strategy.

M = measurable

There is an old IBM saying—*What Gets Measured is What Gets Done.* If you cannot measure it, you cannot manage it. The goal statement is a measure for the succession/transition/exit project. If the goal is accomplished, the project is a success. Here are a couple of examples of measurable goals:

- Successfully retire and exit the practice by December 31, 2015, by selling the practice to a qualified law firm for $300,000 or more, effectively transitioning clients, and providing ongoing employment for existing staff members.
- Hire a lateral attorney and begin grooming him or her to take over the practice no later than January 1, 2017.

Measuring progress helps you stay on track and reach milestones and target dates.

A = attainable

Goals should have an element of stretch, but they also should be attainable. Goals that are not attainable—that are too far out of reach—will stifle rather than motivate goal accomplishment behavior.

R = realistic

Realistic goals are goals that are doable and can be achieved. While a realistic goal may push you and other people assigned to the project, it should not break your backs. The goal needs to be realistic to where you are at the moment.

T = timely—on a timeline.

Smart goals must have a timeline for goals and endpoints, which provides clear project targets. Without a project timeline there will be no commitment, as project participants will feel they can begin at any time and then never seem to get around to it. There is simply no urgency or reason to start now. The timeline must be measurable, attainable, and realistic.

A goal is the ongoing pursuit of a worthy objective until it is accomplished. Steps toward achievement of a goal are:

1. Set the goal
2. Make a plan
3. Get to work
4. Stick to it
5. Reach the goal

Project Management Fundamentals and Tools

In the last few years, there has been a lot of press about how project management concepts are being used to manage matters and cases. Legal project books and CLE seminars abound. In fact, one of ABA's most popular books of the past year was *The Power of Legal Project Management* by David A. Rueff Jr. and Susan Raridon Lambreth. Law firms, especially law firms that handle large litigation matters, are effectively using project management tools to manage large-scale high-stakes matters and cases. While a succession/transition/exit project may not rate at the same level as a large-scale litigation matter nor require use of the same tools, it is still a project with moving parts and can benefit from the use of basic project management tools.

It is difficult for lawyers to serve two masters—the firm (non-billable time) and firm clients (billable time). Firm management issues always seem to take a back seat to client priorities. To do otherwise requires lawyers to be focused and effective time managers. Both balls must be balanced at the same time. Law firm administrators often have a similar problem. His or her priorities are frequently focused on day-to-day operations management and there never seems to be time—especially large chunks of time—for long-term projects. Law firms have a hard time getting long-term initiatives or projects such as the following implemented:

1. Firm strategic plan
2. Partnership agreement
3. New partner compensation system

4. Case management system
5. Website
6. Employee handbook
7. Standard Operating Procedures Manual (SOP)

A starting point is to recognize that managing long-term projects such as those listed above requires a different approach and tools than day-to-day operations management. *Projects* involve all the work that is done one time and ongoing operations represents work that is performed repeatedly. Every project has a beginning and an end. They are unique and temporary. Work that is unique and temporary—projects—requires different management disciplines.

Successful projects are those that:

1. *Schedule*—Are completed on time according to a schedule or timeline
2. *Cost*—Are on budget
3. *Quality*—High-quality, meet expectations

Long-term initiatives must be managed as projects and managed differently than ongoing operations. This also holds true for succession/transition/exit planning projects.

Here is a summary of some of the fundamentals of project management:

- *Milestones*
  A milestone is a target date, representing an important moment or goal in a project such as "complete transition phasedown." Task or category lists, tasks, and sub-tasks help milestones to be achieved.
- *Work Breakdown Structure*
  A work breakdown structure is simply a list of tasks and sub-tasks and who is assigned to them. Tasks are arranged in a logical order, with start and completion due dates to form the project schedule. The schedule is the most visible and important tool used to manage the succession/transition/exit project. In succession/transition/exit projects, I like to use backward scheduling. Set the retirement milestone date and then determine tasks and dates backward from the retirement date.

- *Task List or Category List*
  Task lists or category lists are a way of organizing tasks into groups according to criteria that matters to the project.
- *Tasks and Sub-Tasks*
  Tasks and sub-tasks are assigned to a task list or task category and at a minimum provide the name of the task, person or persons assigned to and responsible for the task, date the task is to start, and completion due date. Sophisticated project management systems will track task priority, task dependencies, projected time to complete the task, time spent on the task, budget, and other resource requirements.
- *Accountability*
  Someone in the firm should be assigned overall project responsibility for the succession/transition/exit project. In a solo or sole owner firm, this will be the owner of the firm. In larger firms, this may be the managing partner, the executive director, or a transition committee. Various individuals should be assigned responsibility for individual tasks and/or sub-tasks. Responsible parties should be held accountable for due dates and staying on schedule.
- *Follow-Up and Control Systems*
  The schedule, calendar, reports, and status meetings are the primary follow-up and control systems that should be used to keep the succession/transition/exit project on track and moving forward.
- *Documentation*
  What is not written down is forgotten. Meeting and status notes, checklists, and other documents should be maintained, filed on a central server, and accessible to all team members—internal and external.

Here is a summary of some of the tools used in project management:

- Simple Excel Spreadsheet
- Microsoft Outlook Task Manager and Calendar
- Microsoft Office OneNote
- Project Reports
- Gantt Charts

- Dedicated project management software such as Microsoft Project
- Online project management systems such as Basecamp—www.basecamp.com or www.teamwork.com.

Most firms will not need to use sophisticated project management concepts or tools. For most firms an Excel spreadsheet or Microsoft Outlook Task Manager will suffice and the work breakdown schedule can be managed from within one or both of these software packages. However, it is important to create a work breakdown schedule, calendar tasks, and assign responsibilities. Samples of some of these tools are provided in the Appendix and are also available online at http://ambar.org/succession.

Our firm uses an online project management portal for all of our client projects and we provide all of our clients "real-time access to their project with full access to the project schedule and calendar, project and task reports, communications, project notes from all meetings, and files and documents involved with the project."

CHAPTER 12

Key Documents and Agreements

Numerous documents and agreements come into play in typical succession/transition/exit planning projects. Initially key documents may be just project plans, calendars, progress checklists, status reports, and so on. As the project moves toward implementation of a specific succession/transition/exit strategy, additional documents and agreements (typically legal agreements) are drafted and executed. The specific documents required are dependent upon the specific strategy.

In succession/transition/exit planning engagements, I often design and draft project plans, checklists and policy documents, and offer content ideas only for legal documents and agreements. Our law firm client or business attorneys retained by our law firm client draft all legal documents and agreements.

In the Appendix, I have provided sample documents and agreements that have been used as content template recommendations in a variety of succession/transition/exit planning projects over the years.

While attorneys prepared the sample legal templates for our use in facilitating discussions, they are not ready-to-use documents or agreements. They are simply provided as "content and format ideas" to stimulate thinking. A business attorney in your state or jurisdiction should prepare any legal documents or agreements.

Here are some key documents and agreements used in succession/transition/exit planning projects either in the initial planning phase or in the implementation phase in which a specific succession strategy is implemented:

Part I—Initial Planning Phase Documents

Succession/Transition/Exit Project Action Plan

A well-designed project action plan sets the stage for the entire succession/transition/exit planning project. It keeps the initiative focused, on schedule, and on track. Appendix A is a sample illustrative partial project action plan that was generated from the project management system that we used for all of our client projects. The project action plan includes:

- Project Milestone Dates
- Task Categories
- Tasks and Sub-Tasks
- Task Start Dates
- Task Due Dates
- Responsible Person(s) for the Task and Sub-Task
- Progress of the Task and Sub-Task
- Status of the Task and Sub-Task
- Completed Tasks
- Tasks with Due Dates Coming Due Within Next Seven Days
- Late Tasks

A less detailed project action plan Excel template is included online at http://ambar.org/succession. Although the Excel template is less sophisticated than the action plan generated from the project management system, it may be all that a firm needs to keep a project on track. Microsoft Outlook using tasks and categories could also be used.

Confidential Descriptive Memorandum

When solo, sole owners, or even larger firms are searching for potential buyers or merger partners, a worthwhile investment of time is to prepare an offer package. This package is provided to other firms. A good offer package consists of the following:

1. A firm profile (without identity for some presentations)
2. Nondisclosure Agreement
3. Confidential Descriptive Memorandum (Offering Memorandum)

The Confidential Descriptive Memorandum tells the firm's story and provides relevant facts that other firms want to know, including:

1. Legal Structure of the Firm
2. Ownership and Governance
3. Key Management Personnel
4. Organizational Chart
5. Client Breakdown
6. Practice Areas/Mix
7. Marketing
8. Historical Financial Performance
9. Potential Growth Opportunities
10. Potential Synergies or Economies of Scale
11. Proposed Deal Structure

The firm profile is the first point of contact with potential buyers/merger partners. It summarizes the key points and describes the firm without revealing any identifying information. If an interested party wishes to go to the next step, a nondisclosure agreement is executed and a confidential descriptive memorandum with more specific information is provided.

Using tools such as these can help you focus your effort, cast your firm in its best light, and reduce wasted effort on the part of all parties.

Equity Ownership (Partnership) Proposal

Solo and sole owner practitioner firms that do not have any equity partners or non-equity partners often have to look, as a first-step strategy, to associates and lateral partner candidates to effect their succession/transition/exit strategy. Solo practitioners will have to look outside the firm and sole owner practitioners may look within the firm by considering on-staff associate attorneys or non-equity partners, or may have to look outside the firm for associate or lateral partner candidates who can been groomed as successors. After initial general discussions, the firm will have to present the future equity candidate a proposal.

Appendix C is an Equity Partnership Proposal for Sample Law Firm. The proposal includes the following:

- Equity ownership offer
- Effective date of equity ownership
- Details and terms
- Client and management transition plan of the present equity owner(s)
- The following supporting documentation
    - Five-year historical financial profile
    - Tax returns and financial statements for the past five years
    - Transition Plan
    - Partnership, Operating, or Shareholder Agreement

Owner (Partner) Transition Plan

In a larger firm with multiple partners, shareholders, or members, succession and transition involves transitioning client relationships and management roles. Such transitions take time. Many larger firms have five-year phasedown retirements for this reason and require equity owners to properly transition clients and management responsibilities. Some firms tie retirement pay or compensation to completing a successful transition program.

Appendix B is an Owner (Partner) Transition Plan for a sample law firm. The plan provides the following:

- The Transition Partner becomes a Transition Partner as of the commencement of the phasedown and begins client and management transition at that time and ending on his retirement date, at which time he retires and withdraws from the partnership. Compensation of the Transitioning Partner is proportionately reduced by the amount of reduction in the Transitioning Partner's present work schedule.

- Transitioning Partner is responsible for the collection of his/her accounts receivable and billing of his/her Work-in-Process throughout the entire transition phase unless delegated to his/her Co-Responsible Partners.
- Transitioning Partner's purchase price (payout) is to be calculated immediately prior to the beginning of the transition period and in the same time and in the same manner in accordance with the Firm Partnership Agreement, and will be paid only upon the completion of the transition period.

The internal succession/transition plan provides a mechanism for the firm to outline a general timeline for a senior partner's retirement, a process to effect an orderly transition of clients and management responsibilities, and a vehicle for starting initial discussions.

Equity Owner (Shareholder) Term Sheet

Sometimes a term sheet is used instead of or before a formal proposal or partnership, operating, or shareholder agreement. A term sheet is a bullet-point document outlining the material terms and conditions of the proposed equity ownership agreement. After a term sheet has been "executed," it guides attorneys in the preparation of a proposed "final agreement." It then guides, but is not necessarily binding, as the signatories negotiate, usually with their attorneys, the final terms of their agreement.

A term sheet implies the conditions of a business transaction, as proposed by a party. It may be either binding or non-binding. Term sheets are very similar to "letters of intent" (LOI) in that they are both preliminary, mostly non-binding documents meant to record two or more parties' intentions to enter into a future agreement based on specified (but incomplete or preliminary) terms. The difference between the two is slight and mostly a matter of style: an LOI is typically written in letter form and focuses on the parties' intentions; a term sheet skips most of the formalities and lists deal terms in bullet-point or similar format. There is an implication that an LOI only refers to the final form. A term sheet may be a proposal, not an agreed-to document.

The term sheet is analogous to a letter of intent, a nonbinding outline of the principal points, which the Partnership Agreement, Operating Agreement, or Shareholder/Stock Purchase Agreement and related agreements will cover in detail. The advantage of the abbreviated term sheet format is, first, that it expedites the process. Appendix D is a sample Equity Owner (Shareholder) Term Sheet.

Merger/Acquisition/Of Counsel Term Sheet

When two law firms are contemplating a merger, acquisition, or an "Of Counsel" relationship, a term sheet can often be a good starting point and can help facilitate and expedite the process. A well-crafted term sheet for a merger, acquisition, or "Of Counsel" relationship can have the same benefits as the Equity Owner (Shareholder) term sheet discussed in the prior paragraph. Appendix E is a sample Merger Term Sheet.

There are numerous steps that law firms must take when considering an acquisition or merger and it is not the intent of this book to be a definitive guide to mergers and acquisitions. The ABA-published book *Anatomy of a Law Firm Merger* (Hildebrandt 2004) is an excellent reference for any law firm contemplating a merger or acquisition.

Part II—Implementation Documents/Agreements

Special Counsel/Of Counsel Agreement

More and more law firms are using "Of Counsel" relationships as either an initial "pilot test" Phase I exploratory relationship or as a permanent succession/transition/exit mechanism. If you think adding an Of Counsel will enhance your law practice, the first step is to find one with the particular experience or expertise you believe will benefit your firm and your clients. Once a suitable candidate is identified, the relationship should be described and put in writing in the form of an Of Counsel agreement. Ensure that any such agreement complies with the rules of professional conduct for your state.

Typical terms that are included in Of Counsel agreements are the term of the agreement, the duties of both the Of Counsel and the firm, malpractice insurance coverage, the mechanism that will be used to collaborate on cases, conflict of interest, compensation, and other rights and liabilities of both parties.

Appendix F is a Special (Of Counsel) Counsel Agreement that was proposed as a succession/transition/exit strategy.

Practice Sale Agreement

One succession/transition/exit strategy used more and more by solo and sole owners is the selling of the practice to another attorney or law firm. Most (but not all) sales of legal practices proceed along the following steps: initial negotiations between the prospective seller and purchaser, signature of an asset purchase agreement (practice sale agreement), notification to the clients of the seller, due diligence, and actual sale of the assets of the legal practice.

Appendix G is a Practice Sale Agreement that was proposed as part of a succession/transition/exit strategy.

Merger Agreement

Often a merger is a drawn-out process over a period of months or sometimes years leading up to a "go" or "no-go" decision. In the case of a larger firm, this involves a formal vote of the entire equity partnership, membership, or shareholders. For solo and sole owners, the decision rests with them and the process moves much quicker. In both situations, once a decision to merge is made and agreed upon, legal documents are prepared by attorneys to acknowledge and document the terms of the merger. Typically, the first document is either a simple letter of intent, term sheet, or a merger agreement that is executed between the two law firms. Items that are usually covered in a merger agreement include:

- Name of the merged firm
- Effective date of the merger
- Management and governance structure
- Compensation system and any deferred benefits
- Capital contributions and required capital accounts
- Retirement policy

- Retirement payouts for founders
- Other matters

Partnership/Operating/Shareholder Agreement

I am often amazed at how many law firms, especially smaller firms, do not have written agreements such as partnership, operating, or shareholder agreements in place. When they do exist, many do not do an adequate job of spelling out details concerning succession/transition/exit planning and retirement. Details concerning valuation of the firm, withdrawal, and payouts are sketchy at best.

Appendix H is a sample partnership agreement for a law firm partnership and Appendix I is a sample operating agreement for a limited liability company. Both of these templates address partner succession/transition/exit and buyout of equity owner interests.

Agreement to Acquire Ownership Interests upon an Owner's Retirement

Usually when an associate attorney is offered an equity interest in a law firm the relationship and arrangement is spelled out in the partnership, or operating or shareholder agreement. However, normally there is a preliminary term sheet or other agreement that is executed prior to these documents.

Appendix J is a sample agreement to acquire ownership interests between an associate attorney and a retiring equity owner.

Buy–Sell Agreement

Law firms operating under a corporate structure will either outline terms for acquisition and disposition of equity owner interests in a shareholder agreement or a separate buy–sell agreement.

Appendix K is a sample buy–sell agreement to acquire and sell equity interests in a law firm organized as a professional corporation.

As I mentioned earlier in this chapter, the appendix includes sample documents and agreements that have been used as content template recommendations in a variety of succession/transition/exit planning projects over the years. While attorneys prepared the sample legal templates for our use in facilitating discussions, they are not ready-to-use documents or agreements. They are simply provided as “content and format ideas” to stimulate thinking. A business attorney in your state or jurisdiction should prepare any legal documents or agreements.

CHAPTER 13

Ethical Issues

A book on succession/transition/exit planning would not be complete without a general discussion of some of the ethical pitfalls, nor without pointing the reader to resources concerning the professional ethics regarding some of the various landmines that he or she may run into while considering various transition/exit options and strategies. A practice is a business and as such, one of its primary aims is to make a profit, but unlike other businesses, the profit motive is not the only and primary concern. As officers of the court, attorneys have other responsibilities and obligations, and must satisfy the ethical requirements of their respective state's rules of professional conduct. These requirements not only affect the profit motive and the pricing of legal services, but also influence how and where services are delivered, who can deliver services, and so on.

Summary of Key ABA Rules of Professional Conduct That Impact Succession/Transition/Exit Strategies

As a law firm management consultant—not legal ethics counsel—I can simply point out that such rules exist and point out some of the areas that a solo, sole owner, or larger law firm should review as they consider various options and strategies. A few of the key rules that may affect a succession/transition/exit strategy involve:

- Lawyer competence
- Conflict of interest
- Sale of law practice
- Professional independence of a lawyer
- Unauthorized practice of law
- Restrictions on the right to practice
- Communications concerning a lawyer's services
- Advertising
- Firm names and letterheads

A good starting point is the ABA Model Rules of Professional Conduct and, more importantly, the rules for your particular state or jurisdiction. Since this book focuses on a national/international readership, I point you to the ABA Model Rules and list here a brief summary of some of the pertinent rules that may pertain to succession/transition/exit situations. Here is a link to the ABA Model Rules website: http://www.americanbar.org/groups/professional_responsibility/publications/model_rules_of_professional_conduct/model_rules_of_professional_conduct_table_of_contents.html

Rule 1.1: Competence

A lawyer shall provide competent representation to a client. Competent representation requires the legal knowledge, skill, thoroughness, and preparation reasonably necessary for the representation.

Rule 1.10: Imputation of Conflicts of Interest: General Rule

a. While lawyers are associated in a firm, none of them shall knowingly represent a client when any one of them practicing alone would be prohibited from doing so by Rule 1.7 or 1.9, unless

1. the prohibition is based on a personal interest of the disqualified lawyer and does not present a significant risk of materially limiting the representation of the client by the remaining lawyers in the firm; or
2. the prohibition is based upon Rule 1.9(a) or (b) and arises out of the disqualified lawyer's association with a prior firm, and
   i. the disqualified lawyer is timely screened from any participation in the matter and is apportioned no part of the fee therefrom;
   ii. written notice is promptly given to any affected former client to enable the former client to ascertain compliance with the provisions of this Rule, which shall include a description of the screening procedures employed; a statement of the firm's and of the screened lawyer's compliance with these Rules; a statement that review may be available before a tribunal; and an agreement by the firm to respond promptly to any written inquiries or objections by the former client about the screening procedures; and
   iii. certifications of compliance with these Rules and with the screening procedures are provided to the former client by the screened lawyer and by a partner of the firm, at reasonable intervals upon the former client's written request and upon termination of the screening procedures.

b. When a lawyer has terminated an association with a firm, the firm is not prohibited from thereafter representing a person with interests materially adverse to those of a client represented by the formerly associated lawyer and not currently represented by the firm, unless:
   1. the matter is the same or substantially related to that in which the formerly associated lawyer represented the client; and
   2. any lawyer remaining in the firm has information protected by Rules 1.6 and 1.9(c) that is material to the matter.
c. A disqualification prescribed by this rule may be waived by the affected client under the conditions stated in Rule 1.7.
d. The disqualification of lawyers associated in a firm with former or current government lawyers is governed by Rule 1.11.

Rule 1.17: Sale of Law Practice

A lawyer or a law firm may sell or purchase a law practice, or an area of law practice, including goodwill, if the following conditions are satisfied:

a. The seller ceases to engage in the private practice of law, or in the area of practice that has been sold, [in the geographic area] [in the jurisdiction] (a jurisdiction may elect either version) in which the practice has been conducted;
b. The entire practice, or the entire area of practice, is sold to one or more lawyers or law firms;
c. The seller gives written notice to each of the seller's clients regarding:
   1. the proposed sale;
   2. the client's right to retain other counsel or to take possession of the file; and
   3. the fact that the client's consent to the transfer of the client's files will be presumed if the client does not take any action or does not otherwise object within ninety (90) days of receipt of the notice. If a client cannot be given notice, the representation of that client may be transferred to the purchaser only upon entry of an order so authorizing by a court having jurisdiction. The seller may disclose to the court in camera information relating to the representation only to the extent necessary to obtain an order authorizing the transfer of a file.
d. The fees charged clients shall not be increased by reason of the sale.

Rule 5.4: Professional Independence of a Lawyer

a. A lawyer or law firm shall not share legal fees with a non-lawyer, except that:
   1. an agreement by a lawyer with the lawyer's firm, partner, or associate may provide for the payment of money, over a reasonable period of time after the lawyer's death, to the lawyer's estate or to one or more specified persons;
   2. a lawyer who purchases the practice of a deceased, disabled, or disappeared lawyer may, pursuant to the provisions of Rule 1.17, pay to the estate or other representative of that lawyer the agreed-upon purchase price;

3. a lawyer or law firm may include non-lawyer employees in a compensation or retirement plan, even though the plan is based in whole or in part on a profit-sharing arrangement; and
4. a lawyer may share court-awarded legal fees with a nonprofit organization that employed, retained, or recommended employment of the lawyer in the matter.

b. A lawyer shall not form a partnership with a non-lawyer if any of the activities of the partnership consist of the practice of law.

c. A lawyer shall not permit a person who recommends, employs, or pays the lawyer to render legal services for another to direct or regulate the lawyer's professional judgment in rendering such legal services.

d. A lawyer shall not practice with or in the form of a professional corporation or association authorized to practice law for a profit, if:
   1. a non-lawyer owns any interest therein, except that a fiduciary representative of the estate of a lawyer may hold the stock or interest of the lawyer for a reasonable time during administration;
   2. a non-lawyer is a corporate director or officer thereof or occupies the position of similar responsibility in any form of association other than a corporation; or
   3. a non-lawyer has the right to direct or control the professional judgment of a lawyer.

Rule 5.5: Unauthorized Practice of Law; Multijurisdictional Practice of Law

a. A lawyer shall not practice law in a jurisdiction in violation of the regulation of the legal profession in that jurisdiction, or assist another in doing so.

b. A lawyer who is not admitted to practice in this jurisdiction shall not:
   1. except as authorized by these Rules or other law, establish an office or other systematic and continuous presence in this jurisdiction for the practice of law; or
   2. hold out to the public or otherwise represent that the lawyer is admitted to practice law in this jurisdiction.

c. A lawyer admitted in another United States jurisdiction, and not disbarred or suspended from practice in any jurisdiction, may provide legal services on a temporary basis in this jurisdiction that:
   1. are undertaken in association with a lawyer who is admitted to practice in this jurisdiction and who actively participates in the matter;
   2. are in or reasonably related to a pending or potential proceeding before a tribunal in this or another jurisdiction, if the lawyer, or a person the lawyer is assisting, is authorized by law or order to appear in such proceeding or reasonably expects to be so authorized;
   3. are in or reasonably related to a pending or potential arbitration, mediation, or other alternative dispute resolution proceeding in this or another jurisdiction, if the services arise out of or are reasonably related to the lawyer's practice in a jurisdiction in which the lawyer is admitted to practice and are not services for which the forum requires pro hac vice admission; or
   4. are not within paragraphs (c)(2) or (c)(3) and arise out of or are reasonably related to the lawyer's practice in a jurisdiction in which the lawyer is admitted to practice.

d. A lawyer admitted in another United States jurisdiction or in a foreign jurisdiction, and not disbarred or suspended from practice in any jurisdiction or the equivalent thereof, may provide legal services through an office or other systematic and continuous presence in this jurisdiction that :
   1. are provided to the lawyer's employer or its organizational affiliates; are not services for which the forum requires pro hac vice admission; and, when performed by a foreign lawyer and requires advice on the law of this or another jurisdiction or of the United States, such advice shall be based upon the advice of a lawyer who is duly licensed and authorized by the jurisdiction to provide such advice; or
   2. are services that the lawyer is authorized by federal or other law or rule to provide in this jurisdiction.

e. For purposes of paragraph (d), the foreign lawyer must be a member in good standing of a recognized legal profession in a foreign jurisdiction, the members of which are admitted to practice as lawyers or counselors at law or the equivalent, and are subject to effective regulation and discipline by a duly constituted professional body or a public authority.

Rule 5.6: Restrictions on Right to Practice

A lawyer shall not participate in offering or making:

a. a partnership, shareholders, operating, employment, or other similar type of agreement that restricts the right of a lawyer to practice after termination of the relationship, except an agreement concerning benefits upon retirement; or
b. an agreement in which a restriction on the lawyer's right to practice is part of the settlement of a client controversy.

Rule 7.1: Communications Concerning a Lawyer's Services

A lawyer shall not make a false or misleading communication about the lawyer or the lawyer's services. A communication is false or misleading if it contains a material misrepresentation of fact or law, or omits a fact necessary to make the statement considered as a whole not materially misleading.

Information about Legal Services

Rule 7.2: Advertising

a. Subject to the requirements of Rules 7.1 and 7.3, a lawyer may advertise services through written, recorded, or electronic communication, including public media.
b. A lawyer shall not give anything of value to a person for recommending the lawyer's services except that a lawyer may
    1. pay the reasonable costs of advertisements or communications permitted by this Rule;
    2. pay the usual charges of a legal service plan or a not-for-profit or qualified lawyer referral service. A qualified lawyer referral service is a lawyer referral service that has been approved by an appropriate regulatory authority;
    3. pay for a law practice in accordance with Rule 1.17; and

4. refer clients to another lawyer or a non-lawyer professional pursuant to an agreement not otherwise prohibited under these Rules that provides for the other person to refer clients or customers to the lawyer, if
   i. the reciprocal referral agreement is not exclusive, and
   ii. the client is informed of the existence and nature of the agreement.

c. Any communication made pursuant to this rule shall include the name and office address of at least one lawyer or law firm responsible for its content.

Rule 7.5: Firm Names and Letterheads

a. A lawyer shall not use a firm name, letterhead or other professional designation that violates Rule 7.1. A trade name may be used by a lawyer in private practice if it does not imply a connection with a government agency or with a public or charitable legal services organization and is not otherwise in violation of Rule 7.1.
b. A law firm with offices in more than one jurisdiction may use the same name or other professional designation in each jurisdiction, but identification of the lawyers in an office of the firm shall indicate the jurisdictional limitations on those not licensed to practice in the jurisdiction where the office is located.
c. The name of a lawyer holding a public office shall not be used in the name of a law firm, or in communications on its behalf, during any substantial period in which the lawyer is not actively and regularly practicing with the firm.
d. Lawyers may state or imply that they practice in a partnership or other organization only when that is the fact.

States That Have Adopted or Modified the ABA Model Rules

Alabama
Alaska
Arizona
Arkansas
Colorado
Connecticut

- Delaware
- District of Columbia
- Florida
- Georgia
- Hawaii
- Idaho
- Illinois
- Indiana
- Iowa
- Kansas
- Kentucky
- Louisiana
- Maine
- Maryland
- Massachusetts
- Michigan
- Minnesota
- Mississippi
- Missouri
- Montana
- Nebraska
- Nevada
- New Hampshire
- New Jersey
- New Mexico
- New York
- North Carolina
- North Dakota
- Ohio
- Oklahoma
- Oregon
- Pennsylvania
- Rhode Island
- South Carolina
- South Dakota
- Tennessee
- Texas
- Utah
- Vermont
- Virgin Islands
- Virginia
- Washington
- West Virginia
- Wisconsin
- Wyoming

Before charging off on a specific succession/transition/exit strategy, ensure that you review and are up on the rules of professional conduct in your specific state and/or jurisdiction. Do not spend massive amounts of time until you know the rules for your state or jurisdiction. I have had clients that charged off in a particular direction, only to find out later that a particular strategy was not in accordance with their state's rules and they then had to abandon their strategy and do a different direction. This resulted in wasted time, effort, and resources.

CHAPTER 14

Key Chapter Takeaways

In the book, I have covered a lot of material with many specific details. This chapter provides key takeaways and a short summary of the key theme of each of the chapters. You may want to keep these takeaways in mind as you contemplate your succession, transition, exit, and retirement.

Chapter 1

Reasons for Early Retirement and Succession Planning

Many small and midsize law firms are setting up formal succession plans to ensure that:

- The firms have the leadership and management in place to continue on to the next generation;
- The firms are able to retain existing client and referral relationships and sources of business and revenue for the firm; and
- The firms are willing and able to finance their buyouts.

Succession is not limited to a single course of action. It involves evaluating different aspects of the firm and identifying systems, processes, and policies that need improvement in order to position your firm or practice succession regardless of your exit strategy. Options for succession/transition/exit typically include:

- Selling or merging the firm or practice;
- Internal transition;
- Practice continuation with other firms; and
- Turning out the lights and closing the practice.

Chapter 2

Coming to Terms with Aging

An essential aspect of retirement planning involves coming to terms with aging. This is the starting point. The more difficult components of retirement include:

- Coming to terms with aging and the fear of getting older;
- Deciding how to spend your time once you quit working;
- Identifying other interests;
- Preserving your self-esteem after retirement;
- Planning your retirement; and
- Dealing with the stress of retirement.

Retirement planning begins with taking the time to think about how you will use your time. Start by creating an interest activity list, a time plan, and then DECIDE, PLAN, and ACT.

Chapter 3

What Other Firms Are Doing

A decade ago, only the more proactive, well-managed law firms had programs and provisions for senior partner succession and transition in place. A majority of firms simply had not addressed or even given serious thought to the eventual retirement and exit of their senior partners. However, in the last five years I have seen a lot of interest in succession, transition, and exit planning. The avalanche of baby boomers reaching retirement age has fueled this interest. Firms from the largest to the smallest are getting proactive and actively addressing succession and transition of senior partners. Some are putting in place formal programs, while others are at least addressing succession and transition informally using ad hoc approaches. The case studies in this chapter illustrate succession/transition/exit strategies that law firms are taking.

Chapter 4

Where and When to Start

The most important ingredient of a successful succession, transition, and exit strategy is to start early. To retire and exit successfully, you need:

A plan—a roadmap that outlines the process and helps you decide on where you want to go and how you will get there.

Timeline—a disciplined implementation timetable keyed to your succession/transition/exit plan.

Start Early—Getting ready for exit takes time. Start early—five to eight years before you are ready to retire or exit.

Decide—When do you want to leave the practice?

Decide—How much cash you will need when you exit.

Decide—To whom you want to transfer the practice.

Chapter 5

Firm Size. Challenges, Issues, and Impact upon Succession and Transition

The size of the firm presents different retirement succession, transition, and exit challenges. Firm size affects the number of moving parts, specific steps that a firm will have to take, and the overall timeline. Solo practitioners and sole owners will have the most moving parts and face the greatest challenges.

Chapter 6

Strategies and Approaches

The biggest challenge for many firms is finding the right WHO.

The *who* dictates the *what*—the actual succession/transition/exit strategy. In other words, many law firms find that they start down one path and end up on another. Not all non-equity partners and associates want to own a law firm. Not all lateral and merger candidates will be a good fit for your firm and culture. The key is the right relationship and sometimes that takes the form of making someone at the firm a partner, bringing in a seasoned lateral, merging with another firm, or selling the practice.

Chapter 7

Finding Candidates and Opportunities

The WHO often dictates the WHAT and this is for some, especially solo practitioners and sole owners, the most time consuming and difficult part of the process. For some larger firms this may also be true as well. The search and grooming process takes time and patience. For some practitioners, finding the right transition candidate—the right WHO—may mean the difference between successfully transitioning the practice and closing the doors.

Successful candidate searches often take a year or longer. Start the process early and allow ample time for conducting the search, vetting the candidates, and performing appropriate due diligence. This applies to all transition candidates, whether they be present or future associate candidates, lateral candidates, merger candidates, or "Of Counsel" candidates.

Chapter 8

Valuation

Whether the firm is considering equity ownership for a non-equity partner, associate, or lateral hire, the firm will have to address the question of value. The same will be true if the firm is considering merger or practice sale. In other words, what is the firm worth? As a firm considers its succession/transition/exit goals and strategies, the firm should perform, or have performed, a valuation of the practice, whether a formal valuation or simply an initial estimate. This will give the firm a feel for the value of the practice. A comprehensive valuation is one of the cornerstones of the succession/transition/exit planning process. Without a good idea of what your firm is worth, it is impossible to make informed succession/transition/exit planning decisions. Without a valuation, you will not be able to plan for retirement, do comprehensive tax planning, formulate a good estate plan, or understand the full extent of various exit options.

Chapter 9

Buy-In/Buyout/Compensation

In Chapter 8, I discussed valuation and the various approaches taken based upon different situations. Valuation should determine a new partner's/shareholder's buy-in as well as buyouts of partners/shareholders, and also play a role in compensation. However, this is not always the case. A few illustrations are provided.

Buy-In

Equity Partner/Shareholder/Member Admission

Law firms and other professional service firms are different from a typical closely held company. Their stock-in-trade is the skills and abilities of their professionals and their assets are their intellectual capabilities. Acquiring or retaining an attorney's talent, skills, and book of business is usually more important than the monetary buy-in. The number of shares (partnership interest) initially offered as well as additional shares (interest) offered in the future is tied to the value that the attorney contributes to the firm from the sweat of their brow. An attorney earns ownership interests through work. Capital contribution, if required at all, is tied to these ownership interests. The remainder of the chapter provides a summary of typical arrangements for new equity partners, shareholders, or members admitted to a partnership, professional, or other corporation, or limited liability company.

Chapter 10

Developing the Plans

Succession/transition plans have to be flexible and often the key is not to get stuck in creating complex succession plans at the onset. Establish timelines, outline a general course of action, generate some momentum, and see where that takes you. Then build the plan when you can see where the firm is headed.

The type of plan will depend upon where you are in the process, size of your firm, type of clients—institutional versus individual clients, and whether you have associates or other non-equity or equity owners in the firm. Here is a general outline and discussion of some of the plans that we have used with client law firms.

Succession/Transition/Exit Project Action Plan

In larger firms where there are heirs apparent, other equity owners, the starting point may be simply writing an internal succession/transition plan and commencing its implementation. In smaller firms with no heirs apparent, the starting point is often a succession/transition/exit project action plan. The key is to approach succession and transition like managing a project or a litigation case using project management concepts and tools. Effective project management is the discipline of getting things done and requires a different approach than managing current operations. A project such as succession and transition happens only one time and has a clear beginning and end. A successful project is completed on time and according to a schedule and it has a clear definition, a plan, and a control system. A project plan is a document with milestone and due dates, start dates, tasks and action items, required resources, and names of those responsible for different tasks and action items. The plan is then used to manage the succession/transition/exit project and related processes. The key is to have a continuous flow, generate momentum rather than fits and starts, and have assigned responsibilities and accountability. A project action plan is designed to accomplish this. An illustration of the format of such a plan is provided.

Internal Succession/Transition/Exit Plan

The succession/transition/exit project action plan provides the roadmap for keeping things moving and managing the overall project. However, in a larger firm with multiple partners, shareholders, or members, succession and transition involves transitioning client relationships and management roles. Such transitions take time. Many larger firms have five-year phasedown retirements for this reason and require equity owners to properly transition clients and management responsibilities. Some firms tie retirement pay or compensation to completing a successful transition program.

Practice Continuation Arrangement/Plan

While many lawyers and law firms are beginning to think about long-range succession issues and the need for long-range succession plans, many have not yet addressed the shorter-range issues. I find that often solo and sole owner practitioners are in a "reactionary mode" and have not adequately prepared backup plans in the event that, in the short term, prior to retirement, something would happen to them.

Chapter 11

Implementation of the Strategies and Plans

Strategies, plans, and ideas are great but useless if not implemented.

Here is a summary of some of the tools that can be used to manage succession/transition/exit planning projects:

- Simple Excel Spreadsheet;
- Microsoft Outlook Task Manager and Calendar;
- Microsoft Office OneNote;
- Project Reports;
- Gantt Charts;
- Dedicated project management software such as Microsoft Project; and
- Online project management systems such as Basecamp (www.basecamp.com) or www.teamwork.com.

Most firms will not need to use sophisticated project management concepts or tools. For most firms an Excel spreadsheet or Microsoft Outlook Task Manager will suffice and the work breakdown schedule can be managed from within one or both of these software packages. However, it is important to create a work breakdown schedule, calendar tasks, and assign responsibilities. Samples of some of these tools are provided in the Appendix and are also available online at http://ambar.org/succession.

Chapter 12

Key Documents and Agreements

Numerous documents and agreements come into play in typical succession/transition/exit planning projects. Initially key documents may be just project plans, calendars, progress checklists, status reports, and so on. As the project moves toward implementation of a specific succession/transition/exit strategy, additional documents and agreements (typically legal agreements) are drafted and executed. The specific documents required are dependent upon the specific strategy. Sample documents are included in the Appendix.

Chapter 13

Ethical Issues

A book on succession/transition/exit planning would not be complete without a general discussion of some of the ethical pitfalls, nor without pointing the reader to resources concerning the professional ethics regarding some of the various landmines that he or she may run into as they consider various transition/exit options and strategies.

A few of the key rules that may affect a succession/transition/exit strategy involve:

- Lawyer competence;
- Conflict of interest;
- Sale of law practice;
- Professional independence of a lawyer;
- Unauthorized practice of law;
- Restrictions on the right to practice;
- Communications concerning a lawyer's services;
- Advertising; and
- Firm names and letterheads.

Here is a link to the ABA Model Rules website: http://www.americanbar.org/groups/professional_responsibility/publications/model_rules_of_professional_conduct/model_rules_of_professional_conduct_table_of_contents.html.

CHAPTER 15

Last Words—Starting Your Journey

As I stated in the introduction to this book, many solo and sole owner attorneys as well as larger law firms are in *reactionary mode* and have not adequately prepared for transition of clients, firm leadership, and management. Your firm's very survival may very well depend upon coming to terms with succession and transition and doing so early.

I hope that this book has helped get you thinking about aging and mortality as well as what you are going to do with your life and your practice after you retire. I asked you to come to terms with aging and accept, rather that deny, the fact that with each passing day, you have less time left on this earth and eventually you will retire from the practice of law, either voluntarily or involuntarily.

Succession and transition planning is all about getting "unstuck" and getting your head out of the sand. I presented present demographics and case studies designed to help you feel a sense of urgency and a desire to begin formulating specific goals and action plans for your life and law practice.

While this book can help get you get started down the path of succession and transition, you may need professional help along the way from professional advisors such as accountants/tax advisors, law firm management consultants, financial planners, insurance agents, business attorneys, spiritual advisors, and accountability coaches or partners. Do not try to take this journey alone. Obtain professional help and guidance along the way.

Throughout this book, I highlighted the demographics of the profession, the importance of early succession planning, and the implications and consequences of failure to address succession and transition. I discussed both challenges and how to come to terms and face aging and eventual retirement as well as what other law firms have been doing and provided stories and case studies of firms that have failed to address succession as well as firms that have successfully addressed succession and transition. I outlined and discussed:

- Where and how to start succession planning;
- Firm size, issues, and impact upon succession and transition;
- Finding candidates and opportunities;
- Strategies and approaches;
- Valuation;
- Buy-in/buyout/compensation;
- Developing the succession and transition plans;
- Implementation of the strategies and plans;
- Key documents and agreements; and
- Ethical issues.

My purpose in this book was to help guide solo practitioners, sole owners, and members of larger law firms on their succession journey and provide tools and resources to help them on their way. I discussed pitfalls to avoid, provided case studies, sample action plans, sample succession plans, sample agreements, and other documents.

An effective succession and transition strategy involves coming to terms with aging and retirement, developing a timeline, and identifying transition candidates—either internally or externally. An old saying at

IBM—what gets planned and what get measured is what gets done. You have worked hard to build your practice. Your practice may or may not have value depending upon the steps you take and when you take them. Start early.

It was my intention and desire that readers would find this book a useful toolkit that helps get senior attorneys and their respective law firms *unstuck* and coming to terms with retirement, succession, and transition by beginning to think about the issue and having open discussions, both at home with family members and at the firm with partners and other stakeholders.

I hope I have succeeded.

APPENDIX A

Sample Law Firm

Project Report: Succession/Transition/Exit Project Action Plan

Samples found in the Appendices are also available online at http://ambar.org/succession.

Project Report: Succession/Transition/Exit Project Action Plan - Sample Law Firm

Completed | Upcoming (next 7 days) | Late

Milestones and associated tasks

Milestone	Description	Date Due	Responsible	Status	Days Late	Date Completed
Begin Transition		01 Jan (2015)	John O.	Complete		07 May (2015)

Milestone	Description	Date Due	Responsible	Status	Days Late	Date Completed
Complete Transition and Practice Exit		31 Dec (2020)	John O.	Upcoming		

Tasks not associated with a milestone

Determine Transition/Exit Strategy (Tasklist)

Task	Description	Start Date	Date Due	Assigned To	Date Created	Priority	Progress	Status
Determine Dates for Full Retirement/Practice Exit and Beginning Phasedown		01 Jan (2015)	31 Mar (2015) (37 days ago)	Client F.	07 May (2015)		0%	Not started
Determine a Rough Estimate of What the Firm Is Worth		01 Jan (2015)	31 Mar (2015) (37 days ago)	Client F.	07 May (2015)		0%	Not started
Determine How Much You Would Like to Get Out of the Practice and How		01 Jan (2015)	31 Mar (2015) (37 days ago)	Client F.	07 May (2015)		0%	Not started
Implement an Equity Partner Consideration/Admission Program		01 Mar (2015)	31 Mar (2015) (37 days ago)	Client F.	07 May (2015)		0%	Not started
Determine How Much Cash or Annual Cash Flow You Will Need When You Exit the Practice		01 Mar (2015)	30 Apr (2015) (7 days ago)	Client F.	07 May (2015)		0%	Not started
Fund a Retirement Plan (if Not Already Done) and Project How Much Income It Will Generate at Various Exit Points		01 Mar (2015)	30 Apr (2015) (7 days ago)	Client F.	07 May (2015)		0%	Not started
Determine if Existing Associates Are Equity Partner Material		01 Mar (2015)	30 Jun (2015)	Client F.	07 May (2015)		0%	Not started
Admit New Partners if Appropriate		01 Jan (2017)	01 Jan (2017)	Client F.	07 May (2015)		0%	Not started

	Task	Description	Start Date	Date Due	Assigned To	Date Created	Priority	Progress	Status
	If Existing Associates Are Not Partner Material - Begin Pursuing a Lateral Strategy		01 Jan (2017)	31 Mar (2017)	Client F.	07 May (2015)		0%	Not started
	If Associate or Lateral Strategy Not Successful - Begin Pursuing a Merger Strategy		01 Jan (2017)	31 Dec (2017)	Client F.	07 May (2015)		0%	Not started
	Establish Date When to Begin Transition Internally (Make Associates Partners) or Bring in Laterals/Merge		01 Jan (2017)	31 Dec (2017)	Client F.	07 May (2015)		0%	Not started
	Decide - To Whom to Transfer the Practice		01 Jan (2017)	31 Dec (2017)	Client F.	07 May (2015)		0%	Not started
	Admit New Partner - Associate or Lateral - If Appropriate		01 Jan (2018)	01 Jan (2018)	Client F.	07 May (2015)		0%	Not started
	Begin Phasedown/Transition		01 Jan (2018)	01 Jan (2018)	Client F.	07 May (2015)		0%	Not started
	Retire and Exit Practice		31 Dec (2020)	31 Dec (2020)	Client F.	07 May (2015)		0%	Not started

Implement Strategies for Enhancing the Future Value of the Firm (Tasklist)

	Task	Description	Start Date	Date Due	Assigned To	Date Created	Priority	Progress	Status
	Improve Profitability - Improve ROI on Marketing Investments		01 Jan (2016)	01 Jan (2016)	Client F.	07 May (2015)		0%	Not started
	Improve Profitability - Improve Staff Performance - Reduce Headcount Ratio if Possible		01 Jan (2016)	01 Jan (2016)	Client F.	07 May (2015)		0%	Not started
	Begin Implementing Management Strategies That Will Maximize the Future Value of the Firm - Before You Exit and Afterward		01 Jan (2016)	01 Jan (2016)	Client F.	07 May (2015)		0%	Not started
	Institutionalize The Firm So It Is Not Uniquely the Firm Owner - Bring Others Up or In		01 Jan (2016)	01 Jan (2016)	Client F.	07 May (2015)		0%	Not started
	Diversify/Increase the Client Base to Reduce Client Dependence on Just 3 Main Multiple Matter Clients		01 Jan (2016)	01 Jan (2016)	Client F.	07 May (2015)		0%	Not started
	Transition Future Equity Partners into Client Relationships and Firm Management		01 Jan (2018)	01 Jan (2018)	Client F.	07 May (2015)		0%	Not started
	Develop a Long-Range Strategic Plan to Focus the Firm's Future Direction		01 Jan (2018)	01 Jan (2018)	Client F.	07 May (2015)		0%	Not started
	Developing a Marketing Plan and Budget to Focus Marketing Activities		01 Jan (2018)	01 Jan (2018)	Client F.	07 May (2015)		0%	Not started
	Develop a Firm Operation Budget		01 Jan (2018)	01 Jan (2018)	Client F.	07 May (2015)		0%	Not started
	Stay Abreast and Implement Appropriate Technologies as Required		01 Jan (2018)	01 Jan (2018)	Client F.	07 May (2015)		0%	Not started

Task	Description	Start Date	Date Due	Assigned To	Date Created	Priority	Progress	Status
Try to Maintain an Associate to Owner Ratio of 3-4 Associates to One Equity Owner		01 Jan (2018)	01 Jan (2018)	Client F.	07 May (2015)		0%	Not started

Administrative Matters (Tasklist)

Task	Description	Start Date	Date Due	Assigned To	Date Created	Priority	Progress	Status
Develop a Partnership Agreement		01 Jan (2018)	01 Jan (2018)	Client F.	07 May (2015)		0%	Not started
Incorporate Founder Retirement Plan in Partnership Agreement or Separate Document		01 Jan (2018)	01 Jan (2018)	Client F.	07 May (2015)		0%	Not started
Develop a Partner Compensation Plan		01 Jan (2018)	01 Jan (2018)	Client F.	07 May (2015)		0%	Not started
Develop Key Financial Dashboard Charts re: Key Financial Metrics		01 Jan (2018)	01 Jan (2018)	Client F.	07 May (2015)		0%	Not started
Implement a Document Management System -May Be Part of a Case Management System		01 Jan (2018)	01 Jan (2018)	Client F.	07 May (2015)		0%	Not started
Implement a Case Management System		01 Jan (2018)	01 Jan (2018)	Client F.	07 May (2015)		0%	Not started
Move to a Paperless Office		01 Jan (2018)	01 Jan (2018)	Client F.	07 May (2015)		0%	Not started

Generated for John Olmstead at 11:20AM 05.07.2015

APPENDIX B

Sample Law Firm

Partner A Transition Plan

Samples found in the Appendices are also available online at http://ambar.org/succession.

I: PURPOSE & OBJECTIVE

A. Partner A has announced his intention to transition and retire from the practice of law.

B. Partner A plans on starting his client and management transition on January 1, 2015, continuing to work full time during 2015 and 2016, gradually phasing down his workload in 2017, substantially phasing down in 2018, and being completely retired on December 31, 2020.

C. The purpose of this plan is to serve as an accountability tool for Partner A and the other partners and help plan, focus, and guide work and efforts during the next five years, all of which is designed to ensure a successful client and management transition.

II: EFFECTIVE DATE

The effective date of commencement of transition is on or around January 1, 2015, and ending on December 31, 2020.

III: PLAN OVERVIEW

A. Partner A shall become a Transition Partner as of January 1, 2016, and he will begin client and management transition at that time and ending on December 31, 2020, at which time he will retire and withdraw from partnership. The transition period shall constitute a reduction in work and transfer of responsibility over a period of five years.

B. Compensation of the Transitioning Partners shall be proportionately reduced by the amount of reduction in the Transitioning Partner's present work schedule. For example, if a Transitioning Partner works a reduced work schedule of 75 percent of his/her present work schedule, then his/her compensation shall be reduced by 25 percent. The Transitioning Partner shall report to the executive committee no later than December 1, what his/her work schedule for the preceding year shall be and the executive committee, after setting the draw of all partners, including the Transitioning Partner, shall then reduce the draw/compensation of the transition partner accordingly. This schedule may be re-evaluated quarterly at the discretion of either the Transitioning Partner or the Executive Committee.

C. Transitioning Partner shall be responsible for the collection of his/her accounts receivable and billing of his/her Work-in-Process throughout the entire transition phase unless delegated to his/her Co-Responsible Partners.

D. Transitioning Partner's purchase price (payout) shall be calculated immediately prior to the beginning of the transition period and in the same time and in the same manner in accordance with the Firm Partnership Agreement, and will be paid only upon the completion of the transition period.

IV: CLIENT TRANSITION

Successful client transition—moving clients from one generation to the next—is a major challenge for all law firms. Shifting clients is not an individual responsibility, but a firm responsibility. To effectively transition clients the individual lawyer, with clients, must work together with the firm to ensure the clients receive quality legal services throughout the transition process. Both the individual lawyer and the firm must be committed to keeping clients in the firm when the senior attorneys retire. Potential obstacles include:

- The firm's complacency regarding the relationship between the responsible attorney and the client.
- Clients who are uncomfortable with other lawyers in the firm doing their legal work.
- Other lawyers in the firm not being familiar with the client's business.
- Senior attorneys who do not include younger attorneys in meetings with clients.
- The point lawyer not identifying the appropriate lawyer successor to the client to work with.

Transitioning client relationships effectively can and, where possible, should, take a number of years—typically not less than three years.

The following client transition plan is designed to effectively transition client relationships over the next two years and nine months.

A. Top Client Lists for Transitioning Partners will be reviewed and a detailed action and milestone plan put in place for each significant client.
B. Transitioning Partner, in consultation with the Firm Executive Committee, shall designate one or more Co-Responsible Attorney(s) for each existing client, and each new client as to which Transitioning Partner is the Responsible (Primary) Attorney. Transitioning Partner, in consultation with the Firm Executive Committee, may for cause adjust or amend the Co-Responsible Attorney(s) designation as to any Transitioning Partner client. The stated goal in designating one or more Co-Responsible Attorneys for each client is to facilitate the transition and retention of Transitioning Partner's clients upon Transitioning Partner's retirement and phase-out from the practice of law. Transitioning Partner agrees to introduce the Co-Responsible Attorney(s) to

the client when the Transitioning Partner is reasonably available, and work with the Co-Responsible Attorney(s) to transition the client and client matters to the Co-Responsible Attorney(s). Transitioning Partner and the Co-Responsible Attorney(s) shall meet to discuss and evaluate the timing for the transition of each client. However, notice to clients shall be solely at Transitioning Partner's discretion. The Co-Responsible Attorney(s) may, at Transitioning Partner's discretion, prepare all invoices for legal services rendered. Transitioning Partner shall review and approve all invoices unless he/she agrees to the contrary in writing. The client's wishes shall be paramount in the designation or selection of any Co-Responsible Attorney(s) and client satisfaction shall at any time allow for change of the designation of same.

C. Transitioning Partner will perform such duties as the Firm Executive Committee of the Firm may from time to time determine to be in the best interest of the Firm and which are agreeable to Transitioning Partner. Transitioning Partner will agree that his/her professional procedures will be in accordance with the rules and regulations promulgated by the Firm Executive Committee. Transitioning Partner will also maintain the records as reasonably required by the Firm Executive Committee.

D. Of Counsel. After December 31, of the final transition year, the parties may enter into an "Of Counsel" relationship with Transitioning Partner and the Firm. In that event, Transitioning Partner would be listed as "Of Counsel." The relationship would be subject to both parties agreeing on the terms and conditions of the "Of Counsel" relationship.

E. New equity partners will develop and submit for approval by the Executive Committee an annual individual personal skill and client development plan.

V: MANAGEMENT TRANSITION

Successful management transition—moving management and leadership from one generation to the next—can also be a major challenge.

The following management and leadership activities are designed to effectively transition management and leadership roles over the next two years and nine months.

A. New equity partners will be invited to serve as members on the executive committee, Chair of the Executive Committee, other committees, or assigned direct responsibility and oversight for a specific management function such as:
   1. Client development/marketing
   2. Human resources/personnel
   3. Financial management
   4. A specific project
B. New equity partners will participate in development of the firm annual budget and financial plan.
C. New equity partners will participate in performance reviews of non-equity partners, associates, and staff.
D. New equity partners will have access to all firm financial records and reports.
E. New equity partners will attend all partner meetings.
F. New equity partners will be invited to attend meetings with the firm's accountants and other advisors.
G. New equity partners will participate in the recruitment and hiring of attorneys and staff.
H. New equity partners will be rotated into a variety of management and leadership roles over the two-year nine-month transition period.

APPENDIX C

Sample Law Firm

Equity Partnership Proposal Lawyer A

Samples found in the Appendices are also available online at http://ambar.org/succession.

Exhibits

	Exhibit
Financial Profile Spreadsheet—2010–2014	A
Capital Account Analysis	B
Calculation of Ownership Percentage Illustration	C
Transition Plan	D
Transition Plan—Action Plan and Milestones	E
Tax Returns—2010–2014	F
Partnership Agreement	G
Office Leases	H
Capital Note	I

I: PURPOSE & OBJECTIVE

A. The firm is pleased to provide this proposal for admission to equity partnership to Lawyer A to become effective on or around April 1, 2015.

B. The overall goal of equity partnership is to reward and provide an enhanced career path for outstanding associates who have worked hard, provided top quality services to firm clients, and worked to maximize the goals of the firm.

C. Lawyer B and Lawyer C have announced their intention to transition and retire from the practice of law.

D. Lawyer B and Lawyer C plan on starting their client and management transition on April 1, 2015, continuing to work full time during 2015, gradually phasing down their schedules in 2016, substantially phasing down in 2017, and being completely retired on December 31, 2017.

II: EFFECTIVE DATE

The effective date of admission to equity partnership is on or around April 1, 2015.

III: WHAT EQUITY PARTNERSHIP WILL MEAN

A. Opportunity to become an equity owner in a law practice that has been extremely successful, profitable on a level with boutique downtown big city firms, and stable.

B. Additional peer and client recognition.

C. More control and direction of your career and your professional future.

D. Opportunity for greater compensation.

E. Initial minority ownership interest (capital) percentage. Additional ownership interest (capital) percentage after Lawyer B and Lawyer C retire and withdraw from the practice.

F. Compensation based upon partnership agreement. Currently the partnership agreement provides compensation to be based upon ownership (capital) interest.

G. Monthly draw against budgeted firm profit in accordance with ownership (capital) interest percentage.

IV: DETAILS AND TERMS

A. Initial minority ownership interest (capital) percentage of eight percent (8%). Additional ownership interest (capital) percentage may be obtained upon or after Lawyer B and Lawyer C's retirement on December 31, 2017, per agreement at that time with the remaining equity partner Lawyer D.

B. Compensation based upon partnership agreement. Currently the partnership agreement provides compensation to be based upon ownership (capital) interest. Based upon the current compensation system, your compensation (earnings) would be eight percent (8%) of firm net profit. You will be required to file your own estimated tax payments and pay your own self-employment tax and pension contributions.

C. Initial capital contribution of $25,000. Five thousand dollars ($5,000.00) payable upon admission to equity partnership with the balance of twenty thousand dollars ($20,000.00) payable within twelve (12 months). You will be asked to sign a "no interest" Capital Note regarding payment of the twenty thousand dollar ($20,000.00) balance. Additional future contributions in accordance with ownership (capital) interest.

D. Monthly draw against budgeted firm profit in accordance with ownership (capital) interest percentage of eight percent (8%).

E. Sign the partnership agreement and a Capital Note.

F. Sign as a signatory with other partners a lease for office space in the existing office.

G. Sign as a signatory with other partners on any firm lines of credit required.

H. Together with Lawyer D, pay Lawyer B and Lawyer C, upon retirement, their cash-based capital accounts and their share of accounts receivable and work in process in accordance with the withdrawal provisions of the partnership agreement. At such time in the future that Lawyer D should decide to retire or otherwise withdraw from the partnership you, in addition to other partners at the time, will pay Lawyer D his cash-based capital accounts and his share of accounts receivable and work in process in accordance with the withdrawal provisions of the partnership agreement.

I. In the event that you withdraw from the partnership, you will be entitled to a payout of your ownership interest (capital) in accordance with the terms outlined in the partnership agreement.

V: CLIENT AND MANAGEMENT TRANSITION PLAN

We the existing partners (Lawyer B, Lawyer C, and Lawyer D) realize that we must take an active role regarding client and management transition. A successful transition of Lawyer B and Lawyer C clients and management responsibilities will require proactive planning, focus, and work during the next three years on the part of the three existing equity partners (especially Lawyer B and Lawyer C) as well as new equity partners being admitted to partnership. The attached Client and Management Transition Plan is designed to focus and guide these efforts.

VI: SUPPORTING DOCUMENTATION

The following supporting documents are attached to this proposal as exhibits:

Financial Profile Spreadsheet—2010–2014—Exhibit A

A financial profile spreadsheet is attached illustrating financial performance from 2010 through 2014. Financial performance has been on par with downtown big city boutique firms and predictable and stable over the five-year period.

Capital Account Analysis—Exhibit B

A capital account analysis is attached reflecting the capital account balances as of December 31, 2014—both on a cash basis and on a modified accrual basis with accounts receivable and work in process included.

Calculation of Ownership Percentage Illustration—Exhibit C

The attached Calculation of Ownership Illustration reflects the analysis that was used to arrive at your initial ownership interest (capital) percentage. Expenses such as self-employment tax and pension have been taken into account in your initial ownership interest (capital) percentage.

The profit pool has been adjusted to illustrate what it would have been had you been an equity partner in 2013–2014.

Transition Plan—Exhibits D and Exhibit E

A transition plan will be implemented to focus client and management transition. While this plan will be fluid and a work in progress, a draft plan is attached outlining key elements and initially providing for the following:

A. Client Transition
    1. Top Client List (Top 20 Clients)
    2. Top Client Transition Plan
    3. Top Client Co-Relationship Partner Assignments
    4. Client Meetings/Visits
    5. Monthly Client Plan Review/Monitoring
    6. New Equity Partner Individual Skill, Personal Brand, and Client Development Plan

B. Management Transition
    1. Membership of new equity partners on the executive committee, other committees, serving as Chair, Executive Committee, or assigned direct responsibility and oversight for a specific management function such as:
        a. Client development/marketing
        b. Human resources/personnel
        c. Financial management
        d. A specific project
    2. Participation in the development of the firm annual budget and financial plan
    3. Participating in performance reviews of non-equity partners, associates, and staff
    4. Access to all firm financial records and reports
    5. Attend all partner meetings
    6. Attend meetings with the firm's accountants and other advisors
    7. Participation in the recruitment and hiring of attorneys and staff
    8. Rotating management roles and assignments for new equity partners over a three-year period.

Tax Returns—2010–2014—Exhibit F

The partnership tax returns for tax years 2010–2014 are attached for your review and reference.

Partnership Agreement—Exhibit G

The partnership agreement is attached for your review and reference.

Office Leases—Exhibit H

Capital Note—Exhibit I

Should you decide you pay your capital contribution over a 12-month period rather than in full, upon admission to equity partnership a zero interest Capital Note will be required. A copy of a Capital Note is attached.

VII: NEXT STEPS

After you have a chance to review this proposal and attached supporting documents, please advise us if you are interested in pursuing or if you have questions and would like to meet with the equity partners to discuss the proposal with you in detail.

We encourage you to also run this past your personal financial and legal advisors as well.

We look forward to you joining the firm as an equity partner.

APPENDIX D

Equity Owner—Shareholder Term Sheet

Memorandum of Agreement for the Admission as Equity Shareholder Lawyer A

Samples found in the Appendices are also available online at http://ambar.org/succession.

1. Effective Date. The effective date of shareholder admission will be January 1, 2016.

2. The name of the firm will be ______________.

3. A shareholder's agreement and buy–sell agreement will be drafted to give effect to the details and terms of the equity shareholder relationship.

4. Lawyer A will be admitted as an equity shareholder with an initial twenty-five percent (25%) shareholder interest. Shareholder interests may increase or decrease over time depending upon personal production and overall contribution to the firm based upon mutual agreement as Lawyer B works less and Lawyer A contributes more. Shareholder

interests will also be dependent upon whether other attorneys are admitted as shareholders. Initial target goals for shareholder interests are:

Years 1–2	Lawyer B 75% - Lawyer A 25%
Years 3–4	Lawyer B 60% - Lawyer A 40%
Years 5–6	Lawyer B 50% - Lawyer A 50%
Years 7–8	Lawyer B 45% - Lawyer A 55%
Years 9–10	Lawyer B 40% - Lawyer A 60%

5. Lawyer A will contribute capital in cash or in kind at a level in accordance with his/her shareholder interest. Upon admission, Lawyer A will contribute $75,000—25% of the cash-based book value plus the value of accounts receivable and unbilled work in process. ($3,000 per share or percentage point—assuming 100 shares.)

6. Lawyer A will be a signatory on the firm credit line and lease.

7. Compensation will be based upon the shareholder compensation plan, which will provide for an individual performance/contribution component and a shareholder component providing for sharing of residual net profit in accordance with a shareholder's ownership share. Lawyer B and Lawyer A each will be paid a scheduled salary and bonuses as cash flow permits. Residual profit allocated based upon ownership shares.

8. The firm will strive to manage by firm by consensus. In the event of a stalemate and the necessity for a formal vote, voting rights will be based upon ownership interests (shares).

9. In the event of withdrawal by either shareholder from the firm, the departing shareholder will be paid their respective share of the cash-based net book value plus accounts receivable and unbilled work in process. In addition, Lawyer B will be paid a founder benefit for the goodwill and firm brand that she has created in the amount of a multiple of .5 times the average past five years annual gross revenue at the time of his/her withdrawal paid in monthly installments over five

years without interest. For example, based upon a five-year average fee revenue of \$1,306,531 × .5 – \$653,266 – \$130,653 per year (\$10,888 per month) for five years.

10. Key Person Life Insurance. The firm shall obtain life insurance and disability policies in the amount of \$____________payable to the other shareholder (or their estate) in the event of death or disability for any portion remaining due under the buy-sell or other agreements.

________________________ ____________

Firm Date
Sample Law Firm
By: Lawyer B

________________________ ____________

Lawyer A Date
By: Lawyer A

APPENDIX E

Merger Term Sheet

Memorandum of Agreement for the Merger of Lawyer a Doing Business as Sample Law Firm and Lawyer B

Samples found in the Appendices are also available online at http://ambar.org/succession.

1. Name. The name of the merged firm will be ____________, LLC. A DBA named __________________will be obtained for Lawyer B's office location.
2. Effective Date. The effective date of the merger will be July 1, 2015.
3. A new LLC will be formed. Articles of Membership and Operating Agreement will be drafted to give effect to the terms of the merger. On the effective date, the parties will be admitted as equity members with the following capital percentage interests:

   Lawyer A - %
   Lawyer B - %

4. Each member will continue to operate primarily out of their respective existing office locations and each member will be set up as a separate profit center in the LLC. Fees and expenses will be allocated to each profit center.

5. Management Committee. The Management Committee for the merged firm will consist of the two members.
6. Decisions Reserved to Members. The two members will each have oversight and manage the day-to-day affairs of their respective profit centers with full authority to make all decisions not specifically reserved for the members. The following decisions are reserved to the members:
   - Admission or expulsion of members.
   - Change of firm name
   - Dissolution of the firm
   - Establishment of the firm's line of credit
   - Approval of all firm (not profit center) expenditures in excess of $1,000.00 not provided for in the firm's budget
   - Election of the Management Committee. (If firm grows)
   - All matters relating to death, disability, retirement, voluntary withdrawal, and expulsion
   - Merger
   - Opening or closing branch offices
   - Change in the compensation system
   - Change in the firm's capital structure
7. Voting Percentages. Each member will have one vote for each ownership share.
8. Compensation. The compensation system will be based upon profit center performance. Two profit centers will be set up in the accounting system. (Office A and Office B) Fees will be allocated to each profit center. Expenses will be allocated to each profit center (primarily allocated by office). However, if staff time is used to service clients in the other office, their expenses will be allocated to the other office based upon timesheets. Other expenses that benefit both profit centers (and previously agreed to by both members) will be allocated to each profit center. Each member's compensation and share of firm profits will be the profit of their office location's profit center.

ILLUSTRATIONS:

9. Member's Draws. The equity members of the merged firm will receive monthly draws against their anticipated profit center net earnings.

The total monthly draw will be allocated pro rata among the equity members in accordance with profit center profit. Supplemental distributions to partners may be declared from time to time by the members if the firm's cash position permits.

10. Members' Capital Accounts. Total initial membership capital for the merged firm will be $___________. Each member will be required to maintain equal capital accounts. Members who have a negative capital balance will be required to contribute additional capital within three months of the effective date of merger. Members whose capital position is above the required amount will be reimbursed in accordance or paid interest on the excess amount at the rate of the current U.S. Treasury Bills.
11. Work in Progress and Accounts Receivable. (Old Business) Each prior firm's accounts receivable and work in progress will be remain with the prior firm and billed and collected through that firm if possible or billed and collected in the merged firm with the proceeds collected returned to the respective prior firms.
12. New Business. All work done by either party on either prior client matters or new clients and or new matters for existing clients will be billed and collected through the merged firm.
13. Income from Law-Related Sources. Any and all that income from law-related sources such as director's fees, teaching salaries, etc., will be paid to the merged firm and allocated to the appropriate profit center.
14. Staff Compensation and Benefits. A determination will be made as to appropriate personnel policies with respect to staff compensation, benefits, and other matters that will apply to the merged firm. The merged firm will in good faith address any inequity that this may cause to either prior firm's personnel.
15. Administrative Systems and Equipment. On the effective date, the accounting system, time and billing system, and contact management systems will be integrated to facilitate one system for accounting and billing at Office A. Remote access will be provided, so both offices have access to the systems. Profit centers as described previously will be established in the accounting system to support the compensation system.

16. Practice Management. It is anticipated that each office will initially each maintain their respective client files, systems, protocols and procedures, and approaches to document generation and management.
17. Marketing. It is anticipated that each profit center will continue individual approaches to marketing and client development as well as joint firm approaches such as a firm website, seminars, etc. Profit center marketing investments will be allocated to the respective profit center and firm investments will be shared and allocated to each profit center.
18. Withdrawal/Retirement Policies. It is anticipated that Lawyer B will retire within the next couple of years. The operating agreement will provide for "buy-out" of Lawyer B's interest that will provide for a return of his/her cash-based capital account, if any, and 20% of collected practice revenue from Office B for five years.
19. Employment of Lawyer B's paralegal. The MERGED FIRM agrees to employ Lawyer B's paralegal who has been a long-term employee of Lawyer B under the terms and conditions to be determined prior to closing, but in all events The MERGED FIRM agrees to exercise all good faith in employing Lawyer B's paralegal upon a minimum of the same terms and conditions she is employed by Lawyer B.
20. The operating agreement will provide for a "buy-out" of member's, other than Lawyer B, interests in the event of retirement, death, disability, or withdrawal.

    The continuing firm shall pay in cash to a retired or otherwise withdrawing member (or their estate) who has satisfied eligibility requirements the following amounts to be paid at the times indicated.

    The value of the Member's capital interest in firm capital as computed and disbursed in accordance with firm policy.

    plus

    The value of the Member's percentage interest in undistributed net income for the current year, which shall be disbursed within sixty (60) days of the close of the year in which the member retired or withdrew;

plus

A full withdrawal payout, calculated and payable as follows, in lieu of any ownership interest in inventory or other assets of the firm:

A members' full withdrawal payout shall be an amount equal to 150% of the average of the highest three years K-1 income (Or Schedule C) in the most recently completed five years' service as a member of prior firm and the merged firms. Payments will be made over five (5) years in monthly installments.

21. Office Leases. The firm will continue to operate from the two existing office locations. The lease obligations will be assigned and assumed by the merged firm. The monthly lease for each office will be charged to each profit center.
22. Professional Liability Insurance. The members of the merged firm shall insure that the insurance carrier, retention and limits, and prior acts coverage, as well as any so-called tail policy coverage, is adequately addressed and covered.

________________________________ ______________

Lawyer B Attorney at Law | Date
By: Lawyer B

________________________________ ______________

Attorney | Date
Lawyer A
DBA Sample Law Firm
By: Lawyer A

APPENDIX F

Special Counsel

Agreement

Samples found in the Appendices are also available online at http://ambar.org/succession.

This Agreement is made effective ____________________, 2015 for a period of six months expiring on ______________ unless renewed by the parties, between LAWYER B, Attorney at Law ("LAWYER B") and LAWYER A, Attorney at Law doing business as LAWYER A ("LAWYER A").

WHEREAS, LAWYER B and LAWYER A are both attorneys duly licensed to practice law in the State of ______________, and

WHEREAS, LAWYER B is exploring options for the eventual succession and transition of ownership of his/her practice and desires to form a six-month (unless extended) exploratory relationship with LAWYER A regarding a possible merger or other combination of the two law firms, and

WHEREAS, LAWYER B and LAWYER A desire to form a "Special Counsel" relationship in order to become familiar with each other to determine compatibility and fit and whether additional steps should be taken in the future regarding possible merger or other combination of the practices, and

WHEREAS, LAWYER B desires from time to time to use LAWYER A to work on Firm matters while LAWYER A also works on his/her own client matters, attorneys desire to collaborate on some matters while continuing to practice law separately.

The parties mutually desire that LAWYER A establish a "Special Counsel" relationship with LAWYER B in the practice of law. Accordingly, the parties desire to set forth the terms and conditions by which that relationship shall be governed. Therefore, it is agreed between the parties as follows:

1. ***Employment.*** LAWYER B shall retain the services of LAWYER A as an independent contractor, not as an agent or employee, in a "Special Counsel" relationship to the LAWYER B.

2. ***Term.*** The "Special Counsel" relationship with LAWYER A shall commence upon the effective date of this Agreement and shall continue until such time as either party terminates the Agreement pursuant to Section 15 hereof.

3. ***Duties.*** During the term of this Agreement, LAWYER A, subject to his/her availability and upon the request of LAWYER A, shall: (a) assist the LAWYER B with client legal engagements primarily within the areas of estate planning, succession business planning, retirement planning and legacy planning (b) review client files for the purpose of consulting on and recommending transaction strategy and documents; (c) assist LAWYER B with the documentation of transactional matters; (d) in LAWYER A's discretion, and with the agreement of the LAWYER B, assume responsibility for negotiation, drafting, and closing of transactional matters and related events; (e) in LAWYER A's discretion, and with the agreement of LAWYER B, assume responsibility for handling of administrative

matters, and (f) engage in other activities relating to the development and client development for LAWYER B in his/her law practice.

4. ***Time Requirements.*** LAWYER A agrees to commit twenty (20) hours (Minimum Time Commitment) of professional time per month to LAWYER B. However, in addition to the Minimum Time Commitment, LAWYER A shall devote such time as may be necessary to handle and complete in an ethical and professional manner those matters which he undertakes for LAWYER B or for which LAWYER A's services are engaged by clients of the LAWYER B, and otherwise discharge his/her duties as set forth in Paragraph 3 of this Agreement. The Minimum Time Commitment is not a guarantee of any minimum payment per month by LAWYER B to LAWYER A.

There may be professional matters that LAWYER B desires to refer to LAWYER A to on a "client referral" basis, and for those matters LAWYER B shall be entitled to receive twenty percent (20%) ("Referral Fee") of any fee charged by LAWYER A as LAWYER B would remain involved in the rendition of service to the client. Furthermore, LAWYER B would receive the Referral Fee for all matters completed by LAWYER A for the client for a period of five (5) years from the date of the referral so long as LAWYER B participates in the rendition of service to the client.

5. ***Compensation, Professional Liability Insurance, and Benefits.***

5A: LAWYER B shall pay LAWYER A as fees for services rendered to clients of LAWYER B, an hourly rate equal to ______________ Dollars ($_________) per hour for time that is charged to any particular client or matter for drafting of legal documents, research or attendance at court calls and hearings. LAWYER A's payment from the LAWYER B shall not be contingent on payment of the bill or receipt of fees by the LAWYER B.

5B: LAWYER B shall name LAWYER A as an insured party upon the Professional Liability Insurance Policy of the LAWYER B with limits no less than: ________________ Dollars ($________________) per claim, ________________ Dollars ($________________) in the aggregate and a deductible of ________________ Dollars ($________________) .

5C: LAWYER A will not be covered under the various life, health, dental, and disability plans currently or hereafter offered by LAWYER B. LAWYER A will not be enrolled nor participate in ERISA programs, if any.

6. ***Expenses.*** LAWYER B shall reimburse LAWYER A for mileage that is chargeable to the client file or is incurred in connection with services provided for clients of LAWYER B, at the Internal Revenue Service (IRS) reimbursable allowable rate. LAWYER A shall submit his/her reimbursable expenses to LAWYER B on the last day of each month or if that day falls on a weekend or holiday, on the business day just preceding that date.

7. ***Records.*** LAWYER A shall keep records of all time spent and expenses incurred in the same manner and in the same form as is prescribed by LAWYER B. Such time shall be entered in the firm's billing system as time is expended on a client matter. LAWYER A shall be subject to the rules and regulations pertaining to the entry of time as determined by LAWYER B from time to time.

8. ***Billing.*** It shall be the obligation of LAWYER B to prepare and mail all bills to clients to whom LAWYER A renders service or expends costs in the manner and form generally utilized by LAWYER B.

9. ***Payment.*** All fees and reimbursement of expenses due LAWYER A pursuant to Paragraphs 5 and 6 of this Agreement shall be paid by LAWYER B to LAWYER A within thirty (30) days of LAWYER A submitting a statement of fees, or if that day falls on a weekend or holiday, on the business day just after that date.

10. ***Taxes.*** It shall be LAWYER A's sole responsibility to pay such federal, state, and local taxes (including but not limited to income taxes and

FICA taxes) as may be imposed or levied upon the income earned or derived by him/her under this Agreement. It is expressly understood and agreed that LAWYER B shall not withhold any such taxes from the compensation paid to LAWYER A.

11. ***Support.*** LAWYER B shall provide LAWYER A with necessary and suitable office space, office supplies, and office furniture. In addition, LAWYER B shall provide LAWYER A with nonexclusive secretarial and clerical services. LAWYER A shall be entitled to perform services in a "remote" work format so long as he/she makes all reasonable efforts to spend a minimum of one afternoon per week at LAWYER B's offices.

12. ***Legal Directories.*** During the term of this agreement, LAWYER B may, at its sole expense, cause LAWYER A's name to be listed as "Special Counsel" on LAWYER B's directory of attorneys, stationary and other publications, advertising and marketing materials, and to the extent that LAWYER B lists the names of individual attorneys in the Martindale-Hubbell (or similar) Directory, ________Bar Association, and/or the ____________, telephone, and in other listings or directories, LAWYER B may list LAWYER A as "Special Counsel" to the LAWYER B in such directories and listings.

13. ***Announcements and Cards.*** LAWYER B may, at its sole expense, cause announcements of LAWYER A's association with LAWYER B to be printed and sent to such persons or organizations, including the use of e-mail and website announcement, as LAWYER B may designate. Further, LAWYER B, at its sole expense, shall provide LAWYER A with business cards indicating his/her association with LAWYER B in the form and style generally utilized by LAWYER B.

14. ***Indemnification.*** LAWYER A, individually, agrees to indemnify LAWYER B for any liability suffered by LAWYER B, its principle, employees, or agents arising from any breach of the terms and conditions of this Agreement, as well as his acts or failure to act from a professional liability claim that is not covered by LAWYER B's professional indemnity insurance; such indemnity shall include, but not be limited to, LAWYER A's deductible or self-insured retention under any such policy of insurance. LAWYER B agrees to indemnify LAWYER A for any liability which he/she may suffer arising from any breach of the terms and conditions of this Agreement, as well as the acts or failure to act from a professional liability claim of any of LAWYER B's principles, associates, employees, or agents, which is not covered by LAWYER B's indemnity insurance; such indemnity shall include, but not be limited to, LAWYER B's deductible or self-insured retention under any such policy of insurance.

15. ***Termination.*** This Agreement may be terminated at the discretion of either party, with or without cause, upon the party wishing to terminate the Agreement and giving the other party at least sixty (60) days' advance written notice of the termination. If this Agreement is terminated, LAWYER A shall be entitled to receive from LAWYER B payment of all sums that may thereafter become due for services performed by him/her during the term of this Agreement. Notwithstanding the preceding termination provision, this Agreement may be terminated by either party immediately upon twenty-four (24) hour written notice for cause if any of the following circumstances occur: If LAWYER B, OR LAWYER A (a) are suspended or barred from the practice of law, sanctioned or disciplined by the Supreme Court of ________and/or the ____________ ____________________; (b) is charged with the commission of a felony or misdemeanor involving honesty or moral turpitude by any jurisdiction with the ability to bring such charges whether State of Federal; (c) commits an act of dishonesty or breach of trust as between each other and/ or the clients of LAWYER B; (d) abuses alcohol to excess or abuses prescription drugs or uses illegal drugs of any type; (e) is disrespectful to clients, is derelict in carrying out usual and customary duties to clients, or so conducts himself/herself so as to cause clients to raise legitimate concerns of professional competence with LAWYER B; (f) commits an act of professional negligence that causes a claim to be made by a client, and said claim is not reported to the Professional Liability Insurance Carrier of LAWYER B pursuant to policy terms, or fails to disclose to LAWYER B any act of professional negligence that the offending party should know or could result in a claim being made against LAWYER B; (g) accepts any case where there is a conflict of interest as between LAWYER B, any attorney assigned to the matter and/or the client or any adverse party; (j) files for a reorganization or liquidation under the United States Bankruptcy Code, makes any assignment for the benefit or creditors, or has any assets attached by any creditor action to collect a debt by any third party.

16. ***Death.*** In the event of the death of LAWYER A during the term of this Agreement, all sums that are then payable to LAWYER A or thereafter become payable to him/her for services rendered prior his/her death shall be paid to LAWYER A or the personal representative of LAWYER A in accordance with the ______________Supreme Court Rules of Professional Conduct as in effect at the time. In the event of the death of LAWYER B, LAWYER A shall have a claim against the Estate of Lawyer B, provided however, the executor of Lawyer B's Estate shall make all efforts to accommodate payment as soon as said executor becomes qualified and has made arrangements for the termination and winding down of the law practice of LAWYER B. All payments shall be made in accordance with the __________Supreme Court Rules of Professional Conduct in effect at the time.

17. ***Binding Effect.*** This Agreement shall be binding upon the heirs, personal representatives, administrators, executors, and assigns of each of the parties.

18. ***Partial Invalidity.*** It is expressly understood and agreed by the parties that should any paragraph or any provision or portion of this Agreement be held invalid, illegal, or void, then and in such event, any paragraph, provision, or portion so held to be invalid, illegal, or void shall be deleted from this Agreement, and this Agreement shall be read as though such invalid, illegal, or void paragraph, provision, or portion was never included herein, and the remainder of such Agreement excluding such invalid, illegal, or void paragraph, provision, or portion shall nevertheless subsist and continue with force and effect.

19. ***Integration.*** This Agreement contains the complete understanding of the parties.

20. ***Disclosure of Information.*** Following the termination of this Agreement, in the absence of authorization, neither party, their shareholders, officers, directors, or principles shall disclose to or use for the benefit of any person, partnership, corporation or other entity, any files, trade secrets, or other confidential information obtained by either party during the term of this Agreement.

21. ***Arbitration.*** Any dispute between the parties arising out of this Agreement or any actions taken or failed to have been undertaken in connection with the negotiation and performance of this Agreement shall be settled by arbitration in either ___________ or _____________ County, ___________according to the commercial arbitration rules of the American Arbitration Association, before a single arbitrator who shall be an attorney with experience in a law firm with at least 10 partners/shareholders, and who shall have been a member of the ____________ Bar for at least thirty (30) years. Judgment upon any arbitration award may be entered and enforced in any court of competent jurisdiction. Each party shall bear their own costs.

22. ***Governing Law.*** This Agreement shall be construed in accordance with the laws of the State of __________________.

23. ***Modification of Agreement.*** No modification or amendment of this Agreement shall be binding unless executed in writing by all parties. No waiver of any provision of this Agreement shall be deemed a waiver of any other provision, nor shall any waiver constitute a continuing waiver.

24. ***Effect of Headings.*** The subject headings of the paragraphs and subparagraphs of this Agreement are included for purposes of convenience only, and shall not affect the construction or interpretation of any of the provisions of this Agreement.

25. ***Right of First Refusal to Purchase the LAWYER B's Practice:*** So long as this Agreement remains in effect, LAWYER A shall possess a Right of First Refusal (ROFR) to acquire the law practice of Lawyer B under the terms and conditions set forth on the Attached Exhibit A. The terms and conditions of the ROFR are as follows:

a. The ROFR shall remain in effect as long as this Agreement is effective as between the parties, and it shall terminate immediately when one party gives notice of a termination of this Agreement pursuant to the terms and conditions of this Agreement either with or without cause. This ROFR may not be assigned without permission of LAWYER B.

b. The terms and conditions of the Law Practice Acquisition Agreement are set forth in the attached Exhibit A, and Exhibit A shall be executed within twenty-four (24) hours of LAWYER A providing written notice to LAWYER B that LAWYER A desires to exercise the ROFR.

c. Should LAWYER B desire to retire, sell, or liquidate his/her law practice, LAWYER B shall first give thirty (30) days' notice (Notice) to LAWYER A in writing of his/her intention, and LAWYER A shall within the said thirty-day period either agree to exercise the ROFR or decline to exercise the ROFR. A failure to respond to the Notice in writing shall be deemed a declination to exercise the ROFR. Should LAWYER B become disabled and/or die during the term of this Agreement, then the executor for the estate of LAWYER B or his/her legal guardian in the event of disability, shall provide the required Notice to LAWYER A, and LAWYER A shall retain the rights granted under the ROFR as if LAWYER B had not suffered a disability or death. The Notice period shall begin once an executor or guardian is qualified for the decedent or disabled adult, and the required written Notice is given to LAWYER A.

26. Breach of Terms and Conditions of Agreement: In the event of either party's default under any of the provisions of the Agreement the nondefaulting party shall be entitled to the remedies available by law or equity including injunctive relief is applicable, as well as, the recovery of reasonable attorney fees and costs incurred in the pursuit of any remedies

SIGNATURE PAGE FOLLOWS

______________________________ _______________

LAWYER B, INDIVIDUALLY Date:

SAMPLE LAW FIRM

By: ___________________________ _______________

LAWYER A, INDIVIDUALLY Date:

APPENDIX G

Exhibit A

Agreement: Sale of Law Practice

Samples found in the Appendices are also available online at http://ambar.org/succession.

THIS AGREEMENT, made and entered into, in duplicate, this ______________day of ________________, 20__, by and between **LAWYER B**, residing at ________________________________ ______________________________________, ______________, ______________, ___________(Zip) and with law office located at ____ ___________ hereinafter referred to as the SELLER and **LAWYER A** doing business as SAMPLE LAW FIRM, residing at ________________ ____and with law office located at ____ ___________, hereinafter collectively referred to as the BUYER.

WITNESSETH:

WHEREAS, SELLER has maintained a law practice in ________ ______________________ for a continuous period of ____ years preceding the execution hereof, and BUYER has maintained a separate law practice in ________________________ for a period of ___ years;

WHEREAS, SELLER desires to sell and BUYER to purchase the law practice of SELLER and specifically the assets thereof, under the terms herein recited;

WHEREAS, SELLER is willing to assist BUYER in the transitional phase of the transfer of his practice and assets thereof by providing advice and consultation so long as he/she does not actively participate in the practice of law on a fee representation basis after the closing date as hereinafter defined; and

WHEREAS, the Parties intend to fully comply with all requirements of ________________________ Supreme Court Rule of Professional Conduct 1.17 (Rule 1.17) in the structure and implementation of this transaction, and any provisions herein that may be in conflict therewith shall be modified to achieve such compliance.

NOW THEREFORE, the SELLER agrees to sell and the BUYER agrees to purchase the assets of the law practice (hereinafter collectively referred to as "the Assets") as hereinafter described, under the following terms and conditions:

1. ***PURCHASE PRICE, PAYMENT, ASSETS, EXCLUDED ASSETS, AND ASSUMED LIABILIES***:
   A. Purchase Price: The Purchase Price shall be a payment of twenty percent (20%) of the "Gross Professional Practice Revenue" received by Buyer from clients of the acquired practice of Seller for a period of five (5) years from the date of closing. These payments are designated The Practice Revenue Payments. Payments shall be made as follows:
      i. At Closing, Buyer shall pay to Seller a non-refundable sum of Fifty Thousand Dollars ($50,000). This payment shall be identified as the Practice Revenue Credit.

ii. Once the Gross Professional Practice Revenue exceeds in the aggregate the sum of \$250,000 (20% × \$250,000 = \$50,000 − Practice Revenue Credit), The Practice Revenue Payments shall commence and be paid to Seller as set forth below.

iii. The Practice Revenue Payments shall be made to Seller, a trust established by Seller, or Seller's Estate as the case may be no later than the fifth day of the close of each month in which a payment is due to Seller. The payment shall be accompanied with an accounting of the payment and the client to which the payment relates.

"Gross Professional Practice Revenues" is defined as the actual client fee collections from all clients of the law practice for the applicable computation period excluding advance cost collections, and administrative or actual expenses charged to the client.

B. Assets Included in the Sale:
   i. All client files, lists, records, and information related to the Sellers' practice of law;
   ii. All equipment, supplies, and furniture and fixtures scheduled on Exhibit A;
   iii. All Goodwill of the Professional Practice;
   iv. The telephone number, website, facsimile number, and email addresses of the Professional Practice; and
   v. All library and professional books as scheduled on Exhibit A-1.

C. Excluded Assets—The following Assets are excluded from this transaction:
   i. Existing accounts receivable, billed and unbilled, for completed professional services of SELLER;
   ii. Cash in SELLER'S checking and other accounts;
   iii. Deposits and refunds of any type or description;
   iv. The personal items of the Seller listed on the attached Exhibit B; and
   v. Advanced Costs of the Seller for client matters.

D. Assumed Liabilities: No liabilities of the Seller are assumed by the Buyer unless Scheduled on Exhibit C.

2. ***DUTIES OF PARTIES***: SELLER shall serve in advisory or consulting capacity to BUYER as requested by Buyer, and shall be available to BUYER a minimum of eight (8) hours per week (excluding vacation periods) for six (6) months after the closing (Consulting Period). BUYER will furnish Seller office space to enable SELLER to function as such consultant, and shall pay SELLER a consulting fee of ____________________dollars per hour ($______ during the Consulting Period Buyer shall bear no responsibility for insuring Seller under any professional liability policy or reimbursing Seller for any premiums on coverage that Seller may elect to buy.
3. ***TITLE TO ASSETS:*** SELLER represents and warrants to BUYER that all Assets shall be free and clear Assets to be transferred to BUYER.
4. ***TRANSITIONAL ACTIVITIES***:
   a. Clients of SELLER shall be properly notified of this sale, and while SELLER shall use his best efforts to preserve select clients for BUYER, both Parties recognize and acknowledge the clients' right to retain other counsel and to take possession of their respective files.
   b. Parties further agree that representation agreements for clients of SELLER shall be honored according to their terms and conditions, and that there will be no increase in professional fees for the matters so transferred to BUYER by this Agreement for purposes of paying for the Purchase Price stated herein. The confidentiality of client information will be strictly preserved.
   c. The Parties shall use good faith and best efforts to fairly allocate legal fees from SELLER'S clients accruing after execution hereof, it being understood and agreed that SELLER shall retain fees for his/her legal services completed and billed prior to closing; shall share equitably in fees for his/her services rendered before but completed and billed thereafter; and shall not participate in fees for BUYER'S services rendered prior to or after closing.
   d. The Parties agree that the Rule 1.17 Notices will be sent to all clients current or former who will have a client file transferred to the BUYER (for purposes of this Agreement, "current clients"

as referred to in Rule 1.17 shall be defined to be all active and inactive clients of Seller for which it is proposed to have a file transferred to BUYER). The Parties specifically recognize that former client files contain Attorney Client Privileged information that may only be transferred upon due notice to the former client.

e. The BUYER shall be entitled to conduct due diligence upon the individual client files to be transferred as each client consents to the transfer by either verbal or written communication to the SELLER'S office (see, procedure for creation of a Client Contact Log below Section 5). Any clients that fail to take any action for 90 days after being given due notice pursuant to Rule 1.17 shall be presumed to have consented to the transfer, and BUYER shall at that time be entitled to review the files for due diligence purposes. All file transfers shall comply with Rule 1.17 sub-part (f) relating to the Ethical Standards of the Profession. The due diligence review shall be made for the purpose of ascertaining any conflict of interest and/or the professional competency of the BUYER to complete the client matter. Should the BUYER determine that a conflict of interest exists with a client or particular client matter, or that the BUYER does not possess the requisite professional expertise to complete a client matter, the SELLER shall notify the client to obtain other counsel to handle the matter, and a transfer shall be made pursuant to the client's instructions.

5. ***RULE 1.17 NOTICE AND CLOSING DATE:*** The parties shall fully comply with Rule 1.17, which requires the mailing of a Notice to all "current clients" as defined in Section 4. The notices shall be sent certified mail return receipt requested at SELLER'S COST. The responses shall be notated, secured, and filed by SELLER, and copies of the return receipts placed in each client file, with the originals to be placed in a central file relating to the sale transaction. SELLER shall keep a written log of each client call or contact (Client Contact Log) that may result from the notices, and shall appropriately notate the Client Contact Log as to any respective client's consent or client request for a transfer of the file to a new attorney. The respective Client

Contact Log reflecting client consent to transfer shall be placed in each client file that is transferred to BUYER, and a copy of each Client Contact Log shall be placed in a central file relating to the sale transaction. The Client Contact Log reflecting any clients desire to transfer a file to another attorney shall be maintained by SELLER, and the files shall not be transferred to BUYER.

The parties shall determine a mutually agreeable closing date, which shall be not earlier than 120 days following SELLER'S mailing of client Notices pursuant to Rule 1.17(c).

6. ***REPRESENTATIONS AND WARRANTIES:*** Each of the Parties represents and warrants to the other that:
   a. Neither party has knowledge of any claims or liabilities arising from her law practice, whether absolute or contingent; nor is she aware of any condition or any event which could reasonably be expected to give rise to any liability to herself or the BUYER; and they will indemnify and hold harmless the other party from any such liability.
   b. To the best of their knowledge and belief, neither party is in default under or in violation of any applicable statute, law, ordinance, decree, order, rule, regulation or license of any governmental body, authority or agency having authority over her which may result in an adverse effect upon this transaction or the handling of any client matter, and has not received any notice of any violation of any of the foregoing.
   c. To her best knowledge and belief, there is no suit, arbitration, claim, investigation, action or proceeding now pending or threatened, before any court arbitrator, administrative or regulatory body, or any governmental agency to which she is a party, and which may result in any judgment, award, order, decree, liability, injunction, restraining order or other determination which will or could have any adverse effect upon this transaction.
   d. Both parties have maintained insurance to protect themselves against the types of liabilities, including professional malpractice,

customarily insured against by persons engaged in the operation of similar practices, and all premiums due on such policies have been paid.

e. Neither party will act or represent themselves in an agency capacity or relationship with the party, as either principal or agent, so as to create any liability on their part; and will indemnify and hold harmless the other party from any claim or liability resulting as a result of any representation.

f. Buyer assumes no liability for the conduct of Seller's law practice prior to the date of closing including without limitation account payables, leases of equipment, service contracts, license fee's, employee benefit plan payments of any type, real estate leases, creditor claims of any type or nature, trust account activity (unless the specific account is transferred to BUYER pursuant to Section 11, below) professional liability claims, tort claims, and any other claim of any type or description, and Seller agrees to fully protect, indemnify, and save Buyer harmless from any such liability, including the payment of any attorney's fees and court costs incurred by BUYER in defending any such claims.

g. That there is not now pending nor does either party have any notice of any pending complaint with the Attorney Registration Disciplinary Commission (ARDC) of the ________________ Supreme Court, and that both parties are and will remain licensed attorneys in the State of ________________through the date of closing.

7. ***CONFORMITY WITH SUPREME COURT RULE 1.17***: This sale shall be consummated in strict compliance with Supreme Court Rule 1.17. After closing, SELLER shall no longer be actively engaged in the private practice of law on a fee representation basis, and her sole responsibility hereunder shall be the rendition of in-house consultation services to BUYER to facilitate the transfer of assets, clients, and files pursuant to this Agreement. SELLER'S private law practice in ________________________, and the surrounding geographic area shall completely cease and become inactive on the closing date hereof.

8. *COVENANT TO RETIRE FROM PRACTICE OF LAW:* SELLER covenants and agrees that upon completion of the transaction that SELLER will be completely retired from the practice of law, and will not compete with the BUYER in the practice of law within _____________ and __________(Covenant Counties) in ________________for a period of five years from the date of closing. SELLER shall not engage in the practice of law offering services to the general public within the Covenant Counties. The Seller may act as a lawyer on the staff of a public service law entity offering services to the indigent, or act as in-house counsel to a business. Any violation or attempted violation of this covenant shall allow the BUYER to seek injunctive relief from a court of appropriate jurisdiction, and the BUYER shall also be entitled to a recovery of damages for any violation of this covenant not to compete.
9. *DEFAULT:* In the event of either party's default under any provision of this agreement, including without limitation the Representations and Warranties of Section 6 hereof, the other party shall have all the remedies available by law, including reimbursement for reasonable attorney fees and costs incurred in the pursuit thereof.
10. *MISCELLANEOUS PROVISIONS:*
    a. This Agreement, together with all documents to be delivered pursuant hereto, shall set forth the entire understanding and supersede all prior oral and written agreements between the Parties hereto relating to the subject matter contained herein and all prior and contemporaneous negotiations or discussions between the Parties hereto are merged herein. No Party hereto shall be bound by any definition, condition, representation, warranty, covenant, or provision other than as expressly stated in this Agreement, or as hereafter set forth in a written instrument executed by such Party.
    b. If any provision of this Agreement is determined unenforceable for any reason, such provision shall be modified to the extent necessary to make it enforceable or, if necessary shall be deemed inoperative, and the remainder of this Agreement shall remain binding upon the Parties hereto.

c. Every notice or other communication required, contemplated, or permitted by this Agreement by any Party shall be in writing and shall be delivered either by personal delivery, telecopy, private courier service, or certified or registered mail with return receipt requested, addressed to the Party to whom intended at the following address:

   i. If to **LAWYER B**: ______________________________, ______________________________

   ii. If to **LAWYER A**: ______________________________ ______________________________

   or at such other address as the intended recipient previously shall have designated by written notice.

d. This Agreement may be executed in any number of counterparts, and each counterpart shall constitute an original instrument, but all such separate counterparts shall constitute one and the same agreement.

e. No remedy conferred by any of the specific provisions of this Agreement is intended to be exclusive of any other remedy, and each and every remedy shall be in addition to every other remedy given hereunder or now or hereafter existing at law or in equity or by statute or otherwise. The election of one or more remedies by any Party hereto shall not constitute a waiver of the right to pursue other available remedies.

f. This Agreement shall be construed and interpreted, and the rights of the Parties determined, in accordance with the laws of the State of __________.

g. This Agreement shall be binding upon and shall inure to the benefit of the Parties hereto and their respective heirs, executors, administrators, personal representatives, successors, and assigns.

h. The parties agree that SELLER shall be entitled to store his/her closed files which are not being transferred to BUYER upon the BUYER'S premises for a period of five years without charge so long as BUYER has appropriate space available for such storage. Removal of all records to and from BUYER'S premises shall be at SELLER'S cost and expense.

i. BUYER agrees to employ __________, who has been a long-term employee of SELLER under the terms and conditions to be determined prior to closing, but in all events BUYER agrees to exercise all good faith in employing ______________upon a minimum of the same terms and conditions he/she is employed by Seller.

11. ***TRUST ACCOUNT TRANSFER***: To the extent any clients whose files are being transferred to BUYER have funds held in the SELLER'S Trust Account, said funds shall be accounted for on a Trust Fund Transfer Schedule at Closing, and an appropriate transfer of funds shall take place at Closing to BUYER. SELLER shall certify the Trust Fund Transfer Schedule as true and accurate, and BUYER shall acknowledge receipt of the funds being transferred all to be deposited into BUYER'S Trust Account, which shall be in compliance with Supreme Court Rules related to the Trust Funds of clients.
12. ***USE OF SELLER'S NAME***: The BUYER and any successor to BUYER shall be entitled to use the SELLER'S name in BUYER'S Law Firm Name as long as the SELLER is designated as "Retired," or in the event of SELLER'S death, "Deceased." The BUYER shall have the absolute right to include the SELLER'S name as part of BUYER'S law firm name as long as such use comports with all ethical considerations of the Supreme Court Rules of Professional Conduct.
13. ***CLOSING***: This Agreement shall have a Closing on the thirtieth (30th) day, or the first business day thereafter should the thirtieth day fall on a weekend or holiday, following the date of the Rule 1.17 Notice, unless another date is agreed upon by the Parties. Closing shall take place at SELLER'S office at 1:30 p.m. on the Closing date. At Closing, the parties shall provide the following:
    a. Seller:
        i. Bill of Sale and Assignment in good form for the transferred Assets;
        ii. Executed Copy of this Agreement;
        iii. Transfer of Trust Account Funds for the benefit of the Clients;

iv. Such other documents and receipts necessary to effect the Closing as are approved by Seller's Counsel; and

v. Possession of all Assets.

b. Buyer:

i. Executed Copy of this Agreement;

ii. $50,000 in certified funds (The Practice Revenue Credit);

iii. Buyers Certificate of Authority to Practice Law with the ________ Supreme Court and Certificate of Authority to transact business within ________________;

iv. Buyer's Directors Resolution authorizing this transaction; and

v. Such other documents and receipts necessary to effect the Closing as are approved by the Buyer's Counsel.

14. *CONDITIONS PRECEDENT TO CLOSING*: The following are Conditions Precedent to the BUYER'S and /or SELLER'S obligation to close pursuant to the terms and conditions of this Agreement:

a. That, each party is licensed to practice law in __________ at Closing;

b. That, there is not pending an ______________BAR/ARDC complaint against either party at Closing; and

c. That, there has been no material change to Rule 1.17 that would prohibit or impact the Closing in a material manner.

IN WITNESS WHEREOF, the Parties hereto have hereunder set their hands and seals, all on the day and year first above written.

SELLER:

____

LAWYER B____

____________________BUYER:

SAMPLE LAW FIRM____

____________________BY:

LAWYER A

APPENDIX H

Partnership Agreement for Sample Law Firm

Samples found in the Appendices are also available online at http://ambar.org/succession.

The undersigned parties hereby agree to confirm that they are Equity Partners and have been engaged as such in a law partnership under the name SAMPLE LAW FIRM and desire to continue the business and affairs of such partnership in accordance with the provisions hereinafter set forth.

Article I-GENERAL

1.1. Parties. The undersigned parties (hereinafter called the "Equity Partners") to this Agreement are all of those persons listed on the Signature Page(s) attached hereto and made a part hereof and are as follows:

Lawyer A - 1/3;
Lawyer B - 1/3; and
Lawyer C - 1/3.

1.2. Effective Date. The effective date of this Agreement shall be _____, _____. All accounts receivable and payable as well as work in process not yet billed through _______, ______ shall remain the property of Lawyer A and Lawyer B along with the responsibility to pay the previously agreed percentages of Lawyer C on his/her respective share of such accounts receivable.

1.3. Name. The Partnership name is SAMPLE LAW FIRM (hereinafter called the "Partnership" or the "Firm").

1.4. Purpose. The purpose of the Partnership is to engage in the practice of law and to conduct all types of business incident thereto.

1.5. Location. The principal place of business of the Partnership shall be at __________ in the State of _________. This location may be changed and/or additional offices maintained at such places as may be determined by the Executive Committee. Such location, changes, or additions may be made without formal written amendment of this Agreement.

1.6. Term. The Partnership shall continue until terminated in accordance with the terms of Article Nine of this Agreement.

Article 2-GENERAL DEFINITIONS

2.1. Defined Terms. As used in this Agreement, the following terms shall have the following respective meanings:

(a) "Capital Account" of each Equity Partner shall be the amount set forth opposite the Equity Partner's name on Schedule E hereto, plus the amount of any cash contributions which may hereafter be made by such Equity Partner to the capital of the Partnership.

(b) "Capital Note" shall mean the promissory note issued by an Equity Partner to the Partnership in connection with his admission to the Partnership.

(c) "Equity Partner" shall mean those Equity Partners identified as such on the Signature page(s) annexed hereto, as the same may be amended from time to time, together with such other or additional persons as shall hereafter become Equity Partners as provided herein.

(d) "Former Equity Partner" shall mean at any time each individual (not then an Equity Partner under this Agreement) who shall have been an Equity Partner under this Agreement or under any prior Partnership

Agreement, and whose status as such an Equity Partner, shall have terminated for any reason.

(e) "Liable Equity Partners" shall mean, with respect to (i) any particular indebtedness or contractual obligations of the Partnership or (ii) any particular debts and obligations of the Partnership arising from errors, omissions, negligence, incompetence, or malfeasance committed in the course of the Partnership business.

(f) The "Partnership" shall mean the law firm as now organized and the continuing firm, however named and reconstituted from time to time, notwithstanding the termination of the membership of any Equity Partner.

(g) The "Partnership Termination Percentage" of an Equity Partner, calculated as of any Termination Date (as described in Section 8.1 hereof) is the amount which (i) the average of such Equity Partner's Total Income (as hereinafter defined) for the immediately preceding three (3) calendar years (or such lesser number of calendar years as the Equity Partner shall have had Total Income) ("Average Income") bears to (ii) the sum of the Average Incomes of each of the persons who are Equity Partners at such Termination Date; provided, however, that except in the event of the termination of the Partnership, the number of calendar years over which Total Income is averaged under the preceding clause (ii) shall not exceed the number of calendar years which Total Income is averaged under the preceding clause (i); and provided, further, that for the calendar year of his admission to the Partnership, an incoming Equity Partner shall have a Partnership Termination Percentage equal to his Partnership Interest, and the Partnership Termination Percentages of the other Equity Partners shall be adjusted on a pro rata basis, in accordance with their Partnership Termination Percentages.

(h) "Practice" shall mean the activities of the Partnership as authorized by this Agreement and by law, and shall include all those activities of the Equity Partners, the income from which, by the terms hereof, belongs to the Partnership.

(i) The "Total Income" of an Equity Partner for any calendar year shall be one-third of the profit from the firm as determined herein.

2.2. Other Definitions. The definitions contained in other sections of this Agreement shall apply throughout this Agreement unless otherwise specified.

2.3. Gender. All pronouns and any variations thereof used in this Agreement shall be deemed to refer to the masculine, feminine, neuter, singular and plural, as the context requires.

Article 3-DUTIES OF EQUITY PARTNERS

3.1. Full-Time Efforts. Each Equity Partner shall devote his full-time ability, energy, and best endeavors, to be used and employed in common among the Equity Partners, in furtherance of the Practice, except as otherwise herein provided.

3.2. Vacations. Equity Partners may take such reasonable vacations as may be agreed upon by the Executive Committee.

3.3. Expense Reimbursement. The general requirements regarding and the procedures for the establishment and maintenance of Equity Partner Business Expense Reimbursement are set forth in a separate policy schedule.

3.4. Outside Interests. Subject to the provisions of Section 3.1 hereof, any Equity Partner may participate or be interested in any business venture or enterprise other than the Practice; provided, however, that the same shall not (a) be conducted under the present, past or future name of the Partnership (or any predecessor of the Partnership) or a name which bears a similarity thereto, (b) involve the private practice of law, or (c) adversely affect the operations of the Partnership. The proceeds of any such venture or enterprise, other than those included in items (a), (b), and (c) of this section, shall belong to such Equity Partner, and the Partnership shall not participate in any income, profits, or losses therefrom or in connection therewith by virtue of this Agreement. If any legal services are rendered by the Partnership or such Equity Partner in connection therewith, such Equity Partner shall pay or cause to be paid to the Partnership the fair and reasonable value of the services so rendered.

3.5. Leaves of Absence. Leaves of absence shall be allowed at the discretion of the Executive Committee pursuant to the terms of Paragraph 4.1.

3.6. Code of Professional Responsibility. Each Equity Partner at all times shall comply with all of the applicable provisions of the Code of Professional Responsibility and with the statutes, rules and regulations covering all professional services that the Equity Partner shall render.

3.7. Partnership Obligations. No Equity Partner shall incur, in the Partnership name (or in the name of any other Equity Partner), any obligation, make or endorse any note, become a guarantor or surety for any person whomsoever, or sell, assign, transfer, pledge, mortgage, encumber or otherwise dispose of any of the business or assets of the Partnership or the other Equity Partners, as the case may be, without the consent of the Executive Committee.

Article 4-MANAGEMENT

4.1. Executive Committee. The management and governance of the Partnership and implementation of this Agreement shall be vested in an Executive Committee (Executive Committee), consisting of three partners, which shall manage the day-to-day operations of the partnership and shall have the power and authority:

(a) To approve and incur unbudgeted capital expenditures.

(b) To make all decisions and take all required actions concerning any Partnership sponsored retirement plan (hereinafter called "The Partnership Retirement Plan").

(c) To formulate and administer Partnership billing policies and practices and to formulate write-off policies and practices.

(d) To recommend to the Partnership the amount of the capital contributions to be made by new Equity Partners.

(e) To make recommendations to the Equity Partners respecting major changes in the scope or nature of the Practice, including, without limitation, recommendations regarding (i) acquisition or disposal of premises; (ii) the merger with other law firms or the making of changes in the structure of the Partnership; (iii) upon advice and recommendation from the Department chairpersons, the introduction of new Equity Partners from within or without the Firm; (iv) the restructuring of any existing Department not contemplated in the budget; (v) the branching or affiliation of the Firm with another law firm.

(f) To permit or prohibit any Equity Partner or employee from serving as a director of any organization or acting as a trustee, executor, or other fiduciary (other than acting as escrow agent, or acting as a fiduciary for such person's family members).

(g) To consider other matters as determined by the Equity Partners.

4.2. Members of Executive Committee. The initial members of the Executive Committee shall be Lawyer A, Lawyer B, and Lawyer C.

4.3. The Managing Equity Partner (Chairman). The Chairman shall be Chairman of the Executive Committee and Managing Equity Partner of the Partnership and will preside at all meetings of the Executive Committee (Management Committee), and of the Partnership and be elected by a majority vote of the Equity Partners. The Chairman may call Executive Committee meetings at any time and will be a nonvoting ex officio member of all Committees of which he is not otherwise a member. The Chairman will have a one-year term and at the end of each term, there will be a subsequent nomination by the Executive Committee which will be submitted at the time of the relevant Annual Election to the Equity Partners for election by a majority vote of the Equity Partners.

4.4. Binding Effect. All actions of the Executive Committee shall be binding upon the Partnership.

4.5. Exculpation. The Partnership shall indemnify the members of the Executive Committee for actions taken by such members in good faith on behalf of the Partnership.

4.6. Authority to Deal with Property and Execute Instruments. Without limiting the scope of the foregoing, the Executive Committee shall have the authority to buy, sell, deposit, withdraw and transfer, in the name of the Partnership, property of every kind and character, and to execute all such instruments as may be necessary to carry on the ordinary and normal business activities of the Partnership including:

(a) Authority to Deal with Leases. All leases for space occupied by the partnership must be approved by the Executive Committee and signed by each Equity Partner. The Equity Partners agree that the executed lease with ________ dated ______ is hereby approved. The

Equity Partners agree that the subleases with _____ and the ______ are hereby approved. The Equity Partners further agree the executed lease for the _____ property located at ____________ and dated ______, is hereby approved. Should an Equity Partner refuse to sign a lease approved by the Executive Committee, such refusal shall constitute the withdrawal of the Equity Partner from the Equity Partnership pursuant to Article Eight hereof.

(b) Authority to Deal with Loans. All loans or lines of credit must be approved by the Executive Committee and thereafter separately approved by each Equity Partner. The existing line of credit in the amount of $_________at ________ is hereby approved. Should any Equity Partner refuse to sign a line of credit or loan approved by the Executive Committee, such refusal shall constitute the withdrawal of the Equity Partner from the partnership pursuant to Article Eight hereof.

4.7. All decisions of the Executive Committee shall be made by a majority in number of the members of the Executive Committee except as to decisions found in 4.8.

4.8. Decisions and Determinations of the Partnership.

(a) Except as otherwise specifically provided in this Agreement, all decisions and determinations of the Partnership not coming within the scope of authority specifically delegated to any Committee shall be made by a majority (in number) of the Equity Partners.

(b) Notwithstanding the foregoing, all decisions and determinations with respect to the following matters shall be made by not less than sixty-seven (67%) percent (in number) of the Equity Partners:

(i) The admission of additional Equity Partners to the Partnership.

(ii) The merger of another law firm or practice with or into the Partnership.

(iii) The change in name of the Partnership.

(iv) The establishment from time to time of a change in each Equity Partner's level of compensation, Non-Accountable Expense Reimbursement, and The Partnership Retirement Plan.

(v) The making of any modifications of, or amendments, to this Agreement.

(vi) Increasing Partnership indebtedness if the aggregate indebtedness in an amount to exceed $50,000.

(vii) Extension or modification of the existing Leases or Subleases if such extension or modification results in substantive change in terms.

4.9. Proxy Vote. An Equity Partner who is not physically present to vote on a decision or determination of the partnership may vote by proxy or by specific written authorization to another Equity Partner to vote for him.

4.10. Partnership Meetings. Monthly meetings of the Partnership shall be held as determined by the Equity Partners. An annual meeting of the Equity Partners shall be held in ___________of each year on a day to be fixed by the Executive Committee. A special partnership meeting may be called on 7 days' notice to the other Equity Partners by any Equity Partner.

4.11. Vote for Removal. The Partnership, by vote of not less than fifty-one (51%) percent (in number) of the Equity Partners, may terminate any Equity Partner's membership in the Partnership for any reason whatsoever, with or without cause. The Equity Partner being removed shall be entitled to be present at the Partnership meeting at which such vote is proposed to be taken and may himself participate in such vote.

Article 5-OPERATIONAL MATTERS

5.1. Bank Accounts. All funds, checks, notes, and drafts received for or on behalf of the Partnership shall be deposited promptly in the account or accounts maintained by the Executive Committee in such bank or banks as shall be determined by the Executive Committee. All Partnership moneys shall be withdrawn only by checks signed by such one or more Equity Partners or/and in such manner as shall be designated by the Executive Committee. The Partnership shall continue to maintain not fewer than two bank accounts in the Partnership name, one of which shall be designated "Special" and shall be for funds deposited in escrow and funds collected, received or held for clients, or for distribution in connection with clients' transactions. The Partnership may maintain other bank accounts for special purposes and may open such additional bank accounts as the Executive Committee shall determine from time to time. The Partnership's banking records and practices shall comply with applicable requirements of the State of ____________and applicable law.

5.2. Equity Partners as Agents. The Partnership, or any Equity Partner on behalf of the Partnership, may endorse and collect any checks, drafts, promissory notes, instruments, or securities constituting Partnership income hereunder, even if received by or payable to any individual Equity Partner. Any mail, which shall be received at the offices of the Partnership, even though addressed to a particular Equity Partner, may be opened by any Equity Partner unless marked "confidential" and/or "personal." Each Equity Partner hereby irrevocably constitutes and appoints each of the other Equity Partners his attorney-in-fact for the aforesaid purposes, which power is coupled with an interest and which power shall survive said Equity Partner's resignation, retirement, death, or incapacity.

5.3. Partnership Income. All fees, salaries, proceeds, commissions, and other compensation earned or received by any Equity Partner (a) for legal services which are substantially similar to those services which said Equity Partner performs on behalf of the Partnership (but excluding any amounts earned or received by any Equity Partner for legal services rendered before the Equity Partner became affiliated with the Partnership), (b) as a holder of political or public office, (c) as a corporate officer or director, trustee, receiver, executor, guardian, administrator, commissioner, master, referee, arbitrator, author, editor, lecturer, teacher, title closer, broker, or finder, (d) as title company or brokerage commissions, (e) from servicing properties or mortgages, or (f) from similar or related professional activities which are substantially similar to those activities which said Equity Partner conducts on behalf of the Partnership shall belong to the Partnership and shall be deposited for and paid over to the Partnership as and when received in exactly in the form received (except for endorsement where required). The foregoing shall not be deemed to require any Equity Partner to pay over to the Partnership any amount received by him if such payment would be in violation of law. Subject to the provisions of Section 3.4 hereof, the foregoing shall not include (i) any fees, commissions, or compensation, coming or arising out of any enterprise, activity or entity controlled, directly or indirectly, by an Equity Partner, his spouse, or his or her family, (ii) commissions received for acting as executor, trustee, or other fiduciary for the benefit of members of the immediate family of such Equity Partner or his or her spouse; provided, however, that the Partnership receives a fair and reasonable fee for all legal services rendered. By way of example, if an Equity Partner is named as the executor of the estate of a personal acquaintance or as the guardian for the child of a deceased personal acquaintance (which type of work is not that which the Equity Partner customarily performs on behalf of the Partnership) and receives a fee for said services, then the Equity Partner shall not be required to pay such fee over to the Partnership.

5.4. Gifts to Equity Partners. It is the general policy of the Partnership that a gift of any value offered to an Equity Partner in lieu of payment for services or disbursements shall not be accepted. This policy is set forth in a separate policy schedule.

5.5. Books and Records. There shall be kept at all times, at the principal office of the Partnership, accurate books of account reflecting all moneys received, paid, advanced, or expended by the Partnership, including the Distributable Income of each Equity Partner. The books of account shall be kept and continually maintained in accordance with generally accepted accounting principles on a cash basis. Any Equity Partner, on reasonable notice, shall have access to the books and records of the Partnership at all reasonable times during regular business hours.

Article 6-DISTRIBUTIONS

6.1. Distributable Income. As used herein, the term "Distributable Income" shall mean (i) the gross receipts (whether or not considered taxable income, including borrowings and capital contributions) of the Partnership from all sources during the calendar year (including checks dated in such year if received through January 15 of the following year), less (ii) the following categories of expenditure paid or reserved for in such calendar year, which shall be referred to as "Partnership Expenses":

(a) All expenditures required for the Practice whether or not deductible for federal income tax purposes;

(b) All funds expended to reduce or retire Partnership indebtedness and interest thereon;

(c) All charitable and political contributions made by the Partnership;

(d) The cost of any insurance maintained by the Partnership;

(e) Salaries paid to Non-Equity Partners and other Partnership personnel;

(f) Fees paid to associates, counsel or other attorneys, whether or not employees of the Partnership;

(g) Fees paid to other professionals such as real estate appraisers, expert witnesses, and process servers;

(h) Expenditures to be reimbursed in accordance with Schedule A hereto;

(i) Contributions made to The Partnership Retirement Plan;

(j) Amounts paid to Former Equity Partners as provided in Article Eight

hereof;

(k) Any amount reasonably set aside as a reserve for contingencies or other purposes, as determined by the Executive Committee.

6.2. Distribution of Distributable Income. Distributable income shall be distributed evenly to the Equity Partners in the following order:

(a) Provided the Partnership can reasonably spare the funds in the opinion of the Executive Committee, each Equity Partner shall be entitled to draw, from time to time, amounts from Distributable Income up to an amount which the Partnership can reasonably spare the funds in the opinion of Executive Committee, each Equity Partner shall be entitled to draw, from time to time, amounts from Distributable Income in equal amounts as is practical.

(b) Any remaining Distributable Income ("Surplus Cash") shall be distributed equally to each of the Equity Partners at such time as is determined by the Executive Committee.

(c) ____________ and __________________shall be entitled to receive repayment on the amounts contributed to their capital account as work in process and account receivables as set forth in Paragraph 1.2 hereof in amounts as determined by the Executive Committee in addition to all other sums in Paragraph 6.2.

6.3. Partnership Losses. In the event that Partnership Expenses in any calendar year shall exceed the gross receipts of the Partnership in such year, each Equity Partner shall be liable for and, if the Executive Committee so determines, shall contribute to the Partnership his equal share of such excess.

6.4. Contribution. Any Equity Partner who has borne more than his share of any Partnership expense shall be entitled to contribution from the other Equity Partners.

6.5. Method of Accounting. Except as otherwise provided herein or as determined by the Executive Committee, the Partnership shall keep its books and records on the cash basis method of accounting used by it pursuant to the federal income tax law. A reference herein to the "profits" of the Partnership shall refer to the Partnership's ordinary income from trade or business activities (currently, for the Equity Partner, Line 1 in the income section of the Schedule K-1 (Form 1065) and, for the Partnership, Line 20a to Schedule K of Form 1065), in each case net of Bonuses (if any) allocated in such fiscal year and the amounts allocated to Non-Equity Partners for such fiscal year. An Equity Partner's percentage of the profits shall be determined by comparing his shares of the profits to the Partnership's total profits, in each case net of Bonuses (if any) allocated in such fiscal year and the amount allocated to Non-Equity Partners for such fiscal year. On every matter concerning the internal affairs of the Partnership and the Equity Partners, there shall be no value assigned to goodwill or client files.

6.6. The Accountant. The Accountant for the Partnership shall be such accountants as the Executive Committee shall select, and such Accountant is referred to in this Agreement as the "Accountant." An annual report shall be prepared from the books and records by the Accountant, and each Equity Partner shall be entitled to a copy of the annual report.

6.7. Fiscal Year. The fiscal year of the Partnership shall be the calendar year. All references to "year" in this Agreement shall be deemed to refer to the calendar year.

Article 7-CAPITAL; THE PARTNERSHIP RETIREMENT PLAN; TAX ALLOCATIONS

7.1. Contributed Capital. Set forth on Schedule D hereto is the outstanding unpaid amount, if any, of each Equity Partner's Capital Note. Except as set forth on such Schedule or as otherwise provided herein, no Equity Partner has agreed to make any additional contributions to capital or shall be required to restore any deficit in his capital account except as set forth otherwise herein. Each Equity Partner who is hereafter admitted to the Partnership shall issue to the Partnership a Capital Note, payable in twelve (12) equal monthly installments (without interest), in an amount to be fixed upon his admission to the Partnership as an Equity Partner, and such amount shall not be adjusted by reason of subsequent variation in either Partnership operations or such Equity Partner's compensation from those contemplated at the time of his admission to the Partnership.

7.2. Capital Accounts. A separate capital account shall be maintained for each Equity Partner. Each such capital account shall be increased by such Equity Partner's capital contributions and share of Partnership income, and shall be decreased by all distributions to such Equity Partner and such Equity Partner's share of Partnership losses. Capital accounts shall, in all events, be maintained and adjusted in accordance with applicable Treasury Department Regulations promulgated under the Internal Revenue Code, as amended from time to time. A list of the Capital Accounts of Equity Partners is set forth in separate schedule.

7.3. Pension Percentages and Pension Adjustments. The Partnership may adopt a partnership retirement plan.

7.4. Tax Allocations and Other Tax Matters.

(a) Except as otherwise provided in this Section 7.4, for Federal, State, and local income tax purposes, the taxable income or loss of the Partnership for any taxable year shall be allocated among the Equity Partners in the following manner:

(i) the aggregate amount of the Equity Partners' Non-Accountable Expense Reimbursement for such year shall be added to the Partnership's net taxable income (or subtracted from the Partnership's net taxable loss) for such year ("Adjusted Allocable Income"). Expense Reimbursement shall be a Non-Accountable Expense

Reimbursement as determined by schedule A as deductible expenses but not chargeable to clients.

(ii) Adjusted Allocable Income shall be allocated to each Equity Partner in the proportion which his Adjusted Allocable Income bears to the aggregate Adjusted Allocable Income of all Equity Partners. Solely for purposes of this Section 7.4, Allocable Income shall include Cash and The Partnership Retirement Plan Account Payments only to the extent actually paid to, or received from an Equity Partner during such year, even if made in respect of a prior year.

(iii) Each Equity Partner's share of the Partnership's taxable income or loss, and all component items thereof, shall be equal to (A) his allocated share of Adjusted Allocable Income (as determined in the preceding clause (ii), minus, (B) his Non-Accountable Expense Reimbursement for such year to the extent actually deducted by the Partnership in computing its taxable income or loss for such year.

(b) In the event of the termination of the Partnership as provided in Article Nine hereof, the Partnership's books shall be closed as of the date of such termination, and all items of Partnership income, gains, losses, deductions, and credits for all periods subsequent to such date shall be allocated among the Equity Partners in proportion to their respective Partnership Termination Percentages.

(c) In the event an Equity Partner receives payments of a Payout Amount (as described in Article Eight hereof), such payments shall first be deemed payments with respect to Partnership property under Section 736(b) of the Internal Revenue Code of 1986, as amended ("IRC") to the extent of his capital account, and the remainder shall be deemed guaranteed payments under IRC Section 736(a)(2).

Article 8-CHANGES AS TO EQUITY PARTNERS

8.1. Termination Date. An Equity Partner's membership in the Partnership shall be terminated under the circumstances set forth below and the effective date of such termination shall be hereinafter referred to as the "Termination Date":

(a) In the event of the death of an Equity Partner, on the last day of the calendar month in which death occurs.

(b) In the event of the mental or physical disability of an Equity Partner, within the meaning of any disability income insurance policy maintained by the Partnership or which substantially prevents the Equity Partner from practicing law in his customary manner ("Disability"), on the earlier of (i) the first date on which any payment is made under any such insurance policy to the disabled Equity Partner, or (ii) on the last day of the calendar month which is six (6) months following the date on which the disabled Equity Partner is no longer able to continue the practice of law substantially in his customary manner.

(c) In the event of the retirement, on the last day of the calendar month in which retirement occurs.

(d) In the event of an Equity Partner's voluntary withdrawal from the Partnership, on the date specified in Section 8.2 hereof.

(e) In the event of the removal of an Equity Partner in accordance with Section 4.11 hereof, on such Termination Date as shall be specified by the Partnership.

8.2. Voluntary Withdrawal. Any Equity Partner may voluntarily withdraw from the Partnership on a Termination Date which is the last day of any calendar month and which is at least sixty (60) days after the date the Equity Partner gives written notice to the Executive Committee of his intention to withdraw; provided, however, that the Termination Date may be an earlier date with the approval of the Executive Committee. On the effective date of the withdrawal, the withdrawing Equity Partner shall cease to be an Equity Partner in the Partnership but will remain liable to the Partnership and the other Equity Partners for such Equity Partner's pro rata share of all Partnership liabilities incurred prior thereof; provided, however, that with respect to all other Equity Partners, the Partnership shall not be dissolved but shall continue uninterrupted and undissolved in accordance with the provisions of Section 8.14 of this Agreement.

8.3. Payment of Capital Account and Accrued Draws. An Equity Partner whose membership in the Partnership terminates (or his personal representatives) shall be entitled to receive an amount equal to his capital account as shown on the books of the partnership on the last day of the month in which termination occurs payable in twelve (12) equal monthly installments, without interest, commencing the last day of the month next succeeding the date of termination. In addition, the Equity Partner shall be entitled to receive that portion of his distributed income under 6.2 which has accrued through his Termination Date, but only to the same extent that all remaining Equity Partners have received payment of their 6.2 distributed income through such Termination Date; reduced, however, by the amount of any disability insurance benefits received by the Equity Partner or his personal representative in respect of such period under any group long-term disability insurance policies maintained by the Partnership.

8.4. Payments to or from Former Equity Partners. In addition to the amounts set forth in Section 8.3 hereof, and except as otherwise provided in this Agreement, an Equity Partner whose membership in the Partnership terminates for any reason shall be entitled to receive from the Partnership an amount ("Payout Amount") calculated as:

(a) Such Equity Partner's Partnership Termination Percentage multiplied by Partnership Net Assets (as computed under Section 8.5 hereof); minus

(b) The unpaid principal balance of such Equity Partner's Capital Note, together with any other indebtedness of such Equity Partner to the Partnership. The unpaid principal balance of the Equity Partner's Capital Note need not be accelerated and paid immediately, but shall instead be set off from the amounts due to the Equity Partner from the Partnership under the foregoing subsection (a).

(c) If the Payout Amount so calculated is a negative number, such amount shall forthwith be paid in its entirety by the Former Equity Partner to the Partnership. Payment of the Payout Amount to a Former Equity Partner shall be made in the manner, and over the period specified in Section 8.8 hereof.

8.5. Partnership Net Assets. Partnership Net Assets shall be the sum of the Partnership's assets, less its liabilities, computed as of an Equity Partner's Termination Date employing the following valuation principles:

(a) Except as otherwise provided below, (i) all Partnership assets shall be valued at the values reflected on the balance sheet incorporated as part of the Partnership's Federal tax return (Form 1065 or successor) as filed for its most recently completed fiscal year, and (ii) all Partnership assets not included on such balance sheet (including the unpaid principal balances of Equity Partners' Capital Notes) shall be valued at the values reflected on the Partnership's books and records of account or, in the absence of recorded values, at their fair market values.

(b) The Partnership's accounts receivable and Work-in-Process shall be valued at the following percentages of the amounts recorded on the Partnership's books and records of account:

unapplied retainers): 100

(i) Work-in-Process generated during the preceding 30 days (net of

(ii) All other Work-in-Process (net of unapplied retainers): 75

(iii) Accounts receivable outstanding less than 30 days: 100

(iv) Accounts receivable outstanding between 31 and 60 days: 90

(v) Accounts receivable outstanding between 61 and 90 days: 80

(vi) Accounts receivable outstanding more than 90 days: 50.

(c) The value or liability of any Partnership leasehold interest(s) shall not be taken into account unless, and then only to the extent, so provided in Section 8.6 hereof.

(d) No value shall be ascribed to the cash value of any life insurance policies owned by the Partnership or to any Partnership goodwill or going concern value, or to any other intangible Partnership asset not ascribed a specific value on the books and records of the Partnership.

(e) All Partnership liabilities shall be subtracted and valued at the values reflected on the Partnership's books and records of account or, in the absence of recorded values, at their fair market values. For these purposes, Partnership liabilities shall include, without limitation: (i) unpaid Payout Amounts owed to Former Equity Partners; and (ii) such amount as the Executive Committee deems reasonably necessary to provide a reserve for contingent Partnership liabilities including, without limitation, claims or lawsuits against the Partnership. To the extent such a contingent liability is thereafter discharged or otherwise eliminated at a cost to the Partnership less than the amount originally reserved for, appropriate adjustment shall be made to the remaining installments of the Payout Amount.

8.6. Leasehold Adjustment. In the event of the termination of an Equity Partner's membership in the Partnership for any reason other than death, disability, retirement, or expulsion without cause, there shall not be a net present value or net present cost, established for the leasehold and the former Equity Partner shall not be required to pay such leasehold cost nor receive a value for such leasehold value, of its leasehold interests. The Former Equity Partner shall have no interest in the value, if any, represented by such leasehold interests other than as a deduction against said Equity Partner's taxable income for the period prior to said Equity Partner's termination, to the extent permitted under then existing tax laws, and hereby irrevocably waives all rights, interests, and entitlement thereto, and the Partnership agrees to indemnify and hold harmless the Former Equity Partner from and against all costs, liabilities, or expenses associated with such leasehold interests arising after the Equity Partner's Termination Date.

8.7. Calculation. The calculation of an Equity Partner's Payout Amount shall be made by such outside certified public accountant as shall be selected by the Executive Committee and shall be delivered to the Former Equity Partner, with reasonably detailed backup data if requested, within 90 days after the Termination Date. It shall be accompanied by a written statement of the Chairman on behalf of the Partnership certifying that the calculation was made in accordance with the principles set forth in this Article Eight.

8.8. Time for Payment. Subject to the conditions and limitations set forth in Section 8.9 hereof, payment by the Partnership of the Payout Amount shall be made in equal calendar monthly installments, without interest, commencing three months following the Former Equity Partner's Termination Date over a period of five (5) years. In the event the Partnership shall fail for a period of one hundred twenty (120) days after notice to make any payment required under this Section 8.8, all such payments shall immediately become due and payable; subject, however, in the event of the termination of the Partnership, to the prior payment in full of other Partnership obligations and expenses as set forth in Section 9.4 hereof. Notwithstanding the above, if the Payout Amount is a negative number, such amount shall be paid immediately, in full, by the former Equity Partner to the Partnership.

8.9. Limitations, Conditions, and Deferral. Notwithstanding any provisions of this Agreement to the contrary, payment of Payout Amounts owing by the Partnership to any one or more Former Equity Partners shall be subject to the following additional terms, conditions, and limitations:

(a) All Payout Amounts shall be payable only from and to the extent of Partnership assets, and the Former Equity Partner shall have no recourse to the individual assets of the Equity Partners for payment thereof.

(b) The Partnership's liability on account of the Payout Amounts shall be subordinated in priority to all other Partnership indebtedness incurred, or which may be hereafter incurred, to parties other than Equity Partners and to all Partnership Expenses.

(c) Except in the event of the death or disability of an Equity Partner, no payment of the Payout Amount shall be made by the Partnership to such Former Equity Partner if such payment would result in the remaining unpaid balance of such former Equity Partner's Payout Amount being reduced below the amount of such Former Equity Partner's Adjusted Receivables. A Former Equity Partner's Adjusted Receivables shall be equal to the sum of (a) 85% of Partnership accounts receivable and Work-in-Process on matters handled for clients originated by the Former Equity Partner (or for which the former Equity Partner had billing responsibility) if such write-offs took place with such Equity Partner's consent during the six-month period prior to, or at any time subsequent to, the Equity Partner's Termination Date. In no event will accounts receivable outstanding for more than one year as of such Former Equity Partner's Termination Date be included in the calculation of Adjusted Receivables.

(d) Payments of the Payout Amount to all Former Equity Partners in any calendar year shall not exceed, in the aggregate, 10% of the Partnership's gross receipts for such year. There shall be excluded from this limitation the payments made pursuant to Section 8.10(b) of this Agreement.

(e) Any Payout Amounts the payment of which is restricted by reason of this Section 8.9 shall be deferred and paid, without interest, at the soonest possible time; subject, however, to the continued applicability of the conditions and limitations of this Section 8.9.

(f) The Partnership shall have the right to set off from the Payout Amount owed to any Former Equity Partner any monetary claims it may have against such Former Equity Partner, or any claims it may have against such Former Equity Partner, or any claims for damages, contribution, indemnity or reimbursement which it may have against such Former Equity Partner.

8.10. Insurance Proceeds. The following provisions shall apply to life insurance policy proceeds, if any, paid by virtue of the death of an Equity Partner:

(a) With respect to life insurance proceeds payable directly to the personal representatives or beneficiaries of the deceased Equity Partner under group life or group health insurance policies paid for by the Partnership, no reduction shall be made in the Payout Amount.

(b) With respect to life insurance proceeds paid to the Partnership under individual or "key-man" life insurance policies owned by and paid for by the Partnership, such proceeds shall be included in the computation of Partnership Net Assets for purposes of computing the Payout Amount due to such deceased Equity Partner. Notwithstanding the provisions of Sections 8.8 and 8.9 hereof, payment of the Payout Amount to the estate or personal representatives of such deceased Equity Partner shall be made immediately upon the Partnership's receipt of such proceeds in an amount equal to the lesser of (i) the Payout Amount, or (ii) such insurance proceeds, and the balance of the Payout Amount in excess of such insurance proceeds shall be paid in the manner and over the period otherwise provided in this Agreement. To secure its obligations under this paragraph (b), the Partnership hereby grants to each Equity Partner who is an insured under any such life insurance policy now owned or hereafter acquired by the Partnership, a first and continuing security interest in the proceeds of such policy, and authorizes any member of the Executive Committee to sign on behalf of the Partnership and file any instruments or documents necessary to further evidence or perfect such security interest.

8.11. Entitlement to Fees. All fees or other compensation earned by an Equity Partner while a member of the Partnership that would belong to the Partnership if received during that period (including all the items referred to in Section 5.3 hereof) shall belong to the Partnership even though not received until after he shall have ceased to be an Equity Partner. Any such amounts received by the Former Equity Partner, his personal representatives, or successors in interest shall be held in trust by the recipient for the benefit of the Partnership and shall be accounted for and paid over to the Partnership.

8.12. Prohibition on Transfer. No Equity Partner, without the consent of the Equity Partners, shall have the right or power to, nor shall he, sell, assign, transfer, pledge, mortgage, encumber of otherwise dispose of his interest in the Partnership or any distributions from the Partnership, except to the extent that the same shall pass to his personal representatives upon his death or adjudication of incompetence.

8.13. Use of Names. The Partnership shall have the absolute right to use the name of a deceased, retired, or disabled Equity Partner either as part of the firm name or under the firm name listing in a professional directory or in any other dignified manner, together with a notation of his death, disability, or retirement whenever required, and to notify clients, the public, and the Bar of his death, disability, or retirement.

8.14. Continuation of Partnership. Except as otherwise provided in Article Nine hereof, the Partnership shall not be terminated by the death, resignation, expulsion, retirement, disability, or bankruptcy of an Equity Partner or Equity Partners, but, notwithstanding any technical dissolution, shall be continued by the remaining Equity Partners. Other than as specifically provided in Article Eight hereof (a) no payment shall be made to a Former Equity Partner, his legal representatives and his successors in interest, and (b) no Former Equity Partner shall have any right to have Partnership property applied to discharge its liabilities and the surplus applied to pay the net amount owing to him, nor to have the value of his interest in the Partnership ascertained and paid to him. Each Equity Partner hereby consents to the foregoing on behalf of himself, his legal representative, and his successor in interest, and he hereby consents that the payments specifically provided in Article Eight hereof shall be deemed in settlement of his account in lieu of an accounting. This Agreement shall continue in lieu of an accounting. This Agreement shall continue in full force and effect except that the name of the Former Equity Partner shall be deemed deleted wherever it appears without, however, in any way affecting the ability of the Former Equity Partner or the Partnership to enforce their respective rights under this Agreement.

8.15. Cooperation by Former Equity Partner. Each Former Equity Partner shall cooperate with the Partnership to the extent reasonably requested by the Partnership from time to time in connection with Partnership matters which may arise as a result of legal services rendered by the Partnership prior to the Former Equity Partner's termination of his membership in the Partnership including, without limitation, Partnership billing matters.

8.16. Client Files. A Former Equity Partner shall not be entitled to possession of nor access to files and documents pertaining to the matters of any clients of the Partnership, even those matters on which the Former Equity Partner worked, unless and until such clients so direct, and possession of any such files and documents by the Former Equity Partner without such a direction having been given shall be considered a breach of this Agreement.

8.17. Confidential Information. In addition to any applicable ethical considerations and any applicable statutes, rules, and regulations governing conduct of attorneys, no Equity Partner or Former Equity Partner, without the prior written consent of the Partnership, shall disclose to any person or entity not lawfully entitled thereto, including but not limited to the press, other media or any public body, in the absence of a court order or some other administrative or regulatory directive, any confidential information relating to the business, affairs or financial condition of the Partnership, including the contents of this Agreement, as well as the compensation and capital accounts of the Equity Partners and any and all payments made to an Equity Partner upon his withdrawal, removal, retirement, disability, or death.

8.18. Indemnification of Former Equity Partner. Except as otherwise provided in this Agreement (including, without limitation, the provisions of Article Nine hereof), the Partnership shall hold harmless and indemnify each Former Equity Partner from and against (a) debts and liabilities of the Partnership incurred after his Termination Date, and (b) debts and liabilities of the Partnership, to the extent that the amounts thereof were taken into account in computing his Payout Amount; provided, however, that the foregoing shall not apply (i) with respect to Partnership debts or liabilities, or claims made against the Partnership, attributable to unauthorized actions or omissions by such Former Equity Partner, or (ii) if any portion of the payout Amount owed by such Former Equity Partner to the Partnership is not paid promptly when due.

Article 9-DISSOLUTION

9.1. Dissolution. The Partnership may be dissolved at any time by the vote of fifty-one percent (51%) in number, of the Equity Partners (excluding Equity Partners whose membership in the Partnership is in the process of terminating but who have not yet reached their Termination Date) which vote may be taken upon the requests of thirty-three percent (33%) in number, of the Equity Partners. In the event of dissolution, the books of the Partnership shall be closed. In dissolution as in all other matters, there shall be no value assigned to goodwill.

9.2. Alternate Dissolution. The Partnership may not be dissolved, terminated, amended, or modified except by written instrument signed by Equity Partners having percentage participations of at least fifty-one percent (51%) of all such participations.

9.3. Retroactive Dissolution. If any Equity Partner shall voluntarily resign his membership in the Partnership, the remaining Equity Partners may, by a Partnership decision made within ninety (90) days after such Equity Partner's Termination Date, elect to treat the Partnership as having been dissolved and terminated as of the day immediately prior to such Termination Date. In such event, (a) the Partnership shall be wound up and terminated, (b) there shall be deemed to have been no resignation of such Former Equity Partner or of any other Equity Partner purporting to resign after such Former Equity Partner, (c) none of the provisions of Article Eight hereof shall apply, and (d) such Former Equity Partner and subsequently resigning Equity Partners shall be considered (and do hereby agree that they shall continue to be) Equity Partners of the Partnership for purposes of winding up the affairs of the Partnership under this Agreement and applicable law.

9.4. Liquidators. Upon the dissolution of the Partnership, a person or persons selected by the Executive Committee shall act as liquidators to wind up the Partnership. The liquidators shall have full power and authority to sell, assign and encumber any or all of the Partnership's assets, collect by any commercially reasonable means fees due to the Partnership by its clients, engage the services of brokers, appraisers, auctioneers, accountants, counsel, and the professionals and to otherwise wind up and liquidate the affairs of the Partnership in an orderly and businesslike manner, upon such terms and conditions, and for such remuneration, as shall be determined by the Executive Committee. A member of the Executive Committee may serve as a Liquidator.

9.5. Distribution of Proceeds. All proceeds from liquidation shall be distributed in the following order of priority:

(a) to the payment of the expenses of liquidation and the debts and liabilities of the Partnership, including secured debts to Former Equity Partners described in Section 8.9(b) of this Agreement, but excluding all other debts to Farmer Equity Partners:

(b) to the setting up of such reserves as the Liquidators may reasonably deem necessary for any contingent liabilities of the Partnership (including, without limitation, reserves for payment of continuing malpractice insurance coverage, fees for brokers, appraisers, attorneys, accountants and auctioneers, moving expenses, premises restoration obligations, and file storage expenses);

(c) to the Former Equity Partners on account of all Payment Amounts owed to them: subject, however, to the continuing conditions and limitations imposed by Section 8.9 (other than clause (d) thereof);

(d) to each of the Equity Partners, the amount of their contributed Capital;

(e) to the Equity Partners in proportion to, and to the extent of, their Capital Accounts (as determined after the foregoing distributions and after allocation of all taxable income and losses incident to the liquidation); and

(f) the balance, to the Equity Partners in equal proportion.

9.6. Alternate Distribution of Proceeds. For purposes of this section, the following definitions shall apply:

"Case in Progress" shall mean each case in which the Partnership shall have actually received in its possession a retainer or engagement agreement executed by the client on or prior to the date of dissolution.

"Concluded Case" shall mean each case in which an offer of settlement has been notified to the client on or prior to the date of dissolution and which offer then has been or is subsequently accepted; and shall mean each case which has been tried to a conclusion in which a verdict has been rendered in favor of a client for monetary damages on or prior to the date of dissolution.

"Net Fee" shall mean the gross fee actually received by the Partnership on each case, less all disbursements, participation fee to other attorneys, and any and all other actual expenditures paid, incurred or accrued in connection with each case.

In the event of the dissolution of the Partnership by operation of Section 9.1 above or by agreement between the Equity Partners then, and to the extent the Equity Partners shall not have expressly agreed otherwise in writing, the Equity Partners shall each be entitled to receive the following (after payment of all of the liabilities of the Partnership and the expenses of dissolution):

(a) The amount of their respective capital in the Partnership, as of the date of dissolution;

(b) The balance, if any, of their respective pro rata shares of the Net Profits of the Partnership for the then current year of the Partnership, calculated to the date of dissolution, less distributions received on account prior to the date of dissolution;

(c) An amount equal to the net fee on each concluded case divided by the number of Equity Partners on the date of such dissolution; and

(d) An amount equal to all disbursements actually recouped on each Concluded Case divided by the number of Equity Partners on the date of such dissolution;

(e) An amount equal to fifteen percent (15%) of the Net Fee plus one half of all disbursements incurred by the Partnership and subsequently recouped on each Case in Progress as of the date of dissolution, which is received by the other Equity Partner (whether alone or with others) at any time after such date as a result of such case in progress having been transferred to the other Equity Partner (whether alone or with others) with consent or at the direction of the client following the dissolution; and

(f) Any other net amount owing to either Equity Partner on the date of dissolution not included in subsections (a) through (e) above shall be added to, or any net amount owing by him to the Partnership shall be deducted from the total of the amounts otherwise due pursuant to this section.

9.7. Sharing of Losses and Cash Deficits. Upon the dissolution of the Partnership, each Equity Partner shall be responsible for losses and liabilities of the Partnership, and shall promptly contribute cash to the Partnership to alleviate any cash deficiencies experienced by it, in proportion to the Partnership Termination Percentage possessed by such Equity Partner as of the date of termination (as set forth in Section 9.1 or 9.2 as the case may be). Following dissolution of the Partnership, no further changes shall be made to any Equity Partner's Partnership Termination Percentage without the written consent of each Equity Partner affected thereby and no purported resignations of Equity Partners shall be effective for any purpose whatsoever.

9.8. Obligations of Equity Partners to Partnership. In the event of the dissolution of the Partnership, the unpaid principal balance of each Equity Partner's Capital Note, together with all other indebtedness of the Equity Partners to the Partnership, shall become immediately due and payable.

9.9. Unfinished Business. In the event that there shall be any unfinished matters upon termination of the Partnership, the Equity Partners by or through whom such matters came into the Partnership office shall be entitled to complete such matters, and the Partnership shall be entitled to receive as to each such matter as and when fees therefor are collected, a reasonable portion of such fees commensurate with the amount of services rendered by the Partnership in connection therewith.

9.10. Use of Name. Upon the dissolution of the Partnership, the right to use the name of any Equity Partner by any of the other Equity Partners shall cease.

9.11. Records and Storage. Upon the dissolution of the Partnership, to the extent required by applicable law, the Executive Committee shall make appropriate arrangements for the maintenance of the Partnership's records, and compliance with all other applicable State rules and requirements.

Article 10-MISCELLANEOUS PROVISIONS

10.1. Notices. Any notices required under this Agreement shall be in writing and shall be delivered personally or sent by registered or certified mail, postage prepaid, to the recipient at his address as recorded in the Partnership's books and records, or at such other address as may be supplied by similar written notice. The date of personal delivery or mailing shall be the date of such notice.

10.2. Actions. Any action instituted to enforce or to recover damages for breach of this Agreement shall be instituted in the Court of the State of __________, County of ___________. If any action is instituted in any other court or before any other tribunal, all parties hereto consent to removal thereof to the Court of the State of _____________, County of _____________.

10.3. Binding Effect. This Agreement shall be binding upon and inure to the benefit of the parties hereto and their respective heirs, successors and legal representatives.

10.4. Assignment of Interest. Subject to the provisions of Section 10.13 of this Agreement, no Equity Partner shall sell, assign, mortgage, hypothecate, or encumber his interest in the Partnership, nor shall any Equity Partner, which is a professional corporation permit the assignment, mortgage, hypothecation, or encumbrance of its capital stock; provided, however, that such interest or stock may be pledged as security to finance an Equity Partner's capital account, with the consent of the Executive Committee; and provided further, that an individual Equity Partner may assign his interest in the Partnership to a professional corporation of which he is the sole shareholder, with the consent of the Executive Committee. Further, except as provided herein, in advance of actually receiving any distribution of profits or surplus, no Equity Partner's interest in the Partnership shall be subject to execution, garnishment, attachment, charging order, insolvency, bankruptcy or other legal proceedings of any character, or legal sequestration, levy or sale, or in any event be applicable or subject to the payment of such Equity Partner's debts.

10.5. Governing Law. This Agreement shall be governed by and construed in accordance with the substantive law of the State of _________, without giving effect to principles relating to conflict of laws.

10.6. Multiple Copies. This Agreement may be executed simultaneously in one or more counterparts, each of which shall be deemed an original, and all of which shall together constitute one and the same instrument. The terms of this Agreement shall become binding upon each party from and after the time that such party executed a copy thereof. In like manner, and after the time that any party executes a consent or other document authorized or required by the terms of this Agreement, such consent or other document shall be binding upon such parties.

10.7. Third-Party Benefit. None of the provisions of this Agreement shall be construed as existing for the benefit of any creditor of the Partnership or of any of the Equity Partners, nor shall any such provision be enforceable by any party not a signatory to this Agreement other than an Equity Partner's legal representative.

10.8. Headings. Heading and captions are used herein solely for convenience and shall not affect the interpretation of any provision hereof.

10.9. Complete Agreement. This Agreement contains the complete agreement of the Parties concerning its subject matter and supersedes all prior and contemporaneous oral and written agreements among the Parties concerning its subject matter.

10.10. Other Instruments. The parties hereto covenant and agree that they will execute such other and further instruments and documents as are or may become necessary or convenient to effectuate and carry out the terms of this Agreement.

10.11. Invalid Provisions. Any clause, sentence, provision, or section or article of this Agreement held pursuant to the procedures set forth in Section 10.2 hereof to be invalid, illegal, or ineffective shall not impair, invalidate or nullify the remainder of this Agreement, but the effect thereof shall be confined to the clause, sentence, provision, section, or article so held to be invalid, illegal, or ineffective.

10.12. Transfer. An Equity Partner may, with the prior approval of the Executive Committee, transfer from one office to another of the Partnership or may perform services for more than one office of such Partnership, and such situation shall in no way change or alter the terms of this Partnership Agreement with respect to such Equity Partner or any other Equity Partner.

10.13. Offset. The Partnership may offset any debt or obligation owing by an Equity Partner to the Partnership against an Equity Partner's capital account and any amounts payable by the Partnership to such Equity Partner.

10.14. Security Interest. Each Equity Partner hereby grants to the Partnership a security interest in his total contribution to its capital, his total distribution of income (as determined in accordance with Section 6.2 of this Agreement) and his interest in the Partnership to secure any and all obligations of the Equity Partner to the Partnership whether arising under this Agreement or otherwise.

10.15. Bankruptcy. If a court of competent jurisdiction enters a decree or order appointing a receiver, assignee, trustee, liquidator, sequestrator, or other similar official of an Equity Partner or of any substantial part of the property of the Equity Partner, or orders the winding up or liquidation of the Equity Partner's affairs or approves as properly filed a petition seeking reorganization, arrangement, adjustment, or composition of the Equity Partner under any bankruptcy law or if an Equity Partner files a petition in voluntary bankruptcy under any of the provisions of any bankruptcy law or consents to the filing of any bankruptcy or reorganization petition against the Equity Partner under any such law or (without limitation of the generality of the foregoing) files a petition or answer or consent to reorganize the Equity Partner pursuant to or seeks relief under any bankruptcy law or makes any assignment for the benefit of creditors or admits in writing the Equity Partner's inability to pay debts as they generally become due or consents to the appointment of a receiver, assignee, trustee, liquidator, sequestrator, or other similar official of the Equity Partner or any substantial part of the Equity Partner's property, and if the Partnership incurs costs, expenses, or losses in connection with complying with court orders relating to such procedure or other action which the Partnership takes with respect to such procedure, the Equity Partner agrees to indemnify and hold the Partnership harmless for all such costs, expenses, and losses.

10.16. Exclusion of Coverage. Each Equity Partner understands and agrees that the Partnership's professional liability insurance policy shall not cover claims against an individual if the act, error or omission giving rise to the claim occurred prior to the date such individual (or such individual's controlled professional corporation) became an employee, Equity Partner, member, or shareholder of the Partnership. For purposes of this paragraph, the term "such individual's controlled professional corporation" shall mean a corporation of which the individual is an employee or principal shareholder.

10.17. Professional Liability Insurance. Pursuant to Schedule "A," the Partnership shall provide to all licensed attorneys, including the Equity Partners, professional liability insurance in an amount approved by the Executive Committee.

10.18. Admission of New Equity Partners. Each new Equity Partner (Equity and Non-Equity) shall be admitted to the Partnership as an Equity Partner pursuant to a separate Memorandum of Understanding. The Memorandum of Understanding shall be executed by the New Equity Partner and by the Chairman of the Executive Committee. Besides executing a Memorandum of Understanding, each new Equity Partner shall agree to the terms of this Agreement by execution of a counterpart of this Agreement. When new Equity Partners are admitted to the Partnership, it shall not be necessary for the existing Equity Partners to re-execute this Agreement.

10.19. Waiver of Provisions-Amendment. Except as otherwise stated herein, any provision of this Agreement may be waived, in writing, by the affirmative vote of fifty-one (51%) percent in number of Equity Partners at that time. The failure to insist upon the strict performance of any covenant, term, condition, or other provision thereof or default or breach in connection therewith shall not be deemed to be a waiver thereof. The waiver of any covenant, term, condition, or other provision hereof or default or breach hereunder shall not affect or alter this Agreement and each and every other covenant, term, condition, or provision hereof. No waiver or amendment with respect to any provision of Article 8 hereof shall have the effect of reducing the amount or altering the terms of any payments then being made to anyone thereunder without the express consent of such individual.

10.20. The parties agree that the employee separation agreement dated ________ entered into with ________________ is approved and shall be considered a liability of the Equity Partners and a part of this agreement.

SIGNATURE PAGE

Each of the undersigned, desiring to enter into the Partnership Agreement of SAMPLE LAW FIRM, dated ________________, hereby (i) agrees to all of the terms and provisions thereof,

(ii) executes the Agreement in the capacity indicated below, and (iii) authorizes this Signature Page, or counterparts thereof, to be attached to the Agreement and all permitted amendments thereof.

________________________________ ________________

(Signature) (Date)

________________________________ ________________

(Signature) (Date)

________________________________ ________________

(Signature) (Date)

APPENDIX I

Sample Law Firm, LLC

Operating Agreement

Samples found in the Appendices are also available online at http://ambar.org/succession.

THIS OPERATING AGREEMENT is made and entered into as of this ________________ day of ________________, ________________, by and between the Members whose signatures appear on the signature page hereof.

WITNESSETH:

WHEREAS, All of the Members are attorneys licensed to practice law in the State of ________________; and

WHEREAS, the Members desire to associate themselves for the general practice of law under the name of "Sample Law Firm, LLC"; and

WHEREAS, Sample Law Firm LLC, is an ______________ limited liability company organized pursuant to ______________ Limited Liability Company Act at ______________, effective as of ______________, ______________; and

WHEREAS, ______________________ is the sole member in ______________, LLC (f/k/a ______________, LLC) ("the ________ Firm"), an ______________ limited liability company, which was organized and has been operated as a law firm engaged in the practice of law, at ______________, ____________________________; and

WHEREAS, ______________ now wishes to continue the practice of law with the other Members under the newly formed limited liability company, Sample Law Firm, LLC, at ______________; and

WHEREAS, the ____________________________ Firm owns the office building commonly known as ______________ ("Office Building") and is willing to lease ______________ in the Office Building to Sample Law Firm, LLC; and

WHEREAS, the ______________ Firm is the owner of all personal property necessary to operate the law practice by Sample Law Firm LLC and is keeping intact the staff of the former law practice owned by the ______________ Firm, of which some of such staff shall be Members under ______________, and the balance of the staff shall become employees of Sample Law Firm, LLC.

NOW, THEREFORE, in consideration of the matters described above, and of the mutual benefits and obligations set forth in this Operating Agreement, the parties agree as follows:

1. **DEFINITIONS.** The following terms used in this Operating Agreement shall have the following meanings:
    1.1. "Act" shall mean the ______________ Limited Liability Company Act at ______________, et seq.

1.2. "Articles of Organization" shall mean the Articles of Organization of Sample Law Firm LLC, as filed with the Secretary of State of ________________, as amended from time to time.

1.3. "Breaching Member" shall have the meaning as set forth in Section 13.

1.4. "Business" shall have the meaning set forth in Section 3.1.

1.5. "Capital Account" as of any given date shall mean the Capital Contribution to the Company by a Member as adjusted up to such date pursuant to Section 10.2.

1.6. "Capital Contribution" shall mean any contribution to the capital of the Company in cash or property by a Member whenever made. "Initial Capital Contribution" shall mean the initial contribution to the capital of the Company pursuant to this Operating Agreement.

1.7. "Cause" shall have the meaning set forth in Section 5.9.

1.8. "Code" shall mean the Internal Revenue Code of 1986 or corresponding provisions of subsequent superseding federal revenue laws.

1.9. "Company" shall refer to Sample Law Firm LLC.

1.10. "Death Valuation Date" shall mean the date a Deceased Member's Capital Account is valued pursuant to Section 12.1.2.

1.11. "Deceased Member" shall mean a Member who has died.

1.12. "Deductible Shortage" shall have the meaning set forth in Section 9.3.

1.13. "Disability Date" shall mean the date a Member first becomes disabled pursuant to Section 12.1.4.

1.14. "Disability Valuation Date" shall mean the date of valuation of the Disabled Member's Capital Account on the last day of the sixth calendar month following the month in which the Disability Date occurs for purposes of Section 12.1.4.

1.15. "Disabled Member" shall mean a Member who is disabled pursuant to Section 12.1.4.

1.16. "Distributable Cash" shall mean all cash, revenues, and funds received by the Company from Company operations, less the sum of the following to the extent paid or set aside by the Company: (i) all principal and interest payments on indebtedness of the Company and all other sums paid to lenders; (ii) all cash expenditures incurred in the normal operation of the Company's Business; and (iii) such Reserves as the Manager deems reasonably necessary for the proper operation of the Company's Business.

1.17. "Dissociated Member" shall mean a Member whose Withdrawal, Expulsion, death, or other event has caused his or her Dissociation.

1.18. "Dissociation" ("Dissociate") shall mean the Withdrawal, Expulsion, or death of a Member or any other event that causes a person to cease to be a Member.

1.19. "Dissociation Date" shall mean, in the case of any Dissociated Member, the date of the event resulting in the Member's Dissociation.

1.20. "Effective Date" shall mean the latter of (i) the date upon which the Articles of Organization is filed with and accepted by the Secretary of State of ________________; and (ii) the date of registration with and acceptance by the ________________ Supreme Court in accordance with Rule ________________of the ________________Supreme Court Rules.

1.21. "Entity" shall mean any general partnership, limited partnership, limited liability company, corporation, joint venture, trust, business trust, cooperative, association, foreign trust, or foreign business organization.

1.22. "Expelled Member" shall mean the Member who has been Expelled.

1.23. "Expulsion" ("Expel" or "Expelled") shall mean a Member's Dissociation as provided in Section 11.3.

1.24. "Expulsion Date" shall mean the date of the Expelled Member's Expulsion from the Company.

1.25. "Expulsion Valuation Date" shall mean the date of valuation of the Expelled Member's Capital Account pursuant to Section 12.1.3.

1.26. "Financial Responsibility" shall have the meaning set forth in Section 9.3.

1.27. "Fiscal Year" shall have the meaning set forth in Section 10.6.

1.28. "Indemnified Person" shall mean each Member and Dissociated Member entitled to indemnification by the Company as provided in Section 15.

1.29. "Insured Death" shall have the meaning set forth in Section 12.1.7(b).

1.30. "Manager" shall mean one or more managers. References to the Manager in the singular or as him, her, it, itself, or other like references shall also, where the context so requires, be deemed to include the plural or the masculine or feminine reference, as the case may be.

1.31. "Member" shall mean each of the parties who executes a counterpart of this Operating Agreement as a Member and each of the parties who may hereafter become Members.

1.32. "Membership Interest" shall mean a Member's entire interest in the Company including the right to vote on, consent to, or otherwise participate in any decision or action of or by the Members granted pursuant to this Operating Agreement and the Act.

1.33. "Net Profits" and "Net Losses" shall mean the income, gain, loss, deductions, and credits of the Company in the aggregate or separately stated, as appropriate, determined in accordance with generally accepted accounting principles employed under the cash method of accounting at the close of each fiscal year on the Company's tax return filed for federal income tax purposes.

1.34. "Operating Agreement" shall mean this Operating Agreement as originally executed and as amended from time to time.

1.35. "Other Member" shall have the meaning set forth in Section 9.4.

1.36. "Paying Member" shall have the meaning set forth in Section 9.4.

1.37. "Percentage Interest" shall mean, for any Member, the Percentage Interest in the Company as set forth on Exhibit A, as may be changed from time to time by the unanimous consent of the Members.

1.38. "Persons" shall mean any individual or Entity, and the heirs, executors, administrators, legal representatives, successors, and assigns of such "Person" where the context so permits.

1.39. "Premium Shortage" shall have the meaning set forth in Section 9.3.

1.40. "Reserves" shall mean funds set aside or amounts allocated to reserves which shall be maintained in amounts deemed sufficient by the Manager for working capital and to pay taxes, insurance, debt service, or other costs or expenses incident to the ownership or operation of the Company's Business.

1.41. "Transfer" shall mean an assignment, conveyance, encumbrance, exchange, pledge, hypothecation, lease, mortgage, sale, or other disposition for consideration, or gift or other disposition for no consideration, whether voluntary, involuntary, by operation of law or otherwise.

1.42. "Treasury Regulations" shall include proposed, temporary, and final regulations promulgated under the Code.

1.43. "Valuation Date" shall mean the date of valuation of a Withdrawn Member's Capital Account pursuant to Section 12.1.1.

1.44. "Withdrawal" ("Withdraw") shall mean a Member's Dissociation from the Company as a result of the Member's withdrawal or resignation as provided in Section 11.2 or a required retirement pursuant to Section 12.1.4.

1.45. "Withdrawal Date" shall mean the effective date of Withdrawal or retirement of a Withdrawn Member.

1.46. "Withdrawn Member" shall mean the Member whose Withdrawal causes his Dissociation from the Company.

1.47. "Work in Process" shall have the meaning set forth in Section 12.1.5.

2. **FORMATION OF COMPANY.** The information concerning the formation of Company is as follows:

2.1. Formation. Sample Law Firm LLC, shall or has been organized as an ________________Limited Liability Company by executing and delivering Articles of Organization to the ________________Secretary of State in accordance with and pursuant to the Act. The Company shall be effective on the Effective Date.

2.2. Name. The name of the Company is Sample Law Firm, LLC.

2.3. Principal Place of Business. The principal place of business of the Company within the State of ________________shall be, ________________. The Company may locate its places of business at any other place or places as the Manager may deem advisable.

2.4. Registered Office and Registered Agent. The Company's initial registered office shall be at the office of its registered agent at ________________, Suite ________________, ________________, ________________, and the name of its initial registered agent shall be Lawyer A. The registered office and registered agent may be changed by filing the address of the new registered office and/or the name of the new registered agent with the ________________Secretary of State pursuant to the Act.

3. **BUSINESS OF COMPANY.** The Business of the Company shall be:

3.1. Business. To operate as a law firm engaged in the practice of law ("Business") under the name Sample Law Firm LLC. The Company shall possess and may exercise all powers and privileges granted by the Act, any other law, or by the Agreement, including incidental powers thereto, to the extent that such powers and privileges are necessary, customary, convenient, or incidental to the attainment of the Company's purposes. The Company shall not engage in any other activity or business without the unanimous consent of the Members.

3.2. Purpose and Title to Property. The Members have formed this Company for the purpose of deriving income from the practice of law. The Members hereby agree that legal title to any and all property, real or personal, acquired by the Company shall be held by the Company in its name.

4. **NAMES AND ADDRESSES OF MEMBERS.** The names and addresses of the Members are set forth on Exhibit A of this Operating Agreement.

5. **RIGHTS AND DUTIES OF MANAGER.**

5.1. Management. The Business and affairs of the Company shall be managed by its Manager. The Manager shall direct, manage, and control the Business of the Company. Except for situations in which the approval of the Members is expressly required by this Operating Agreement or by nonwaivable provisions of the Act, the Manager shall have full and complete authority, power, and discretion to manage and control the Business, affairs, and properties of the Company, to make all decisions regarding those matters and to perform any and all other acts or activities customary or incident to the management of the Company's Business. At any time when there is more than one Manager, any one Manager may take any action permitted to be taken by the Manager, unless the approval of more than one of the Managers is expressly required pursuant to this Operating Agreement or the Act.

5.2. Number, Tenure, and Qualifications. The number of Managers of the Company shall be fixed from time to time by the unanimous vote of the Members, but in no instance shall there be less than one Manager. Each Manager shall hold office until his successor shall have been elected and qualified. A Manager shall be elected by the unanimous vote of the Members. A Manager shall be a Member of the Company and must be licensed to practice law in the State of ________________.

5.3. Initial Manager of Company. Lawyer A shall be the initial Manager of the Company. On matters Lawyer A deems appropriate, he/she will seek advice from and consult with the other Members with the intent of reaching consensus, but in the event of disagreement of the Members, the final decision will be made by Lawyer A. Members shall comply with management decisions and announced rules of practice and operation.

5.4. Certain Powers of Manager. Without limiting the generality of Section 5.1, the Manager shall have power and authority, on behalf of the Company:

5.4.1. To acquire property from any Person as the Manager may determine, whether or not such Person is directly or indirectly affiliated or connected with any Manager or Member;

5.4.2. To borrow money for the Company from banks, other lending institutions, the Manager, Members, or affiliates of the Manager or Members on such terms as the Manager deems appropriate, and in connection therewith, to hypothecate, encumber, and grant security interests in the assets of the Company to secure repayment of the borrowed sums. No debt shall be contracted or liability incurred by or on behalf of the Company except by the Manager, or to the extent permitted under the Act, by agents or employees of the Company expressly authorized to contract such debt or incur such liability by the Manager;

5.4.3. To purchase liability and other insurance to protect the Company's property and Business;

5.4.4. To hold and own Company real and personal properties in the name of the Company;

5.4.5. To invest Company funds in time deposits, short-term governmental obligations, commercial paper, or other investments;

5.4.6. Upon the unanimous consent of the Members, to sell or otherwise dispose of all or substantially all of the assets of the Company as part of a single transaction or plan as long as such disposition is not in violation of or a cause of a default under any other agreement to which the Company may be bound;

5.4.7. To execute on behalf of the Company all instruments and documents, including, without limitation, checks; drafts; notes and other negotiable instruments; mortgages or deeds of trust; security agreements; financing statements; documents providing for the acquisition, mortgage, or disposition of the Company's property; assignments, bills of sale; leases; and any other instruments or documents necessary to the Business of the Company;

5.4.8. To employ accountants, legal counsel, managing agents, or other experts to perform services for the Company;

5.4.9. To enter into any and all other agreements on behalf of the Company, in such forms as the Manager may approve;

5.4.10. Make assignments of cases and other work to Members and staff;

5.4.11. Select office space, art, decoration, and design;

5.4.12. Select and purchase supplies and equipment;

5.4.13. Determine methods of dealing with clients and case control;

5.4.14. Make risk-loss decisions;

5.4.15. Make human resources decisions, including, but not limited to, personnel selection, policies, compensation, and benefits;

5.4.16. Select work methods, office procedures and substantive systems, and safeguards;

5.4.17. File or cause to be filed such statements of authority as shall be appropriate for filing under the Act, including any documentation required by the ________ Supreme Court.

5.4.18. Notwithstanding anything to the contrary contained in this Agreement, to limit or restrict distribution to the Members or their Capital Accounts for such reasons and purposes as the Manager, in his sole discretion, may elect and shall be, in such Manager's reasonable opinion, in the best interest of the Company; and

5.4.19. To do and perform all other acts as may be necessary or appropriate to the conduct of the Company's Business.

Unless authorized to do so by this Operating Agreement or by the Manager of the Company, no attorney-in-fact, employee or other agent of the Company shall have any power or authority to bind the Company in any way, to pledge its credit or to render it liable for any purpose. No Member shall have any power or authority to bind the Company unless the Member has been authorized by the Manager to act as an agent of the Company in accordance with the previous sentence. No Member shall have the right to hold himself or herself out as an agent of the Company in any business or activity other than the Business. No Member shall have the right to hold himself or herself out as an agent of any other Member.

5.5. Liability for Certain Acts. Each Manager shall perform his duties as Manager in good faith, in a manner he reasonably believes to be in the best interests of the Company, and with such care as an ordinarily prudent person in a like position would use under similar circumstances. A Manager shall not be liable to the Company or to any Member for any loss or damage sustained by the Company or any Member, unless the loss or damage shall have been the result of fraud, deceit, gross negligence, willful misconduct, or a wrongful taking by the Manager.

5.6. Unanimous Consent. The following matters shall require the unanimous consent of the Members:

5.6.1. Admission of new Members to the Company and the existing Members shall determine the Percentage Interest in the LLC's Net Profits of a new Member, with each Member contributing his pro rata share of the new Member's Percentage Interest.

5.6.2. Change of the Company name.

5.6.3. Change of the manner of compensation for Members.

5.6.4. Change in this Operating Agreement, or the Articles of Organization of the Company which in any manner shall controvert any of the provisions of this Operating Agreement.

5.6.5. Make, execute, deliver, endorse, or guarantee any commercial paper, nor agree to answer for, nor indemnify against any act, debt, default, or misconduct of any Person or Member.

5.6.6. Other than in the regular course of Company Business, make, execute, and deliver any assignments for the benefit of creditors or any bond, confession of judgment, chattel mortgage, indemnity bond, surety bond or contract of sale or contract to sell its entire personal property.

5.6.7. Hire, lease, purchase, or sell or mortgage any real estate, or interest therein, or enter into any contract for such purpose.

5.6.8. Hire, or agree to hire, any Person for a definite period in excess of one month, or discharge any Person who shall have been hired for a definite period in excess of one month.

5.6.9. Increase in the principal amount of any indebtedness guaranteed by the Members;

5.6.10. Mergers with or into other partnerships, corporations, limited liability companies, or other business entities;

5.6.11. Assign, mortgage, or sell his or her Interest of the Company, nor any part thereof, or enter into any agreement as the result of which any Person may become interested with him or her therein, except as herein provided.

5.6.12. Endorse any notes or become surety or guarantor for any Person upon any obligation whatsoever.

5.6.13. Amendment or waiver of a Member's obligation to make a Capital Contribution.

5.6.14. Expulsion of a Member.

5.6.15. Entering into or modifying the lease of the Company's office facilities.

5.6.16. Establishing new offices of the Company.

5.6.17. Initiation of an action on behalf of the Company against any Member or Dissociated Member.

5.7. Bank Accounts. The Manager may from time to time open bank accounts in the name of the Company, and the Manager or a designee of the Manager shall be a signatory thereon, unless Members unanimously determine otherwise.

5.8. Resignation. Any Manager of the Company may resign at any time by giving written notice to the Members of the Company. The Resignation of any Manager shall take effect upon receipt of notice thereof or at such later date specified in such notice; and, unless otherwise specified therein, the acceptance of such Resignation shall not be necessary to make it effective. The Resignation of a Manager who is also a Member shall not affect the Manager's rights as a Member and shall not constitute a withdrawal of a Member.

5.9. Removal. At a meeting called expressly for that purpose, all or any lesser number of Managers may be removed at any time, with or without cause, by the unanimous vote of the Members. A Manager may be removed at any time for cause or if Disabled by the unanimous vote of all Members excluding the vote of the Manager for whom the removal vote pertains. The removal of a Manager who is also a Member shall not affect the Manager's rights as a Member and shall not constitute a Withdrawal of a Member. The term "Cause" shall mean conviction of a felony or misdemeanor involving dishonesty, fraud, or moral turpitude, the intentional dereliction of duties, the material failure to properly service Company clients or perform duties, the theft or conversion of the property of the Company or a Company client, the performance of employment duties under the influence of alcohol or illegal drugs, the loss of license to practice law, any continuing material failure to comply with the Company's policies, practices or procedures after receiving written notice of such failure from the Company with a failure to cure within 10 days of such notice, and a material breach of this Agreement after receiving written notice of such failure from the Company with a failure to cure within 10 days of such notice.

5.10. Vacancies. Any vacancy occurring for any reason in the number of Managers of the Company may be filled by the unanimous vote of the Members. Any Manager's position to be filled by reason of an increase in the number of Managers shall be filled by the unanimous vote of the Members at a meeting of Members called for that purpose or by the unanimous written consent of the Members; provided, however, if the vacancy has been caused by the removal of a Manager, the unanimous vote or consent of the Members excluding the removed Manager/Member's vote shall be required to fill such vacancy. A Manager elected to fill a vacancy shall be elected for the unexpired term of his predecessor in office and shall hold office until the expiration of such term and until his successor shall be elected and qualified or until his earlier death, resignation, or removal. A Manager chosen to fill a position resulting from an increase in the number of Managers shall hold office until his successor shall be elected and qualified, or until his earlier death, resignation, or removal.

5.11. The Manager shall be held to the same standards of conduct as prescribed for the Members in Sections 6.14 through 6.16.

6. RIGHTS AND OBLIGATIONS OF MEMBERS.

6.1. Limitation of Liability. Each Member's liability shall be limited as set forth in this Operating Agreement, the Act and other applicable law, including ______________ Supreme Court Rules ______________ and ______________.

6.2. Company Debt Liability. A Member will not be personally liable for any debts or losses of the Company beyond any obligation of the Member under Section 9 and Section 10.1.2 to make Capital Contributions, except as otherwise required by law or this Operating Agreement.

6.3. Each Member shall charge reasonably for all professional services rendered by him or her, following generally the policies of the Company as to fees charged. Each Member, however, reserves unto himself the right to finally determine the fee or fees to be charged to clients for which said Member has primary responsibility and may serve professionally without charge or at a reduced charge any Member of his own family, any relative or any other client, in such Member's sole and absolute discretion.

6.4. Each Member shall devote his best efforts to serving professionally the Company and its clients, including the clients of all of the Members and employees ("associates").

6.5. Notwithstanding the foregoing, no Member shall accept representation of any client on a contingent basis with respect to any matter requiring a substantial expenditure of time without prior approval of all Members.

6.6. No Member shall accept an interest in any property, venture, or transaction in lieu of a cash fee without the prior unanimous consent of the Members. The approval of any such fee by the Members shall also include the method in which the interest in any such property, venture, or transaction to be received as a fee shall be allocated among the Members.

6.7. Company Books. The Manager shall maintain and preserve, during the term of the Company, the accounts, books, and other relevant Company documents described in Section 9.9. Upon reasonable written request, each Member shall have the right, at a time during ordinary business hours, as reasonably determined by the Manager, to inspect and copy, at the requesting Member's expense, the Company documents identified in Section __________ of the Act, and such other documents which the Manager, in his discretion, deems appropriate.

6.8. Priority and Return of Capital. Except as may be expressly provided in Section 9, no Member shall have priority over any other Member, either as to the return of Capital Contributions or as to Net Profits, Net Losses, or distributions; provided that this Section shall not apply to loans which a Member has made to the Company.

6.9. Liability of a Member to the Company. A Member who receives a distribution or the return in whole or in part of his

Capital Contribution is liable to the Company only to the extent provided by the Act and this Operating Agreement.

6.10. Exclusive Services and Loyalty to Company. Members shall work full time for the Company and none of the Members shall engage in or have an interest in any other law business other than that benefiting the Company. Legal work should be charged to a client; any pro bono or volunteer legal work must be preapproved by the Manager, which consent shall not be unreasonably withheld. Members shall keep the Manager informed of their legal activities, so that work can be coordinated and liabilities and impact upon firm reputation assessed objectively with full information. Members shall conduct their activities so as to respect the fact that each Member's reputation is affected by the decisions and conduct of the other Members and that loyalty to the Company and each other Member is essential. In addition, prior to Dissociation, each Member agrees that he shall not compete with the Company and that he shall offer all matters that might constitute opportunities for the Company to the Company.

6.11. Costs Advanced and Recovered. Costs advanced for a client or in investigating a case shall be paid as an operating expense and deemed "costs advanced" and "costs recovered." Members shall try to coordinate efforts to minimize and control costs and clear them through the Manager, unless minimal or ordinary and within operating procedures.

6.12. Members' Client Base. Members shall designate which clients they have attracted or produced to the Company. A Member shall declare upon commencement of work for a client that he or she produced the client. Any dispute as to origination of a client shall be settled by the Manager. Generally, a client shall be deemed to have been originated by a Member if the client is attracted to the office by the Member. Repeat work by a Member for a client originated by another Member, or whose work was previously performed by another Member, does not change whose client it is for these purposes. The goal is to gain new clients through new contacts, not to claim a client simply because a return client has asked for a particular attorney or because work is being done for the client. Clients who call in and just ask for "a lawyer" shall be deemed clients of the Company. This is not intended to create unhealthy competition or a petty proprietary attitude among the Members, but is an attempt to monitor and determine who produces what clients and the size of a Member's draw of clients and book of business.

6.13. Time Keeping. Time records shall be kept by Members for purposes of accurate billing, to determine profitability of work, to record a history of the handling of cases, and to monitor the contribution of Members to the Company.

6.14. Fiduciary Duties of the Members and Manager (Generally). The fiduciary duties a Member or Manager owes to the Company and the other Members include the duty of loyalty and the duty of care set forth in Sections 6.14.1 and 6.14.2.

6.14.1. Duty of Loyalty. A Member's or Manager's duty of loyalty to the Company and the other Members includes the following:

6.14.1.1 To account to the Company and hold as trustee for it any property, profit, or benefit derived by the Member or Manager in (i) the conduct and (ii) winding up of the Company Business or derived from a use by the Member or Manager of Company property, including the appropriation of a Company opportunity;

6.14.1.2 To act fairly when a Member or Manager deals with the Company in the conduct or winding up of the Company Business as or on behalf of a party having an interest adverse to the Company; and

6.14.1.3 To refrain from competing with the Company in the conduct of the Company Business before the dissolution of the Company.

6.14.2. Duty of Care. A Member's or Manager's duty of care to the Company and the other Members in the conduct and winding up of the Company Business is limited to refraining from engaging in grossly negligent or reckless conduct, intentional misconduct, or a knowing violation of law.

6.14.3. Obligation of Good Faith and Fair Dealing. A Member or Manager shall discharge the duties to the Company and the other Members under this Operating Agreement and the Act and exercise any rights consistently with the obligation of good faith and fair dealing.

6.14.4. Furtherance of Member's Own Interests. A Member or Manager does not violate a duty or obligation under this Operating Agreement or the Act merely because the Member's or Manager's conduct furthers the Member's or Manager's own interest.

6.15. Transacting Business with the Company. A Member may lend money to and transact other business with the Company, and as to each loan or transaction the rights and obligations of the Member are the same as those of a person who is not a Member, subject to other applicable law.

6.16. Confidentiality of Company Information. Each Member and Manager agrees to maintain all Business information with respect to the Company in confidence, and agrees not to use or disclose any Business information, trade secrets, processes, or confidences of the Company in competition with the Company. This obligation of confidentiality shall survive the Dissociation of any Member.

6.17. Standards of Conduct in Winding up Company. This Section 6 applies to a person winding up the Company Business as the personal or legal representative of the last surviving Member as if the person were a Member.

6.18. Modification of Standards of the Act. Except as expressly set forth herein, the Members agree to be bound by 805ILCS180/15-3.

7. LEASE
   7.1. The Sample Law Firm shall lease the office space at, ________________, ________________and the contained personal property, to the Company pursuant to the lease attached hereto as Exhibit ________________.
8. MEETINGS OF MEMBERS
   8.1. Annual Meetings. There shall be an annual meeting of the Members at a time and place determined by the Manager.
   8.2. Other Meetings. Other meetings may be called at the request of the Manager or any Member.
   8.3. Notice of Meetings. Members shall be given notice orally, in writing or by e-mail, of any meeting and, to the extent known, the matters to be discussed at the meeting, but no defect in notice shall cause the action taken at such a meeting to be invalid.
   8.4. Meeting of All Members. If all of the Members shall meet at any time and place, either within or outside of the State of ________________, and consent to the holding of a meeting at such time and place, such meeting shall be valid without call or notice, and at such meeting lawful action may be taken.
   8.5. Proxies. At all meetings of Members, a Member may vote in person or by proxy executed in writing by the Member or by a duly authorized attorney-in-fact. Such proxy shall be filed with the Manager of the Company before or at the time of the meeting. No proxy shall be valid after six months from the date of its execution, unless otherwise provided in the proxy.
   8.6. Action by Members Without a Meeting. Action required or permitted to be taken at a meeting of Members may be taken without a meeting if the action is evidenced by one or more written consents describing the action taken, signed by Members or if less than the vote of all Members is required, signed by the Members required to vote.
   8.7. Waiver of Notice. When any notice is required to be given to any Member, a waiver thereof in writing signed by the person entitled to such notice, whether before, at, or after the time stated therein, shall be equivalent to the giving of such notice.

9. MEMBERS' CONTRIBUTION TO THE COMPANY, GUARANTEE OF COMPANY OBLIGATIONS, AND LIABILITY FOR COMPANY OBLIGATIONS
   9.1. Members' Obligation to Contribute in General. Except as expressly set forth in this Operating Agreement, including Sections 9 and 10.1.2, no Member or Dissociated Member shall have any obligation to contribute to the Company. The obligations to contribute as set forth in this Operating Agreement are solely for the benefit of the Members and Dissociated Members and no creditor of the Company or any other person shall have any right to rely upon or enforce any contribution obligation contained in this Operating Agreement. The Members reserve the right to unanimously amend or waive any contribution obligation of any Member with or without consideration at any time, but, except as required by this Operating Agreement or by law, no Member's obligation to contribute shall be increased without that Member's express written consent.
   9.2. Initial Contributions. Each Member shall contribute his share of cash and other assets reflected on Exhibit A. Provided, however, the Members identified on Exhibit ____ may pay such Initial Contribution in installments by directing that a portion of their monthly distribution be retained by the Company in such Member's Capital Account until such time as the Member shall have contributed in full the Initial Contribution. Such election may not be spread over a time period exceeding ____ months. All liabilities shown on the balance sheet of the ___________ Firm dated ___________________, ___________________, as prepared by ___________________ [*Accounting Firm*] shall be assumed by the Company with the exception of ___________________. Each Member and the Firm shall contribute his/its clients to the Company.
   9.3. Maintenance of Insurance. The Members agree to maintain at least the minimum insurance required by Rule _____________ of the _____________Supreme Court. In the event the

Company should have insufficient money to pay insurance premiums for liability insurance ("Premium Shortage") or to pay deductible amounts under any liability insurance policy under which a claim has been made ("Deductible Shortage") or fails to satisfy the proof of financial responsibility provisions of _________Supreme Court Rule _________) ("Financial Responsibility"), each Member agrees to loan the Company an amount equal to that Member's Pro Rata share of such Premium Shortage, Deductible Shortage, or Financial Responsibility. It is understood that all Members agree that the Company will fully comply with the proof of financial responsibility of _________Supreme Court Rule _________).

9.4. Guarantees and Contributions. Upon unanimous written approval of the Members, each Member agrees to execute his personal guarantee of any indebtedness of the Company not to exceed in the aggregate $50,000. The Members shall attempt to structure the guarantee in such a manner as to limit each Member's guarantee to that Member's Pro Rata share of the indebtedness. In the event any Member is required to make any payment with respect to such indebtedness, the Company shall indemnify that Member for all amounts paid or incurred with respect to such indebtedness. In the event any Member (the "Paying Member") is obligated to make a guaranty payment in excess of the Paying Member's Pro Rata share of the indebtedness, each other Member (an "Other Member") shall be obligated to pay to the Paying Member an amount equal to the Other Member's Pro Rata share of the excess of the amount paid by the Paying Member over the Paying Member's Pro Rata share of the indebtedness.

9.5. Obligation of Member or Dissociated Member to Contribute to the Company. Any Member or Dissociated Member whose actions have contributed to the creation of a liability or obligation of the Company with respect to which that Member would not be entitled to indemnification under Section 15 shall contribute an amount sufficient to indemnify the Company against all costs, obligations, and liabilities of the Company arising from such actions (including the obligation to indemnify any other Indemnified Member) except to the extent that obligation or liability is paid or reimbursed under a policy of insurance carried by the Company.

9.6. Liability for Company Obligations. Except as specifically provided in this Operating Agreement, in accordance with Section _________ of the Act, no Member or Manager shall be personally liable or accountable, directly or indirectly (including by way of indemnification, contribution, assessment or otherwise), for debts, obligations and liabilities of, or chargeable to, the Company, or another Member or Members, whether arising in tort, contract or otherwise, solely by reason of being a Member or acting (or omitting to act) in such capacity, which such debts, obligations and liabilities occur, are incurred or are assumed while the Company is a limited liability company.

9.7. Contribution and Indemnity Obligations Controlling Regardless of Liability Protection. The obligation to contribute under Sections _________ and _________shall continue notwithstanding the qualification of the Company as a limited liability company.

10. DIVISION OF PROFITS AND LOSSES; MONTHLY DRAWS; AND CAPITAL ACCOUNTS, ELECTIONS AND REPORTS

10.1. Division of Profits and Losses.

10.1.1. The Net Profits and Net Losses of the Company shall be divided among the Members in the Percentage Interests set forth on an exhibit. Said Percentage Interests shall be reviewed and adjusted annually and confirmed in writing for the next succeeding calendar year by unanimous vote of the Members.

10.1.2. Distribution of Available Cash by Monthly Draws. The available cash of the Company shall be distributed not less frequently than monthly as determined by the Manager. To the extent it is determined at the end of the Company year by the accountants regularly employed by the Company that an adjustment must be made to a Member's Capital Account, such adjustment shall be made and such Member shall recontribute any deficit in his Capital Account.

10.2. Capital Account. An individual Capital Account shall be established and maintained for each Member. Each Member's Capital Account (a) shall be increased by (i) the amount of money and net value of property contributed to the Company and (ii) the Member's allocable share of income and gain allocated pursuant to this Company Agreement, and (b) shall be decreased by (i) the amount of money and fair market value of property distributed to that Member and (ii) that Member's allocable share of deductions and loss allocated pursuant to this Operating Agreement. The Manager shall determine from time to time the minimum equity to be retained by the Company. Each Member's Capital Account shall at a minimum be that Member's Pro Rata share of the minimum equity. To the extent a Member has a deficit Capital Account, the Member will not be entitled to distributions until the deficit is eliminated. Provided, however, a Member may elect to eliminate such deficit by reducing his monthly distribution by such percent as will eliminate such deficit over a time period not to exceed _________ months.

10.3. Valuation of Capital Account. At any particular time each Member's Capital Account shall be the amount as shown from time to time for that Member as "Ending Capital" on the Schedule of Members' Equity-Income Tax Basis as contained in the monthly financial statements of the Company as prepared by the accountants then employed by the Company. The Capital Accounts are equivalent to Members' equity and shall be computed as follows: each Member's Initial Capital Contribution, plus or minus the Net Profits and Net Losses allocated to each Member in accordance with Section 10.1.1 hereof, less all withdrawals and draws made by or for the benefit of that Member to the date of such valuation. The method of valuation of assets shall be on a basis consistent with the method of valuation of assets made in the accountants' statements prepared during calendar year _________for the Firm. Each Member recognizes that fixed tangible assets of the Company are and shall be in the future carried on the books of the Company at depreciated and nominal values, which may be far less than their actual values, and agree that said depreciated and nominal values shall be used in determining values of Capital Accounts of Members. The total amount of "Ending Capital" as reflected on said monthly financial statements shall be determined, fixed and adjusted from time to time, by the Manager, as are the amounts of monthly draws as described in Section 10.1.2 hereof.

10.4. Limitation upon Distributions.

10.4.1. No distributions or return of contributions shall be made and paid if, after the distribution or return of distribution is made either:

10.4.1.1 The Company would be insolvent; or

10.4.1.2 The net assets of the Company would be less than zero.

10.4.2. The Manager may base a determination that a distribution or return of contribution may be made under Section 10.4.1 in good faith reliance upon a balance sheet and profit and loss statement of the Company represented to be correct by the person having charge of its books of account or certified by an independent public or certified public accountant or firm of accountants to fairly reflect the financial condition of the Company.

10.4.3. Except as otherwise provided herein, a Member has no right to demand and receive any distribution in a form other than cash.

10.4.4. Accounting Principles. The Net Profits and Net Losses of the Company shall be determined in accordance with generally accepted accounting principles applied on a consistent basis using the cash method of accounting.

10.4.5. Interest on and Return of Capital Contributions. No Member shall be entitled to interest on its Capital Contribution or to return of its Capital Contribution, except as required by this Operating Agreement.

10.5. Loans to Company. Nothing in this Operating Agreement shall prevent any Member from making secured or unsecured loans to the Company by agreement with the Company.

10.6. Accounting Period. The Company's accounting period shall be the calendar year ("Fiscal Year").

10.7. Records, Audits, and Reports. At the expense of the Company, the Manager shall maintain records and accounts of the operations and expenditures of the Company. At a minimum the Company shall keep at its principal place of business the following records:

10.7.1. A current list of the full name and last known address of each Member setting forth the amount of cash each Member has contributed, a description and statement of the agreed value of the other property or services each Member has contributed or has agreed to contribute in the future, and the date on which each became a Member.

10.7.2. A copy of the Articles of Organization of the Company and all amendments thereto, together with executed copies of any powers of attorney pursuant to which any amendment has been executed.

10.7.3. Copies of the Company's federal, state, and local income tax returns and reports, if any, for the three most recent years.

10.7.4. Copies of the Company's currently effective written Operating Agreement, and copies of any financial statements of the Company for the three most recent years.

10.7.5. Minutes of meetings.

10.7.6. Any written consents obtained from Members for actions taken by Members without a meeting.

10.7.7. Unless contained in the Articles of Organization or the Operating Agreement, a writing prepared by the Manager setting out the following:

10.7.7.1 The times at which or events on the happening of which any additional contributions agreed to be made by each Member are to be made.

10.7.7.2 Any right of a Member to receive distributions that include a return of all or any part of the Member contributions.

10.8. Returns and Other Elections. The Manager shall cause the preparation and timely filing of all tax returns required to be filed by the Company pursuant to the Code and all other tax returns deemed necessary and required in each jurisdiction in which the Company does Business. Copies of such returns, or pertinent information therefrom, shall be furnished to the Members within a reasonable time after the end of the Company's fiscal year upon the Members' written request. All elections permitted to be made by the Company under federal or state laws shall be made by the Manager in his sole discretion.

10.9. Tax Matters Member. Lawyer A is designated the "Tax Matters Member" (as defined in Code Section 6231), and is authorized and required to represent the Company (at the Company's expense) in connection with all examinations of the Company's affairs by tax authorities, including, without limitation, administrative and judicial proceedings, and to expend Company funds for professional services and costs associated therewith. The Members agree to cooperate with each other and to do or refrain from doing any and all things reasonably required to conduct such proceedings.

11. DISSOCIATION OF MEMBERS
    11.1. Effect of Dissociation. The Dissociation of a Member by reason of resignation, Withdrawal, death, or Expulsion shall neither result in the dissolution of the Company nor require the winding up of the Company Business, and the rights of the Dissociated Member and remaining Members shall be determined pursuant to this Operating Agreement.
    11.2. Withdrawal of a Member. A Member may withdraw or resign from the Membership at any time upon _________ days' prior written notice, addressed to the Members. Unless otherwise mutually agreed between the Company and the Withdrawn Member or resigning Member, the Withdrawn Member or resigning Member shall cease to be a Member and shall be Dissociated from the Company _________ days after delivery of the notice of Withdrawal or resignation.
    11.3. Expulsion of a Member. The Company may Expel a Member upon the unanimous consent of the Members. Such Expulsion shall be effective regardless of whether the Expulsion is for cause or otherwise. Upon Expulsion, the Member shall cease to be a Member and shall be Dissociated from the Company.
    11.4. Death or Required Retirement of a Disabled Member or Assignment of a Member's Interest. A Member shall cease to be a Member and shall be Dissociated from the Company on the Member's death, required retirement of a Disabled Member, or upon any purported Transfer of all or any portion of the Member's interest in the Company whether voluntary, involuntary or by operation of law.
12. RIGHTS OF DISSOCIATED MEMBERS
    12.1. Payments to Dissociated Members.
        12.1.1. Withdrawn Member. Upon the Withdrawal of a Member, the Withdrawn Member shall be entitled to receive the Withdrawn Member's Capital Account, which shall be paid to the Withdrawn Member pursuant to Section 12.1.7. The Withdrawn Member's Capital Account, subject to adjustments

as hereinafter provided, shall be valued as of the following dates: (a) the effective date of Withdrawal or retirement, if such Withdrawal Date occurs on the last day of a calendar month or (b) as of the last day of the calendar month immediately preceding the Withdrawal Date, if the Withdrawn Member's Withdrawal Date occurs at any time other than on the last day of a calendar month. The Capital Account as of the Valuation Date shall be reduced by the following: (i) amounts the Withdrawn Member has received as withdrawals and amounts which have been paid for the Withdrawn Member's benefit after the Valuation Date; (ii) the Company's employees' and associates' prorated bonuses and *[add profit sharing or other employee benefit plan name]* plan contributions for the calendar year in which the Withdrawal Date occurs which shall be determined by the following formula:

> Total amount of bonuses and *[add profit sharing or other employee benefit plan name]* contributions for the calendar year prior to the year in which the Withdrawal Date occurs, multiplied by a fraction, the numerator of which is the number of days elapsed from the first day of the calendar year in which the Withdrawal Date occurs through to the Valuation Date and the denominator is 365, multiplied by the Withdrawn Member's Percentage Interest as set forth in Section 10.1.1 hereof, plus the amount of the contribution, if any, to be made to such plan(s) for such calendar year on behalf of the Withdrawn Member.

(iii) in the event the *[insert plan name]* plan contributions for the calendar year prior to the year in which the Valuation Date occurs has not been paid as of the Valuation Date, the unpaid contributions for employees and associates for such prior year multiplied by the Withdrawn Member's Percentage Interest as set forth in Section 10.1.1 hereof, plus the amount of the contribution to be made to such plan(s) for such year on behalf of the Withdrawn Member. In addition, the Withdrawn Member shall be paid pursuant to Section 12.1.7 the Withdrawn Member's Percentage Interest (as set forth in Section 10.1.1 hereof) of accounts receivable actually billed on or before the Valuation Date as and when the same are collected, reduced, and adjusted as follows:

(1) If the Withdrawal Date occurs prior to the date on which the Withdrawn Member has completed 12 months as a Member of this Company or a Member of an Entity which was a predecessor to the Company, he shall not receive any part of his Percentage Interest of accounts receivable.

(2) If the Withdrawal Date occurs upon or after the Withdrawn Member has completed 12 months but prior to the date on which he has completed 24 months as a Member of the Company or a Member of an Entity which was a predecessor to the Company, he shall receive 25% of his Percentage Interest of accounts receivable.

(3) If the Withdrawal Date occurs on or after the Withdrawn Member has completed 24 months but prior to the date on which he has completed

36 months as a Member of the Company or a Member of an Entity which was a predecessor to the Company, he shall receive 50% of his Percentage Interest of accounts receivable.

(4) If the Withdrawal Date occurs on or after the Withdrawn Member has completed 36 months but prior to the date on which he has completed 48 months as a Member of the Company or a Member of an Entity which was a predecessor to the Company, he shall receive 75% of his Percentage Interest of accounts receivable.

(5) If the Withdrawal Date occurs on or after the Withdrawn Member has completed 48 months as a Member of the Company or a Member of an Entity which was a predecessor to the Company, he shall receive 100% of his Percentage Interest of accounts receivable.

For purposes of this Operating Agreement, any accounts receivable that are subject to division with or participation with any Person other than Company shall be considered as an account receivable only to the extent of the net amount of the account receivable collected or retained by Company. In the event a Withdrawn Member's Capital Account as computed pursuant to the provisions of this Operating Agreement reflects a deficit, the amount of the deficit shall be deducted from the first payments required to be paid on collection of accounts receivable and shall be credited to the Withdrawn Member's Capital Account until the Withdrawn Member's Capital Account reflects no deficit. Further, for purposes of this Operating Agreement the xx Firm shall be deemed to be a predecessor to the Company.

12.1.2. Death. Upon the death of a Member, the Deceased Member's widow or widower, or such other person designated by the Deceased Member, or, if the Deceased Member shall not make such designation, the Deceased Member's estate or personal representative, shall be entitled to receive the Deceased Member's Capital Account which shall be paid pursuant to Section 12.1.7. The Deceased Member's Capital Account, subject to adjustments as hereinafter provided, shall be valued as of the following dates: (a) the Deceased Member's date of death, if the date of death occurs on the last day of a calendar month or (b) as of the last day of the calendar month immediately preceding the date of death if the date of death occurs other than on the last day of a calendar month. The Capital Account as of the Death Valuation Date shall be reduced by amounts the Deceased Member received as withdrawals and amounts which have been paid for the Deceased Member's account after the date of death, computed and adjusted on the basis set forth in Section 12.1.1 hereof. In addition, the Deceased Member's widow or widower, designee, estate, or personal representative shall be paid pursuant to Section 12.1.7 the Deceased Member's Percentage Interest of accounts receivable billed on or before the Death Valuation Date as and when collected, adjusted and reduced on the basis set forth in Section 12.1.1 hereof. In addition to the above sums, a Deceased Member's widow or widower, designee, estate, or personal representative shall be paid an amount equal to that certain percentage (as indicated below) of the proceeds of all life insurance policies owned by the Company insuring the Deceased Member's life.

Members % to Widows, Widowers, % to Widows, Widowers, Etc.

12.1.3. Expelled Member. Upon the Expulsion of a Member, the Expelled Member shall be entitled to receive the Expelled Member's Capital Account, which shall be paid to the Expelled Member pursuant to Section 12.1.7. The Expelled Member's Capital Account, subject to adjustments as hereinafter provided, shall be valued on the Expulsion Valuation Date determined as follows: (a) the Expulsion Date, if the Expulsion Date occurs on the last day of a calendar month, or (b) as of the last day of the calendar month immediately preceding the Expulsion Date, if the Expulsion Date occurs at any time other than on the last day of a calendar month. The Capital Account as of the Expulsion Valuation Date shall be reduced by amounts the Expelled Member received as withdrawals and amounts which have been paid for the Expelled Member's account after the Expulsion Date, computed and adjusted on the basis set forth in Section 12.1.1 hereof. In addition, the Expelled Member shall be paid pursuant to Section 12.1.7 the Expelled Member's Percentage Interest of accounts receivable billed on or before the Expulsion Valuation Date as and when collected, adjusted, and reduced on the basis set forth in Section 12.1.1 hereof. The interest of an Expelled Member in the Company property and earnings shall cease as of the Expulsion Date. The Expelled Member shall thereafter have no rights against the Company or the remaining Members as to the property or earnings except as to the payments set forth in this section.

12.1.4. Disability. A Member shall be deemed to be disabled at such time as he cannot perform his ordinary duties as a practicing attorney. Should any dispute arise as to whether or not the Member is a Disabled Member, the decision shall be made by a duly licensed physician or physicians mutually selected by all of the Members (excluding the allegedly Disabled Member) and by the allegedly Disabled Member. Provided the Disabled Member remains disabled, during the period commencing with the date the Member first becomes disabled and ending on the last day of the third calendar month following the Disability Date, the Disabled Member shall continue to receive the monthly draw referred to at Section 10.1.2 hereof and share in the Net Profits and Net Losses of the Company as set forth in Section 10.1.1 hereof. Thereafter, the Disabled Member shall not be entitled to receive such a monthly draw or share in the Net Profits and Net Losses of the Company, but the Disabled Member may receive any and all disability income payments, if any, to which the Disabled Member may then be entitled by virtue of any disability income insurance then owned by the Company; provided, however, that nothing in this Operating Agreement shall be construed to require the Company to purchase or maintain any disability income insurance policies.

Any Disabled Member may be retired from the Company by the unanimous decision of all of the Members (excluding the Disabled Member) effective as of the Disability Valuation Date. In such case the Disabled Member shall be entitled to the value of the Disabled Member's Capital Account as of the Disability Valuation Date, which shall be paid pursuant to Section 12.1.7. The Disabled Member's Capital Account shall be reduced by amounts the Disabled Member received as withdrawals and amounts which have been paid for the Disabled Member's account after the Disability Valuation Date, computed and adjusted on the basis set forth in Section 12.1.1 hereof. In addition, the Disabled Member shall be paid pursuant to Section 12.1.7 the Disabled Member's Percentage Interest of accounts receivable billed on or before the Disability Valuation Date as and when collected, adjusted and reduced on the basis set forth in Section 12.1.1 hereof.

12.1.5. Work in Process Not Payable. Accounts receivable are hereby defined as amounts billed for services rendered and costs advanced. The parties hereto specifically agree that work in process, or work which has been completed, for which invoices have not been sent to clients, shall not be considered as accounts receivable and that the Withdrawn Member, Expelled Member, estate of a Deceased Member, or Disabled Member shall have no interest in, or right to accounting pertaining to, Work in Process.

12.1.6. Payment in Full. All payments made hereunder for Members' Capital Accounts include the Member's interest in the fixed assets and said Member's allocated share of Company earnings, and shall be accepted by the recipient thereof as "payment in full" for all of the Member's interest in the Company.

All payments made pursuant to the provisions of Sections 12.1.1 through 12.1.4 hereof to the extent they apply to accounts receivables as collected shall be payment for services rendered by said Withdrawn Member, Deceased Member, Expelled Member, or Disabled Member and shall be considered an expense to the Company and income to the receiving parties.

12.1.7. Schedule of Payments. All payments to be made hereunder shall be made as follows:

(a) In the case of withdrawal, retirement, expulsion, disability, or death where the Company is not entitled to receive and retain life insurance proceeds by reason of such death in an amount which exceeds the amount of the Deceased Member's Capital Account, payment of the applicable valuation date Capital Account balance determined pursuant to this Section 12, shall be made by paying twenty-five percent (25%) of the Capital Account balance within one hundred twenty (120) days after the applicable valuation date as hereinabove defined, and the balance in eight (8) equal monthly installments thereafter until paid in full.

(b) In the case of death where the Company is entitled to receive and retain life insurance proceeds by reason of such death in an amount which exceeds the amount of the Deceased Member's Death Valuation Date Capital Account balance (hereinafter the "Insured Death"), then the Death Valuation Date Capital Account balance shall be paid in full immediately upon the firm's receipt of such life insurance proceeds.

(c) Payments of accounts receivable shall be made within ninety (90) days from the end of the month in which each individual account receivable is collected by the Company; provided, however, in the case of Insured Death, payments of accounts receivable shall be made (i) for collections made prior to the receipt of the insurance proceeds on or before the earlier of ninety (90) days from the end of the month of collection of each account receivable or on the 15th day of the month following the month insurance proceeds are collected to extent of proceeds retained by the Company; and (ii) for collections of accounts receivable made after receipt of the insurance proceeds on the 15th day of each month following the month of collection.

12.1.8. Determination of Amounts Payable. All amounts payable pursuant to this Operating Agreement shall be determined as, from and by the books, records, and statements prepared and maintained by the accountants then employed by the Company for that purpose, on a basis consistent with the method regularly used by the accountants for the Company.

12.2. Payments Reduced for Amounts Owing from Dissociated Members. The payments due to anyone under this Section 12 may be reduced for amounts owing by said party to the Company, including any damages owing as a result of any breach of this Operating Agreement.

12.3. Rights and Duties of Dissociated Member Under the Operating Agreement. Except with respect to provisions concerning contribution and indemnification and rights to payments under this Section 12, a Dissociated Member shall cease to have rights and duties under this Operating Agreement as of the Dissociation Date.

12.4. Life Insurance. A Dissociated Member (other than a Deceased Member) whose life was insured by an insurance policy owned by the Company shall have the right to purchase said policy from the Company for an amount that is derived by taking a fraction wherein 365 is the denominator and the number of days remaining for the annual prepaid policy period is the numerator, and multiplying such fraction times the annual premium that the Company paid. Similarly, in the event the premium for such insurance is paid on a basis other than annually, the Dissociated Member shall pay the pro rata portion of the premium for the unused premium period.

13. CONSEQUENCES OF VIOLATION OF COVENANTS

If a Member breaches any provision of this Operating Agreement (a "Breaching Member"), then, in addition to all other rights and remedies available to the Company, the Breaching Member shall be liable in damages, without requirement of a prior accounting, to the Company for all costs and liabilities that the Company or any Member may incur as a result of such breach, including reasonable attorneys' fees incurred in connection with the breach and in connection with recovery of damages from the Breaching Member. The Company may apply any distributions otherwise payable to the Breaching Member to satisfy any claims it may have against the Breaching Member.

14. TITLE TO PROPERTY

All real and personal property of the Company shall be owned by the Company as an Entity. No Member shall have any ownership interest in the Company property in his or her own individual name or right.

15. INDEMNIFICATION OF THE MANAGER AND MEMBERS

The Company shall indemnify, defend, and hold harmless each Manager, Member, and Dissociated Member (and their respective heirs, personal representatives, and successors) (an "Indemnified Person") with respect to any Company debt, obligation, or liability of, or chargeable to, the Company or such Indemnified Person and amounts paid in settlement of any of the foregoing, whether arising in tort, contract or otherwise, which such debts, obligations and liabilities occur, are incurred or are assumed in the course of the Company's Business and in accordance with the provisions of this Operating Agreement. Notwithstanding the foregoing sentence, no Indemnified Person shall be entitled to indemnification for (i) any Company debts, obligations, and liabilities resulting from the Indemnified Person's grossly negligent or reckless conduct, intentional misconduct, or knowing violation of the law; or (ii) any personal liability for or Company liability derived from claims arising out of acts, errors or omissions in the performance of professional services by the Member as a lawyer or any person under such Member's direct supervision and control pursuant to __________Supreme Court Rule __________; except to the extent such obligation or liability is paid or reimbursed under a policy of insurance carried by the Company.

16. RESTRICTIONS ON TRANSFER; NEW MEMBERS
    16.1. Nature of Company Interest. Each Member's interest in the Company shall be personal property for all purposes.
    16.2. No Transfer. A Member may not directly or indirectly Transfer the Member's Membership Interest in the Company, nor shall a Member permit the Member's Membership Interest in the Company to be directly or indirectly Transferred. An attempted Transfer of a Member's interest in the Company shall not render the transferee a Member without the unanimous consent of the Members, but shall result in the transferee having only those rights stated in Section _________ and _________of the Act.
    16.3. New Members. No person shall become a Member except with the unanimous consent of the Members and upon execution of a counterpart of this Operating Agreement. No new Members shall be entitled to any retroactive allocation of losses, income or expense deductions incurred by the Company. The Manager(s) may, at their option, at the time a Member is admitted, close the Company books (as though the Company's tax year has ended) or make pro rata allocations of loss, income, and expense deductions to a new Member for that portion of the Company's tax year in which a Member was admitted in accordance with the provisions of Code Section 706(d) and the Treasury Regulations promulgated thereunder.
17. DISSOLUTION AND TERMINATION
    17.1. Dissolution. The Company shall be dissolved upon the occurrence of any of the following events:
        17.1.1. By the unanimous written agreement of all Members; or
        17.1.2. Upon the death, retirement, resignation, expulsion, bankruptcy, or dissolution of the last Member or occurrence of any other event which terminates the continued membership of the last Member in the Company.

17.1.3. (i) The adjudication of the Company as insolvent within the meaning of insolvency in either bankruptcy or equity proceedings; (ii) the filing of an involuntary petition in bankruptcy against the Company (which is not dismissed within ninety (90) days); (iii) the filing against the Company of a petition for reorganization under the Bankruptcy Code (which is not dismissed within ninety (90) days); (iv) a general assignment by the Company for the benefit of creditors; (v) the voluntary claim (by the Company) that it is insolvent under any provision(s) of the Bankruptcy Code; or (vi) the appointment for the Company of a temporary or permanent receiver, trustee, custodian, or sequestration and such receiver, trustee, custodian, or sequestration is not dismissed within ninety (90) days; or (vii) as otherwise required by the Act.

17.1.4. If a Member who is an individual dies or a court of competent jurisdiction adjudges him to be incompetent to manage his person or his property, the Member's executor, administrator, guardian, conservator, or other legal representative may exercise all of the Member's rights for the purpose of settling his estate or administering his property.

17.2. Winding Up, Liquidation, and Distribution of Assets.

17.2.1. Upon dissolution, an accounting shall be made by the Company's independent accountants of the accounts of the Company and of the Company's assets, liabilities and operations, from the date of the last previous accounting until the date of dissolution. The Manager shall immediately proceed to wind up the affairs of the Company.

17.2.2. If the Company is dissolved and its affairs are to be wound up, the Manager shall:

17.2.2.1 Sell or otherwise liquidate all of the Company's assets as promptly as practicable (except to the extent the Manager may determine to distribute any assets to the Members in kind).

17.2.2.2 Allocate any Net Profit or Net Loss resulting from such sales to the Member's Capital Accounts in accordance with Section 10.1.1 hereof.

17.2.2.3 Discharge all liabilities of the Company, including liabilities to Members who are creditors, to the extent otherwise permitted by law, other than liabilities to Members for Distributions, and establish such Reserves as may be reasonably necessary to provide for contingent liabilities of the Company (for purposes of determining the Capital Accounts of the Members, the amounts of such Reserves shall be deemed to be an expense of the Company).

17.2.2.4 Distribute the remaining assets in the following order:

(i) If any assets of the Company are to be distributed in kind, the net fair market value of such assets as of the date of dissolution shall be determined by independent appraisal or by agreement of the Members. Such assets shall be deemed to have been sold as of the date of dissolution for their fair market value, and the Capital Accounts of the Members shall be adjusted pursuant to the provisions of Section 9 of this Operating Agreement to reflect such deemed sale.

(ii) The positive balance (if any) of each Member's Capital Account (as determined after taking into account all Capital Account adjustments for the Company's taxable year during which the liquidation occurs) shall be distributed to the Members, either in cash or in kind, as determined by the Manager, with any assets distributed in kind being valued for this purpose at their fair market value as determined pursuant to Section 17.2.2.4(i). Any such distributions to the Members in respect of their Capital Accounts shall be made in accordance with the time requirements set forth in Section 1.704-1(b)(2)(ii)(b)(2) of the Treasury Regulations or at Manager's sole election.

17.2.3. Subject to the provisions for contribution in this Operating Agreement, upon a liquidation within the meaning of Section 1.704-1(b)(2)(ii)(g) of the Treasury Regulations, if any Member has a Deficit Capital Account (after giving effect to all contributions, distributions, allocations, and other Capital Account adjustments for all taxable years, including the year during which such liquidation occurs), such Member shall have no obligation to make any Capital Contribution, and the negative balance of such Member's Capital Account shall not be considered a debt owed by such Member to the Company or to any other Person for any purpose whatsoever.

17.3. Company Termination. Upon completion of the winding up, liquidation, and distribution of the assets, the Company shall be deemed terminated.

17.4. Manager's Duty. The Manager(s) shall comply with all requirements of applicable law pertaining to the winding up of the affairs of the Company and the final distribution of its assets.

17.5. Articles of Dissolution. When all debts, liabilities, and obligations of the Company have been paid and discharged or adequate provisions have been made therefor and all of the remaining property and assets of the Company have been distributed, articles of dissolution as required by the Act, shall be executed in duplicate and filed with the ____________________ Secretary of State.

17.6. Effect of Filing of Articles of Dissolution. Upon the filing of articles of dissolution with the ____________________ Secretary of State, the existence of the Company shall cease, except for the purpose of suits, other proceedings and appropriate action as provided in the Act. The Manager shall have authority to distribute any Company property discovered after dissolution, convey real estate, and take such other action as may be necessary on behalf of and in the name of the Company.

17.7. Return of Contribution Nonrecourse to Other Members. Except as provided by Law or as expressly provided in this Operating Agreement, upon dissolution, each Member shall look solely to the assets of the Company for the return of its Capital Contribution. If the Company property remaining after the payment or discharge of the debts and liabilities of the Company is insufficient to return the cash contribution of one or more Members, such Member or Members shall have no recourse against any other Member, except as otherwise provided by law or this Operating Agreement.

17.8. Notwithstanding anything herein to the contrary, in the event of the dissolution of the Company for any reason, the Firm will retain the rights of ownership, occupancy and use of the office space at ______________________________, and of the personal property rented to the Company by the ____________________Firm. Any Member other than __________________ceasing membership in the Company shall promptly vacate the office premises.

18. MISCELLANEOUS PROVISIONS

18.1. Notices. Any notice, demand, or communication required or permitted to be given by any provision of this Operating Agreement shall be in writing and shall be deemed to have been duly given (a) on the date of service if served personally on the party to whom notice is to be given, (b) on the day after delivery to Federal Express or similar overnight courier or the Express Mail service maintained by the United States Postal Service, or (c) on the third day after mailing, if mailed to the party to whom notice is to be given, by first class mail, registered or certified, postage prepaid, and properly addressed, return receipt requested. Notices shall be delivered to the Member's and/or Company's address, as appropriate, which is set forth in this Operating Agreement.

18.2. Books of Account and Records. Proper and complete records and books of account shall be kept or shall be caused to be kept by the Manager in which shall be entered fully and accurately all transactions relating to the Company's Business in such detail and completeness as is customary and usual for businesses of the type engaged in by the Company. Such books and records shall be maintained as provided in Section 9.9. The books and records shall at all times be maintained at the principal place of business of the Company.

18.3. Application of __________Law. This Operating Agreement and its interpretation shall be governed exclusively by its terms and by the laws of the State of _________________, and specifically the Act and Supreme Court Rules __________________.

18.4. Retention of Clients. Upon leaving the Company for any reason other than death, a Member shall retain for himself and continue the representation of those clients who choose to remain as his clients, and the Company shall retain those clients who choose to remain as clients of the Company.

18.5. Amendments. This Operating Agreement may not be amended except in writing by the unanimous consent of the Members.

18.6. Execution of Additional Instruments. Each Member hereby agrees to execute such other and further statements of interest and holdings, designations, and other instruments necessary to comply with any laws, rules, or regulations.

18.7. Construction. Whenever the singular number is used in this Operating Agreement and when required by the context, the same shall include the plural and vice versa, and the masculine gender shall include the feminine and neuter genders and vice versa.

18.8. Headings. The headings in this Operating Agreement are inserted for convenience only and are in no way intended to describe, interpret, define, or limit the scope, extent or intent of this Operating Agreement or any provision hereof.

18.9. Waivers. The failure of any party to seek redress for default of or to insist upon the strict performance of any covenant or condition of this Operating Agreement shall not prevent a subsequent act, which would have originally constituted a default, from having the effect of an original default.

18.10. Rights and Remedies Cumulative. The rights and remedies provided by this Operating Agreement are cumulative and the use of any one right or remedy by any party shall not preclude or waive the right to use any other remedy. Said rights and remedies are given in addition to any other legal rights the parties may have.

18.11. Severability. If any provision of this Operating Agreement or the application thereof to any person or circumstance shall be invalid, illegal, or unenforceable to any extent, the remainder of this Operating Agreement and the application there of shall not be affected and shall be enforceable to the fullest extent permitted by law.

18.12. Heirs, Successors, and Assigns. Each and all of the covenants, terms, provisions, and agreements herein contained shall be binding upon and inure to the benefit of the parties hereto and, to the extent permitted by this Operating Agreement, their respective heirs, legal representatives, successors, and assigns.

18.13. Creditors. None of the provisions of this Operating Agreement shall be for the benefit of or enforceable by any creditors of the Company.

18.14. Counterparts. This Operating Agreement may be executed in counterparts, each of which shall be deemed an original but all of which shall constitute one and the same instrument.

IN WITNESS WHEREOF, the parties hereto have caused their signatures, or the signatures of their duly authorized representatives, to be set forth below as of the day and year first above written.

MEMBERS:

____

____

EXHIBIT A

Member	Address	Initial Capital Contribution	Percentage Interest
Lawyer A			___%
Lawyer B			___%

Initial Manager: Lawyer A

APPENDIX J

Agreement to Acquire Initial Ownership Interests in Sample Law Firm and Full Ownership Interest Upon Lawyer A's Subsequent Retirement

Samples found in the Appendices are also available online at http://ambar.org/succession.

THIS AGREEMENT TO ACQUIRE INITIAL OWNERSHIP INTERESTS IN SAMPLE LAW FIRM AND FULL OWNERSHIP INTEREST UPON LAWYER A SUBSEQUENT RETIREMENT (the "Agreement") made and executed on this _ day of _______, 20__, by and between attorneys and partners of Sample Law Firm, LLC hereinafter referred to as "LAWYER B" and "LAWYER C" and "LAWYER A"

W I T N E S S E T H:

WHEREAS, LAWYER A, who owns 100 percent of the interests of Sample Law Firm, desires to retire and sell his/her ownership interests to LAWYER B and LAWYER C, who are currently associate attorneys employed by the firm;

WHEREAS, LAWYER A's final consideration to be paid to him/her from LAWYER B and LAWYER C as members of Sample Law Firm, LLC, in the form of retirement payments is:

$______payable in sixty (60) monthly installments in addition to the value of his/her capital account that by agreement is agreed to be $__________, which will be paid sometime during __________but no later than __________;

WHEREAS, LAWYER A, LAWYER B, and LAWYER C have reached an agreement as to the amount of LAWYER A's interest as of __________ and the manner of payment of such amount to ____________; and

WHEREAS, the amount and manner of the final buyout of LAWYER A's Retirement shall be governed by the terms of this Agreement; and

WHEREAS, LAWYER A has requested that the Law Firm continue to pay him compensation for services performed, and the terms of such continued compensation shall be contained in separate Of Counsel agreement between LAWYER A and the Law Firm.

NOW, THEREFORE, in consideration of the foregoing premises, and for other valuable consideration, the legal adequacy and sufficiency of which is hereby acknowledged by all parties hereto, the parties do covenant and agree as follows:

I: MEMBERSHIP ADMISSION OF LAWYER B AND LAWYER C.

A. The name of the law firm will change to __________, effective ____________.

B. LAWYER B and LAWYER C will pay $______________in cash, payable to the firm on ___________as capital contributions, and the operating agreement will provide that if LAWYER B or LAWYER C leaves the firm prior to five years with the firm as "members" then their capital contribution with be forfeited and retained by the firm.

C. On ________________, LAWYER B and LAWYER C will each be issued a twenty-percent (20%) interest in the firm, and LAWYER A will retain 60 percent (60%)

D. On __________, the date of LAWYER A's planned retirement, his/her ownership interest will be assigned to the firm and LAWYER B and LAWYER C will be allocated this interest equally resulting in LAWYER B and LAWYER C having a one- hundred-percent (100%) ownership interest.

E. The operating agreement will provide that the amount of _____ capital contribution is $____________that will be paid to him at any time during __________by LAWYER B and LAWYER C, which is the year that he/she will be retired. This amount represents a rough estimated value of items of tangible property owned by the firm.

II: LAWYER A RETIREMENT

A. LAWYER A's retirement date will be __________.

B. In exchange for LAWYER A's ownership interests, LAWYER A shall be a retired member and shall be paid $__________in retirement compensation, with the retirement payments being personally guaranteed by LAWYER B and LAWYER C. The payments will be without interest as long as there is no default in payments. If there is a default in payments, interest will be owned on the delinquent payments at the rate of prime plus five percent (5%).

C. Retirement payments will be paid out on a five-year (60 months) payout in the amount of $__________each calendar year starting in __________, with payments made monthly in the amount of $__________. Prepayments are permitted but are not to exceed $__________ during any calendar year.

D. In the event that LAWYER A would continue to practice law in private practice on his own or with another law firm other than Sample Law Firm, LLC, or its successor, LAWYER A would no longer be entitled to retirement payments under this agreement and payments would stop.

E. In the event that LAWYER A dies while there are payments still due under this agreement, said payments shall be paid to the person or persons designated on the latest Beneficiary Designation Form submitted to the law firm while LAWYER A was still employed by the firm.

III: COMPENSATION, BENEFITS, AND DUTIES OF MEMBERS

A. Compensation percentages will be used rather than ownership interests to determine compensation.
   1. During _____ the percentages will be as follows:
      LAWYER A –%
      LAWYER B –%
      LAWYER C –%
   2. During _____ the percentages will be as follows:
      LAWYER A –%
      LAWYER B –%
      LAWYER C –%

B. Employee Benefits
   1. A _____ SEP contribution will be made to eligible employees for _____ tax year to be paid by Sample Law Firm, LLC.
   2. LAWYER A will be entitled to compensation of at least $_____ from the firm for _______ and if there is enough revenue during __________ after payment of all expenses and compensation, he/she will keep up to $______ in the firm checking account to carryover into ___________ to be ear-marked and used for payment of the __________ SEP contributions to be paid by April 1, ____. If there is enough cash after taking care of these obligations, then LAWYER A will consider making additional payments to himself and bonuses to LAWYER B and LAWYER C at his discretion.

C. Management Duties
   1. During ________ will have duties for managing human resources.
   2. All management duties will be divided between ATTORNEY B and ATTORNEY C to commence on ________, with ATTORNEY A providing management advice and consultation.

IV: ATTORNEY A AS OF COUNSEL TO THE FIRM

A. ATTORNEY's retirement date will be __________ but he/she will continue to work part-time in an Of Counsel capacity as an employee with the firm.

B. As an Of Counsel, an employee of the firm, the firm, while ATTORNEY A is an employee of the firm, will pay for:
   1. ATTORNEY A's license and membership fees
   2. ATTORNEY A's continuing education expenses
   3. ATTORNEY A's insurance
   4. Tailgate malpractice insurance having limits of at least $________ million for ATTORNEY A that will cover his/her liability after he/she is no longer employed by the firm

C. Additional details concerning ATTORNEY A's working arrangement with the firm, compensation for work performed, paid expenses, and other matters will be spelled out in a separate Of Counsel Agreement.

V: MISCELLANEOUS PROVISIONS

A. Upon ATTORNEY A's retirement he will remove certain items of personal tangible property which has been agreed to as follows:
   Insert

B. Office Lease
   1. Sample Law Firm, LLC, known hereafter as "The Firm or Firm," will enter into a three-year lease for the office space with LAWYER A, for $______ per month starting ________with an option to renew for another three years at $___________per month. The landlord will pay property taxes and landlord's insurance. The firm will pay to insure its property plus liability insurance. Lessor shall maintain the roof, exterior, exterior windows and doors, HVAC, plumbing, and electrical. Lessee shall maintain and keep in repair the interior, including repairs and replacements. The lease will provide a right of first refusal to purchase ___________during such time that the lease or any renewal of the lease is in effect and not in default.
   2. Specific details to be outlined in office lease.

C. There will be no public communications about LAWYER A's retirement and no public retirement party.

D. The firm will own the rights to the firm newsletter and other proprietary materials and may continue to use that name in its newsletter, if legally available.

E. The firm will provide LAWYER A legal services for LAWYER A and his/her spouse, parents, and for LAWYER A's children at reduced rates—¼ of the normal fee for LAWYER A and his/her spouse and ½ of the normal fee for LAWYER A's parents and children.

ATTACHED SCHEDULES:

Schedule A.	Of Counsel Agreement
Schedule B.	Office Lease
Schedule C.	Secured Promissory Note
Schedule D.	Security Agreement
Schedule E.	Operating Agreement

THIS AGREEMENT executed by the parties hereto in _______on the date first above written.

_______________________ _______________________________

LAWYER A DATE

_______________________ _______________________________

LAWYER B DATE

_______________________ _______________________________

LAWYER C DATE

APPENDIX K

Cross-Purchase Buy–Sell Agreement with Trustee

Samples found in the Appendices are also available online at http://ambar.org/succession.

This agreement made this ____________day of ___________ by and between ____________, and ______________________, and ____________________as TRUSTEE.

WITNESSETH:

WHEREAS, the above named individuals own stock of SAMPLE LAW FIRM, LTD., a corporation, with its principal office in ____________, in the amounts set forth in Schedule "A" attached hereto and made a part hereof; and

WHEREAS, the stockholders desire to ensure the continuity of harmonious management of the corporation by providing for the purchase of a stockholder's shares of stock by the other stockholder in the event a stockholder dies, becomes disabled, or desires to sell his shares of stock during his lifetime;

NOW THEREFORE, in consideration of the premises and mutual covenants contained herein, it is agreed by and between the parties as follows:

FIRST: In order to facilitate the carrying out of this agreement, each stockholder shall endorse in blank all certificates of stock in the corporation which he now owns or which he may hereafter acquire under the terms of this agreement and shall deposit said certificates with the Trustee to be held by it subject to the terms of this agreement. Each stockholder shall have the right, however, to vote his shares of stock and to receive all dividends thereon.

SECOND: Upon the death of a stockholder, the surviving stockholder shall purchase, and the legal representative of the estate of the deceased stockholder shall sell to, the surviving stockholder all of the shares of stock owned by the deceased stockholder, for the price established in accordance with the provisions of ARTICLE FIFTH and upon the terms and conditions set forth in ARTICLE EIGHTH.

THIRD: Upon the disability of a stockholder for a period of 18 consecutive months, the nondisabled stockholder agrees to purchase all of the shares of stock owned by the disabled stockholder. The disabled stockholder agrees that any shares of stock owned by him shall be sold and transferred to the nondisabled stockholder after he is disabled for a period of 18 consecutive months. The term "disabled" as used in this Article shall mean disability as defined in the disability policy on the disabled stockholder acquired under this agreement. The disabled stockholder shall sell to the nondisabled stockholder all of the shares of stock owned by the disabled stockholder for the price established in accordance with the provisions of ARTICLE FIFTH and under such terms and conditions in ARTICLE EIGHTH.

FOURTH: If a stockholder desires to sell part or all of his shares of stock at any time during his lifetime, he shall first give written notice hereof to the other stockholder and the Trustee, and upon receipt of such notice such other stockholder shall have 60 days to purchase said shares of stock at the price established in accordance with the provisions of ARTICLE FIFTH. The other stockholder shall have the right to purchase all of the shares of stock owned by the selling stockholder. If all the offered shares of stock are not purchased within the aforesaid period, the selling stockholder may dispose of any remaining shares in any lawful manner available to him but not at a price less than that established in accordance with the provision of ARTICLE FIFTH, without first offering to sell such remaining shares to the other stockholder at such lesser price.

FIFTH: Unless and until a new value is established as herein provided, the value of the stock of the corporation for purposes of this agreement is $300.00 per share. Within 30 days after the end of each fiscal year of the corporation, the stockholders shall redetermine the value of the stock of the corporation for purposes of this agreement and shall endorse such redetermined value on Schedule "B" attached hereto and made a part hereof. If the stockholders fail to redetermine the value of the stock of the corporation for a particular year, the last previously established value shall control, except that if the stockholders have not so established a value within three years prior to the death of a stockholder, or within three years prior to an offer to sell by a stockholder in accordance with the provisions of ARTICLE FOURTH, the value shall be determined by the independent certified public accountant regularly retained by the corporation to audit its books. If no such accountant shall be so retained, said value shall be determined by any other certified public accountant selected by mutual agreement of the surviving or remaining stockholder and the selling stockholder or the legal representative of the estate of the deceased stockholder. The value of the stock of the corporation as above stated and as redetermined from time to time hereafter, is and shall be inclusive of the value of goodwill.

SIXTH: In order to assure the availability of funds for the purchase of the shares of stock of a stockholder by the other stockholder, the trustee has purchased insurance on the lives of each stockholder on behalf of the other stockholder and disability insurance, the details of such insurance purchase being set forth in Schedule "C" attached hereto and made a part hereof. The trustee may purchase additional insurance to further the availability of funds for this purpose and, with the joint approval of all stockholders, other policies may be substituted for policies set forth in Schedule "C". Any such additions or substitutions or policies shall be endorsed on Schedule "C".

SEVENTH: The trustee shall be the beneficiary of all policies purchased for purposes of this agreement and shall retain physical custody of said policies. The Trustee shall be the absolute owner of all policies purchased by it for purposes of this agreement, and shall pay all premiums necessary to maintain said policies in force from funds provided by the stockholders. Until the termination of this agreement the trustee shall not surrender any policies owned by it for purposes of this agreement for their cash surrender value, borrow upon said policies, pledge or assign them as security for any loan or indebtedness, nor shall it otherwise modify or impair any of the rights or values in said policies, unless it first has notified and received the written consent of the stockholders.

EIGHTH: Upon the death of a stockholder or disability for 18 consecutive months, the Trustee shall immediately collect the proceeds of each policy on the deceased or disabled stockholder payable to it for the purposes of this agreement and shall apply on behalf of the remaining stockholder as much of its proceeds as may be necessary to purchase the shares of stock of the deceased or disabled stockholder which said remaining stockholder is obligated to purchase under the provisions of ARTICLES SECOND and THIRD at a price established in accordance with the provisions of ARTICLE FIFTH, and shall pay the balance of said proceeds, if any, to said remaining stockholder; however, if the proceeds for purposes of this agreement are not sufficient to purchase all the shares of stock of the deceased or disabled stockholder which said surviving stockholder is obligated to purchase under the provisions of ARTICLES SECOND and THIRD, the balance of the purchase price of said shares shall be paid in one sum, or, at the option of said surviving stockholder, within three years, in equal three payments with interest at the rate of 8% per year, which payment shall be evidenced by a promissory note. Said note shall be subject to prepayment in whole or in part at any time.

Upon payment of the purchase price of all the shares of stock of the deceased or disabled stockholder which the remaining stockholder is obligated to purchase under the provisions of ARTICLES SECOND and THIRD by cash and the delivery of any necessary note as aforesaid, the Trustee shall deliver the certificate for said shares to said remaining stockholder and the legal representative of the estate of the deceased stockholder or the disabled stockholder shall execute and deliver to said remaining stockholder such instruments as shall be necessary to transfer complete title to said shares of stock to said remaining stockholder, provided, however, that said legal representative or disabled stockholder shall have the right to receive from the Trustee and retain as collateral security for the payment of any unpaid payments under said note such number of said shares as will equal in value, as determined by ARTICLE FIFTH, the amount of such unpaid payments.

NINTH: Upon the death or disability of a stockholder, the Trustee shall have the option for 60 days after the appointment of the legal representative of the estate of the deceased stockholder or the determination of disability for a disabled stockholder, to purchase from said party for their cash surrender value the stockholder's beneficial interest in such policies as the Trustee owned on the lives and health of said remaining stockholder for purposes of this agreement. If the Trustee exercises said option, said legal representative shall immediately release all right, title, and interest in said policies to said Trustee.

TENTH: The Trustee shall be entitled to reasonable compensation for his services.

ELEVENTH: This agreement shall terminate and the stock and insurance policies subject hereto shall be released from the terms of this agreement upon the happening of any one of the following events:

(a) The written agreement of all the stockholders;

(b) The bankruptcy or dissolution of the corporation; and

(c) The sale of all of the stock of all but one of the stockholders.

TWELFTH: In the event of the sale of all of his shares of stock during his lifetime, or the termination of this agreement for any cause, a stockholder shall have the right, within 60 days of such sale or termination, to purchase the policies upon his own life which are subject to this agreement upon the same terms and conditions as set forth in ARTICLE NINTH.

THIRTEENTH: This agreement may be amended or revoked in whole or in part at any time by filing with the Trustee a written instrument signed by all of the stockholders, provided, however, that any such amendment, which shall increase the obligations or reduce the rights of the Trustee, shall require its written consent .

FOURTEENTH: No insurance company shall be under any obligation with respect to the performance of the terms and conditions of this agreement, and payment by any insurance company pursuant to the terms of any policies, which are subject to this agreement, shall be a complete discharge of said company from all claims, suits, and demands of all persons whomsoever with respect to said policies.

FIFTEENTH: This agreement shall be binding upon the stockholders individually and their respective heirs, executors, and administrators.

IN WITNESS WHEREOF, the stockholders and ________________, as Trustee herein, have executed this agreement the day and year first hereinabove written.

________________________________ ____________

TRUSTEE DATE

________________________________ ____________

SHAREHOLDER DATE

________________________________ ____________

SHAREHOLDER DATE

SCHEDULE A

The amount of stock in the corporation owned by each stockholder is as follows:

____________________________ 500 Shares

Shareholder A

____________________________ 500 Shares

Shareholder B

SCHEDULE B

This day of ________, ________, 20__the Shareholders have determined the value of the stock of the corporation to be $______________ per share.

SCHEDULE C

Name Policy No: Issued By:

APPENDIX L

Retirement Readiness Assessment

Samples found in the Appendices are also available online at http://ambar.org/succession.

Questions	YES	NO	DNK
1. Are you in a position in your life where you can retire? Describe ________________________________ ________________________________	___	___	___
2. Do you know what you want to do after retirement and how you would use your time? Describe ________________________________ ________________________________ ________________________________	___	___	___
3. Are there personal or work-related issues that you must deal with before you can retire? Describe ________________________________ ________________________________ ________________________________	___	___	___

Questions	YES	NO	DNK
4. Do you have a sense of how far away you are from retirement? Describe ______________________________ ______________________________	___	___	___
5. Do you feel that you are financially ready to retire? When? Describe ______________________________ ______________________________	___	___	___
6. Have you discussed your retirement goals and plans with your family? Describe ______________________________ ______________________________	___	___	___
7. Have you discussed your retirement goals and plans with others in your firm? Describe ______________________________ ______________________________	___	___	___
8. Are you willing to take classes or do some other on-the-job training to learn new interests and skills? Describe ______________________________ ______________________________	___	___	___
9. If you do want to work after retirement, do you know what kind of environment you want to work in and how much time you want to work after retirement? Describe ______________________________ ______________________________	___	___	___
10. Do you want to work at all after retirement? Describe how you will use your time that is freed up: ______________________________ ______________________________	___	___	___

Questions	YES	NO	DNK
11. If you do want to work after retirement, do you want to work for yourself or for an organization? Describe ______________________	___	___	___
12. Describe your ideal retirement. ______________________			
13. Is leaving a legacy important to you? Describe your legacy______________________	___	___	___
14. When do you want to retire? ____________			
15. Comments and Planning Notes __________			

16. Action Items

ACTION ITEM	DUE DATE	PERSON RESPONSIBLE

ACTION ITEM	DUE DATE	PERSON RESPONSIBLE

BIBLIOGRAPHY AND OTHER RESOURCES

Books and References

"A Profile of Older Americans: 2012." Administration on Aging, Administration for Community Living, U.S. Department of Health and Human Services. Accessed December 7, 2014. http://www.aoa.gov/Aging_Statistics/Profile/2012/docs/2012profile.pdf

Avery, Robert B. and Rendall, Michael S., 1993. "Estimating the Size and Distribution of Baby Boomers' Prospective Inheritances." American Statistical Association, Proceedings of the Social Statistics Section: 11–19.

Clay, Thomas, 2013. "2013 Law Firms in Transition—An Altman Weil Flash Survey." Accessed February 2, 2015. http://www.altmanweil.com/dir_docs/resource/2d831a80-8156-4947-9f0f-1d97eec632a5_document.pdf

Cotterman, James, 2004. "Determining the Right Compensation—Altman Weil Web Site." Accessed May 3, 2015. http://www.altmanweil.com/dir_docs/resource/2d831a80-8156-4947-9f0f-1d97eec632a5_document.pdf

Delamontagne, Robert P., 2010. *The Retiring Mind: How to Make the Psychological Transition to Retirement*. Kindle edition.

Giuliani, Peter A., 2013. *Passing the Torch Without Getting Burned*. Chicago: American Bar Association.

Hildebrandt International, 2004. *Anatomy of a Law Firm Merger*. Chicago: American Bar Association.

Kinsella, Kevin, and Wan He, 2009. "An Aging World: 2008." Washington, DC: National Institute on Aging and U.S. Census Bureau, 2009. Accessed December 7, 2014. http://www.census.gov/prod/2009pubs/p95-09-1.pdf

"Lawyer Demographics—2013." American Bar Association. Accessed February 2, 2015. http://www.americanbar.org/content/dam/aba/migrated/market-research/PublicDocuments/lawyer_demographics_2013.authcheckdam.pdf

Mayes, Roger, 2012. *The Art of Successful Retirement*. Kindle edition.

Mecke, Viola, 2013. *Aging Wisely. Facing Emotional Challenges From 50 to 85+ Years*. Kindle edition.

Milne, Derek, 2013. *The Psychology of Retirement*. Malden, Massachusetts: Wiley-Blackwell. Kindle edition.

Mrsnik, Marko, 2010. "Standard & Poor's: Global Aging 2010: An Irreversible Truth—Council on Foreign Relations." Accessed December 7, 2014. http://www.cfr.org/aging/standard-poors- global-aging-2010-irreversible-truth/p23299

"National Organization of Bar Counsel—Association of Professional Responsibility Lawyers Second Joint Committee on Aging Lawyers Final Report—April, 2014." Accessed December 7, 2014. http://barcounsel.org/docs/news/NOBC-APRL-CoLAP-final-report.pdf

Poll, Edward, 2005. *Selling Your Law Practice: The Profitable Exit Strategy.* Venice, CA: LawBiz Management Company.

Powell, Pamela, Susan Goodwin, James McCollom, Ellen Plaza, and Max Wright, 2013. "Aging and Transitioning with Dignity." *Texas Bar Journal* 127–130.

Board Service Opportunity Websites

www.bridgespan.org
www.boardsource.org
www.boardnetusa.org
www.unitedway.org
www.cof.org/locator

Community Service Websites

www.seniorcorps.gov
www.aarp.org—search for experience corps
www.oasisnet.org
www.peacecorps.gov
www.nationalservice.gov
www.reserveinc.org
www.islp.org—International Senior Lawyers Project

Law Practice Management and Other Sites

ABA Law Practice Division www.americanbar.org/groups/law_practice.html

ABA Senior Lawyers Division www.americanbar.org/groups/senior_lawyers.html

ABA Model Rules of Professional Conduct www.americanbar.org/groups/professional_responsibility/publications/model_rules_of_professional_conduct/model_rules_of_professional_conduct_table_of_contents.html

ABA Model Rules of Professional Conduct, Sale of Law Practice, Rule 1.17 http://www.americanbar.org/groups/professional_responsibility/

publications/model_rules_of_professional_conduct/rule_1_17_sale_of_law_practice.html
ABA Solo, Small Firm and General Practice Division www.americanbar.org/groups/gpsolo.html
Olmstead & Associates Legal Management Consultants Resource Sites
www.olmsteadassoc.com
http://blog.olmsteadassoc.com
http://blog.olmsteadassoc.com/olmstead_associates_law_p/successionexit-strategies/
www.olmsteadassoc.com/Services-Provided/Law-Practice-For-Sale.aspx

Volunteer Websites

www.serve.gov
www.volunteermatch.org
www.allforgood.org
www.createthegood.org
www.handsonnetwork.org
www.catchafire.org
www.sparked.com

INDEX

ABOUT THE AUTHOR

John W. Olmstead, MBA, PhD, CMC, is a certified management consultant and president of Olmstead & Associates, legal management consultants based in St. Louis, Missouri.

Olmstead & Associates is a management consulting firm that works with law and other professional service firms ranging in size from 100+ professionals to firms with solo practitioners. Founded in 1984, the firm serves clients across the United States and internationally, assisting them with implementing change and improving operational and financial performance.

John has more than forty-six years of experience working with law and other professional service firms. His assignments have ranged from marketing and strategic planning to other legal management engagements such as organizational change, firm governance, succession and exit planning, implementation of technology, financial management, staff development, partner compensation, and practice management. John has helped clients implement client service improvement programs consisting of client satisfaction surveys, program development, and training and coaching programs. His assignments have covered the spectrum of management issues. However, in recent years, much of his time has focused on engagements helping firms with:

- Succession and Exit Planning
- Sale of Law Practices, Mergers & Acquisitions
- Partnership Admission
- Partner Compensation
- Governance
- Strategy and Competitive Business Models

John has presented at conferences and workshops for bar and other professional associations at the national, state, and local levels. He has also authored numerous articles on law office management in local, regional, and national law office management publications. John is currently serving as editor-in-chief, Thomson Reuters Legal Solutions (formally West Group), The Lawyers Competitive Edge: The Journal of Law Office Economics and Management. John also writes a weekly column on best practice tips for the Illinois State Bar Association's Illinois Lawyer Now Blog. http://iln.isba.org/blog/best-practice-tips.

John has a MBA in marketing and finance as well as a PhD in business in organizational psychology. He is an associate member of the American and Illinois State Bar Associations and a member of the Institute of Management Consultants. John is a past chair and a current member of the Illinois State Bar Association Standing Committee on Law Office Management and Economics. In addition, he is past president and member of the Board of Directors of the Institute of Management Consultants—St. Louis Chapter.

John may be contacted via e-mail at: *jolmstead@olmsteadassoc.com*. Additional articles and information is available at the firm's website: www.olmsteadassoc.com and blog at http://blog.olmsteadassoc.com.